Detroit Kids Catalog

GREAT LAKES BOOKS

DETROIT KiDS CATALOG

THE HOMETOWN TOURIST

Ellyce Field

Wayne State University Press
Detroit

Copyright © 1990 by Wayne State University Press, Detroit, Michigan 48202. All rights reserved. No part of this book may be reproduced without formal permission.
Manufactured in the United States of America.

94   93   92   91   90   5   4   3   2   1

Library of Congress Cataloging-in-Publication Data

Field, Ellyce, 1951–
   Detroit kids catalog : the hometown tourist / Ellyce Field.
    p. cm. — (Great Lakes books)
   Includes index.
   ISBN 0–8143–2202–6 (pbk. : alk. paper)
   1. Detroit Region (Mich.)—Description and travel —Guide-books. 2. Children—Travel—Michigan—Detroit Region—Guide-books. I. Title. II. Series.
F574.D43F54   1990
917.7404′43—dc20   90–12601
                                      CIP

Designer: Mary Primeau

For my husband Steve, my best friend, whose loving support sustained me during this project.

For my parents, Charles and Belle Ruben, who taught me that with hard work anything is possible and supervised my carefree growing up in Detroit.

For my three sons, Jordan, Andrew, and Garrett, who smilingly endured tossed-together dinners, diminished computer time, and school vacations spent zigzagging across Michigan.

CONTENTS

8   Contents

Contents 9

13 Detroit at Work 301

Tours

Animals • Arts & Crafts • Cultural • Ecology •
Farming • Fire & Police • Food • Government •
Industry • Media • Medical Research • Mining •
Theater • Toys • Transportation • Utilities

14 Programs for the Schools 333

A Sampling of Traveling Programs

Animals • Arts & Crafts • Creative Writing • Crime
Prevention • Dance • Drug Education • History •
Magic • Music • Puppets • Science • Space •
Storytelling • Theater • Values

15 Overnight Adventures 351

10   Contents

PREFACE

Born and raised in Detroit and its suburbs, I am the consummate Hometown Tourist.

As soon as my children were portable (a backpack for the firstborn, twin strollers for the next two), my husband Steve and I started searching for sites and experiences that our entire family could enjoy. In 1987, I began writing the *Detroit News* "Kid Stuff" column, and so a quest for memorable family experiences that could be shared with a readership began in earnest.

My family and I have crisscrossed Michigan, exploring new sites and revisiting old favorites. With a growing sense of adventure, we have bucked the crowds at popular area attractions, found pleasure in little-known museums, and spent afternoons all by ourselves in nature centers off the beaten track. We have picked apples, strawberries, and pumpkins; listened to jazz and classical concerts; watched puppet shows, light opera, mime, and drama. We have ridden wild waves, tame ponies, and zooming go-carts. We have cheered for our home teams, lounged at the beach, marveled at laser and Omnimax shows and witnessed the birth of many Made-in-Michigan products. In short, we have discovered the child's world in Metro Detroit.

This book is a collection of all those sights and sounds, a family's guidebook to the city and its environs, a handbook for adults and children who are ready to become Hometown Tourists.

It's my family's way of saying "Welcome! Michigan's yours to explore."

Disclaimer

Sites listed were chosen by the author. No one paid to be included in this book. Every effort was taken to be sure all information in this book was correct when we went to press. However, hours, exhibits, prices and even locations may change from time to time. PLEASE CALL AHEAD.

Symbols

H   handicapped access or programs adapted for the disabled.

PLEASE NOTE: While the symbol "H" is used consistently in Chapters 4, 5 & 6 to indicate handicapped access, it is used only sporadically throughout the rest of the book. Therefore, do not assume that a site is NOT handicapped accessible if it is missing the "H." When going on an outing with a wheelchair or stroller-bound youngster, it is always advisable to call ahead to find out where entrances, ramps, elevators and bathrooms are located.

SP   school programs

T   group tours

1
INTRODUCTION

Who Needs This Book?

■ You grew up in Detroit (but it sure seems like a long time ago). Now your kids are old enough to be introduced to your favorite sites. Do they still exist?

■ It's fall. You have visions of apples, cider, and donuts. Is there a cider mill or U-pick orchard nearby?

■ The grandkids are coming for a week. Are there any more old-fashioned pleasures left? Is is possible to keep busy for a week without spending a fortune?

■ It's summer and the living is easy. Where can you go for a weekend adventure with the kids?

■ You want to show off Detroit to your visiting friends and their children. What's flashy and especially *Detroit?*

■ It's your turn to plan the girl scouts' next field trip or the school's next special assembly. What type of tours or school programs are available?

■ You're a divorced parent and the kids are coming to spend the weekend. You're fortified with G-rated videos, but sooner or later the kids will want to cruise. Where can you take them?

■ You're coming to Detroit for business and decide to bring the kids. What are Detroit's best children's attractions?

■ You're new to Detroit and finally unpacked. It's time to explore the Detroit area and claim it as your own.

If you've ever found yourself in any of these situations, the *Detroit Kids Catalog: The Home-town Tourist* is for you. This book is an annotated list of where to go, what to do, what to see, how to get there, and how to plan your time in Metro Detroit with kids from toddler to teen.

How Is This Book Organized?

I wrote this book for busy parents who, like myself, enjoy traveling around town with their kids, but have very little time to plan out a detailed adventure and would rather have all the information at their fingertips, with all the suggestions and pitfalls mentioned.

Chapters are arranged around a specific theme, for example, museums or parks. Sites are listed in alphabetical order. The most important information (address, phone, location, hours, admission, ages, plan, parking, lunch, and facilities) is listed. A short annotation describes the site and gives you its flavor.

Here are some important facts to remember:

The age designation of a particular site is based on my experience with my children, who are often very mature, cooperative travelers, but at other times are very reluctant, irritable travelers! No one knows your children's needs, interests, and attention span better than you do, so use the age designation as a suggested guideline. However, please respect a specific age requirement for admittance to a site or performance.

Plan refers to how long you should plan on the visit taking. I've indicated *approximate* amounts of time by: "all day visit" (6+ hours), "half day visit" (4+ hours), "short visit" (2+ hours) and "under one hour." Keep in mind that the best laid plans often go awry. If your baby needs a nap, your guest has to get to the airport, or your children become cranky and hungry, your half day visit could turn into a short visit. Come back on a more relaxing day.

Lunch tells you where you can find food on the premises or nearby. If you're going out for the day, it doesn't hurt to pack a snack or a picnic lunch just in case the kids get hungry, which they always do, when you're lost or driving on the expressway.

Facilities includes information about stroller rental, bathrooms, and gift shops.

Chapters 7, 8, 12, and 15 group sites by type or location. Because the sites in chapters 4, 5, 6, 9, 10, 11, 13, and 14 are so various, a brief description of the site or its activities — for instance, "Petting Farm" or "Music & Dance" — appears above the entry in these chapters.

Detroit is the Motor City. Most of us have sturdy wheels and are not afraid to drive from here to there. For this reason, the chapters include sites in the greater Metropolitan Detroit area (Wayne, Oakland, and Macomb counties), plus cities that are within a 1½ hour drive (approximately 100 miles) from Detroit, such as Ann Arbor, Ypsilanti, East Lansing, Lansing, Jackson, Flint, and Port Huron. Sites more than 1½ hours away are listed geographically in the Overnight Adventure chapter.

Enjoy traveling with your kids. With each excursion, you'll develop a core of family memories and a love for Metro Detroit.

2
FIRST THINGS FIRST

Things to Know

The secret to successful family outings is to PLAN AHEAD. Be sure to CALL AHEAD to verify times, prices, directions, and special events whenever you go anywhere with your kids. This way, you'll minimize disappointment and unnecessary frustration. Unless otherwise noted, all phone numbers listed in this chapter are in the 313 area code.

This chapter is designed to help you plan ahead. Listed are: publications that offer calendars of kids' events; telephone information numbers; emergency resources; and information about transportation and tours, Canada and customs, and Detroit's best kid stuff.

Weather and Clothes

Detroit is famous for its changeable weather, its extremes and its surprises. When it isn't doing any of the above, it's safe to say: summer is hot; autumn is cool; winter is snowy cold, and spring is wet. So dress the kids in layers and throw an extra jacket or sweatshirt in the backseat. Take along a sun hat or visor in the summer and carry boots, hats, and mittens in the winter. I always carry a large shopping bag or a backpack to hold the layers as they are peeled off.

Publications

The Detroit News "Kid Stuff" column highlights family entertainment and sites and includes a calendar of kids' events for the coming weekend and week. 222-2300.

The Detroit Free Press offers a "Family Fare" column and a "Seeing & Doing" calendar. 222-6400.

Detroit Monthly, the monthly city magazine, includes a very brief listing of kids' events in its monthly calendar. 446-6000.

All Kids Considered, a monthly parenting newspaper available by subscription, offers a monthly calendar of kids' events. 352-0990.

Telephone Information

General Information

Detroit Visitor Center: 567-1170

Detroit Convention and Visitor Center Main Office: 259-4333 (open Monday-Friday)

Detroit Public Information: 224-3270

"The What's Line": 298-6262 (a 24-hour list of daily events)

Michigan Regional Tourist Associations:
Upper Peninsula: 906-774-5480
West Michigan: 616-456-8557
East Michigan: 517-777-9800

Michigan Travel Bureau: 1-800-543-2937

Michigan Travel Bureau: TDD 1-800-722-8191 (for the hearing impaired)

Michigan State Chamber of Commerce: 517-371-2100 (for the name, address, and phone of a specific city's chamber of commerce)

Time: 472-1212
Ticketmaster: 645-6666
Weather: 1-976-1212
Windsor Convention and Visitors Bureau:
519-255-6530

Emergency Numbers

Babysitting—Hourly Drop-Off:
My Place: 737-5437 (Farmington Hills),
540-5702 (Birmingham)

Dental Referral Service: 559-7900

Doctor's Referral Service: 567-1640

Hospitals:

Beaumont Hospital, Royal Oak:
1-800-633-7377, Emergency 551-2000

Bon Secours of Michigan, Grosse Pointe:
343-1000, Emergency 343-1605

Children's Hospital of Michigan, Detroit:
745-5437, Emergency 745-5206

Henry Ford Hospital, Detroit:
876-2600, Emergency 876-1545

Mt. Carmel Mercy Hospital, Detroit:
Emergency 927-7701, After hours 927-7000

Oakland General Hospital, Madison Heights:
967-7000, Emergency 967-7670

Pontiac General Hospital, Pontiac:
857-7200, Emergency 857-6720

Providence Hospital, Southfield:
424-3000, Emergency 424-3331

St. Joseph Mercy Hospital, Ann Arbor:
572-3456, Emergency 572-3000

St. Joseph Mercy Hospital, Pontiac:
858-3000, Emergency 858-3100,
Pediatric After Hours Center 858-3493

Sinai Hospital, Detroit:
493-5713, Emergency 493-5555

University of Michigan Medical Center,
Ann Arbor:
936-4000, Emergency 936-6666,
Pediatric Walk-In Clinic 936-4230

Medical Societies:
Oakland County Medical Society: 646-5400
Macomb County Medical Society: 463-2101
Wayne County Medical Society: 567-1640

Police, Fire, EMS: 911 in Detroit, Oakland County, Sterling Heights, and Clinton Township in Macomb County, Highland Park and Livonia in Wayne County. All other cities should refer to emergency phone listings on the inside cover of the Ameritech Yellow Pages.

Frequently Used Box Office Numbers

Birmingham Theatre, Birmingham: 644-1096

Cobo Arena: 567-6000, 645-6666 (use Ticketmaster for orders)

Detroit (DIA) Youtheatre: 832-2323

Detroit Symphony Orchestra: 833-3700

Fisher Theatre: 872-1000

Fox Theatre: 567-6000 (office), 645-6666 (use Ticketmaster for orders)

Joe Louis Arena: 567-7474, 567-6000, 645-6666 (use Ticketmaster for orders)

Lydia Mendelssohn Theatre, Ann Arbor: 763-1085

Macomb Center for the Performing Arts, Mount Clemens: 286-2222, 286-2268

Masonic Temple: 832-7100

Meadow Brook Music Festival, Rochester: 377-2010

Michigan Opera Theatre: 874-SING

Michigan Theater, Ann Arbor: 668-8397

Michigan Union Ticket Office, Ann Arbor: 763-TKTS

Music Hall: 963-7680

Orchestra Hall: 833-3700

The Palace, Auburn Hills: 377-8600

The Palace Gardens, Auburn Hills: 377-8600

Pine Knob, Clarkston: 625-0511 (office), 645-6666 (use Ticketmaster for orders)

Power Center, Ann Arbor: 763-3333

Ticketmaster (Order tickets by phone using credit card): 645-6666

Transportation and Tours

Unlike other major cities, Detroit is an automobile town. It is almost impossible to get around town without a car, unless you are staying downtown and visiting only downtown, uptown, and Cultural Center sites. Then you can hop on the People Mover, trolley, and a Woodward bus.

Driving is easy around Metro Detroit. We are a town with well-marked, easy-to-follow freeways. I-75, I-275, and US-10 are the major north-south highways, I-94, I-696, and I-96 are the east-west highways.

Traffic tends to be heavy going downtown during morning rush hour, generally 7:30-9 a.m., and leaving downtown in afternoon rush hour, 4:30-6 p.m. On Friday afternoon during the summer, northbound I-75 is quite dense. Ditto Sunday evening on southbound I-75. This is "Up North" traffic.

If you avoid being in those places at those times, you'll rarely be caught in traffic, with one exception: Detroiters support their sports teams. Plan on lots of traffic after a game. And be sure to buckle up — Michigan has a seatbelt law.

Road Conditions: 256-9639

Bus Lines

People Mover: 962-RAIL

50 cents a ride. Exact change is needed although token machines selling 50-cent coupons for dollar bills are in the works. Monthly, semi-annual, and annual passes are available. Hours are 7 a.m.-11 p.m., Monday-Thursday. 7 a.m.-midnight, Friday. 9 a.m.-midnight, Saturday. Noon-8 p.m., Sunday. *See* People Movers for more information about the People Mover as a tourist attraction.

SMART: 962-5515

The Suburban Mobility Authority for Regional Transportation provides commuter service between Detroit and the suburbs and between suburbs. There are also "connector" buses that provide curb-to-curb service and are useful for the handicapped. Fares vary with routes.

D-Dot: 933-1300

Detroit Department of Transportation has many bus routes throughout the city. Fare is generally $1, plus 10 cents for a transfer.

A mini-bus service connecting major downtown hotels with the business district costs 45 cents.

A doubledecker red trolley operates daily from Grand Circus Park to the Renaissance Center. 7:10 a.m.-5:40 p.m., Monday-Friday. 10 a.m.-5:40 p.m., Saturday, Sunday, and holidays. Fare is 45 cents. Trolley drivers do not give change.

Greyhound Lines: 963-9840

Detroit-Canada Tunnel Bus: 567-4422

Taxis

You'll have the best luck with cabs if you call for one and wait. Some cabs hang around the major downtown hotels, but rarely cruise near attractions. Cabs operate on a meter system. Basic charge is approximatey $1.10 per mile. Meters start at $1.10.

The city's major cab companies are City Cab 833-7060, Checker Cab 963-7000, American Cab 833-3800, Blue Eagle Cab 934-2000, and Detroit Cab 898-0600.

Railroads

Amtrak: 1-800-872-7245 or 222-1000 (Detroit number)

Detroit's Vernor Hwy. and Michigan Avenue station and Dearborn's Michigan Avenue and Greenfield Road station provide service to various parts of the country.

The one-hour train ride to Ann Arbor is a great way to introduce the kids to rail travel. Have a family member drive the family car to Ann Arbor and meet you at the station so you can explore Ann Arbor by car.

Canadian National Railroad: 963-7396 (Detroit number)

Air Travel

Detroit City Airport: 267-6400

Detroit Metropolitan Airport: 942-3685 (airport operations), 942-3550 (lost and found). Call individual airlines for departure and arrival information.

Windsor Airport: 519-969-2430

Northwest Airlines: Detroit's largest carrier 1-800-225-2525 (reservations) or 962-2002 (Detroit office, incoming flight information)

Limousine Service: Commuter Transportation Co. 941-3252. This is the major shuttle service between the airport and downtown hotels. A booth is located in the airport baggage claim area. They also have scheduled pickups from hotel to airport.

Rental Car Agencies

Detroit's largest and best-known national companies are Avis 964-0494, Hertz 759-5200, and National 941-5030.

Organized Tours

Charter Bus Unlimited: 962-3033

Dearborn Trolley: 274-6300

Detroit Department of Transportation: 933-1300

Detroit Historical Society: 833-7934

D-Tours: 855-2740

Kirby Tours: 963-8585

Steward McMillian Tours: 882-9940

Canada and Customs

For a quick trip abroad, take the Detroit-Windsor Tunnel or the Ambassador Bridge into Canada. Traveling through the tunnel and across the bridge will be a great adventure for children. There's plenty to do across the border, and the kids will marvel at the colorful Canadian currency

You can also drive into Canada across the Blue Water Bridge that connects Port Huron to Sarnia, Ontario. Lake Huron is on one side of the bridge; the St. Clair River is on the other.

U.S. citizens should carry with them a driver's license or proof of car ownership, personal identification, and birth certificate or naturalization papers. Landed immigrants should carry their passport. Foreign nationals should consult immigration officals for details on border crossing.

U.S. citizens are permitted to bring back duty-free up to $25 of personal or household merchandise per person. After 48 hours in Canada, the customs' exemption is $400 per person, including children.

There is a toll collected at each side of the Detroit River. It is $1.50 U.S. and $1.75 Canadian for passenger cars at the Detroit-Windsor Tunnel; $1.25 U.S. and $1.50 Canadian for passenger cars at the Ambassador Bridge. The Blue Water Bridge toll is 75 cents in either Canadian or U.S. currency.

U.S. Customs: 226-3138

U.S. Immigration: 226-3290

Canadian Customs: 519-253-7271

Canadian Immigration: 519-253-3006

Be sure the kids are buckled up. Both Michigan and Ontario have a seatbelt law.

Detroit's Best Kid Stuff

No guidebook is complete without a list of the area's best attractions. These sites have a proven track record and have been family favorites for many years. I offer this list knowing full well that when my children were small, they sometimes enjoyed the neighborhood playground more than a visit to Detroit's best children's sites. Apply your discretion in using this list. As your children grow, your family favorites will change. Check the index for a more complete listing.

Ann Arbor Hands-On Museum

Belle Isle Aquarium

Children's Museum (Flint)

Cranbrook Institute of Science

Detroit Historical Museum

Detroit Institute of Arts

Detroit People Mover

Detroit Science Center

Detroit Symphony Orchestra Young People's Concerts

Detroit Youtheatre

Detroit Zoological Park

Ella Sharp Museum

Greenfield Village and Henry Ford Museum

Historic Fort Wayne

Impression 5 Museum

Michigan Historical Museum

Michigan Space Center

University of Michigan Exhibit Museum

During the summer:

Boblo Island

Crossroads Village/Huckleberry Railroad

Four Bears Water Park

Meadow Brook Music Festival

Penny Whistle Place

3
MONTHLY
CALENDAR
OF SPECIAL EVENTS

We Michiganians love to celebrate our seasons, our ethnicity, our children, our products, our arts. Throughout the year, we hold hundreds of festivals and special events just perfect for family outings. Here is a monthly list of the area's best family-oriented annual events. Unless otherwise noted, all phone numbers listed are in the 313 area code. If I missed your favorite festival, please send me the information and we'll try to include it in this book's next edition.

Be sure to check *The Detroit News'* Kid Stuff Calendar weekly for more up-to-the-minute information. And keep a watchful eye on this calendar so you won't miss something special and have to wait an entire year for it to come around again.

January

Brighton Winterfest

If you love winter sports, you'll love this festival located throughout the Brighton area. There are downhill and cross-country ski events, dogsled races, snowmobiling, and a snow sculpture contest. 878-5064 or 227-5086.

Festival of Bands

Community bands from the Metro Detroit area join together for several sound-spectacular shows in Novi's Twelve Oaks Mall. 661-4610 or 661-4604.

North American International Auto Show

Cobo Hall is transformed into a glitzy automobile heaven for nine days beginning the first weekend in January. The kids will enjoy the excitement, the shiny new cars, trucks and vans, and the fun promotions and giveaways. 224-1010.

Parkey's Winter Break

Join Parkey the Panda for breakfast or lunch several times during the year. He entertains young children with games, arts and crafts, and story-telling. The Parkey series includes Valentine's Day, St. Patrick's Day, Easter, and Mother's Day. Sponsored by the Farmington Hills Recreation Department. 474-6115.

Plymouth Ice Sculpture Spectacular

Professional chefs and ice carvers from around the world work in frigid temperatures, wielding chisels and chain saws to create over 200 larger-than-life sculptures. Their ice art lines the streets of Plymouth's shopping district and fills Kresge Park. In order to see everything, dress warmly and put little ones in strollers. The Masonic Temple on Penniman, across from the park, sells hot chocolate and cookies. 453-1540 or 453-1620.

Sesame Street Live!

Cobo Arena hosts the 90-minute show of fast-paced song, dance, and vaudevillian routines performed by larger-than-life Sesame Street characters. Kids preschool to fourth grade will enjoy the heartwarming songs, colorful costumes, and silly shticks. 567-6000. For charging tickets by phone, Ticketmaster 645-6666.

February

African American History Month

Many cultural institutions hold special children's events, workshops, and activities to highlight Black history. Of great interest are the Detroit Institute of Arts (DIA) Youtheatre's Saturday performances by well-known African American theater troupes. Detroit Youtheatre, 833-2323.

Ann Arbor Winter Fest

Grab your cap and celebrate winter in Ann Arbor. The downtown is lined with giant snow sculptures. At William and Main Streets, there is a warming tent, refreshments, and ice-skating pond for the kids (they can "skate" in their boots). The weekend also has a lineup of cultural activities and children's plays. Usually the second weekend in February. Ann Arbor Vistor's Bureau, 995-7281.

Paczki Day

In other cities, the day before Lent might be called Shrove Tuesday or Fat Tuesday, but in Hamtramck the last day to indulge in goodies is called Paczki Day, so named for paczkis (pronounced poonsh-keys), delicious fruit-filled pastries. Bring home a dozen. Hamtramck Chamber of Commerce, 875-7877.

Parkey's Valentine Breakfast

Parkey the Panda is back for a breakfast complete with story and craft. Farmington Parks and Recreation, 474-6115.

Rochester Hills Winter Festival
Snow scuplting, ice fishing, broomball games, and dogsled races. It's time for a little organized winter fun. 656-4673.

Valentine's Day
Check your local library for a Valentine's story hour or craft program. Also many community parks and recreation programs hold father-daughter Valentine's Day dances.

March

Day of Puppetry
The Detroit Puppeteers Guild presents a day of puppet-making workshops and fine puppet performances. 898-6341 or 494-1210.

Detroit Kennel Club Dog Show
North America's largest, one-day, all-breed, benched dog show comes to Cobo Hall. A great opportunity to take the kids dog shopping. Call DKC-SHOW.

Don't Miss the Easter Bunny
The Easter Bunny's March/April calendar (depending on when Easter falls) is packed with special bunny breakfasts, candy egg hunts, storytelling, and songs. Sure, he's at every mall, but you might want to sign the kids up for some of the area's very special Easter Bunny events.
A sampling: "Easter Bunny Breakfasts," Hudson's Restaurants, 443-6247. "Easter Bunny Brunch," Grosse Pointe War Memorial, 881-7511. "Easter Egg Hunt," Melvindale Parks and Recreation, 928-1200. "Mr. Bunny Egg Hunt," West Bloomfield Parks and Recreation, 334-5660. "Easter Spring Fling," Springfield Oaks, 625-8133. "Easter Egg Scramble," Sterling Heights, 977-6200. "Easter Treasure Hunt," Dinosaur Hill, 656-0999. "Parkey's Easter Egg Hunt," Farmington Hills, 474-6115. "Eggstraordinary, Eggciting Eggs," Stony Creek Metropark, 781-4621. "Easter Egg Hunt," Southwest Detroit Parks and Recre-

ation, 297-9337. "Great Marshmallow Drop,"
Elizabeth Park, Trenton, 671-5220. The Easter
Bunny's Mother usually visits the Detroit
Youtheatre during its Easter-week perfor-
mances, 833-2323.

Guernsey Farm Dairy

The dairy in Northville offers a free, once-a-
year tour of its ice cream plant, plus a St. Pad-
dy's Day party. 1-5 p.m., the Sunday before St.
Pat's Day. 349-1466.

The Ice Capades

Ninety dazzling minutes full of showman-
ship, glitz, and talent. For little children, there
are always several numbers with cartoon-cos-
tumed skaters; in 1990 the ice was full of characters from Nintendo's Mario Brothers. Joe
Louis Arena, 567-6000. For charging tickets by
phone, Ticketmaster 645-6666.

Ice Shows—A March Sampling

The ice shows cometh in March and continue through May at area ice arenas. Here's a
chance to see earnest local skaters strut their
stuff in creative and colorful numbers. Your
kids will adore seeing other children perform.
Call for dates and times. Trenton's Kennedy
Ice Arena, 676-7179. Birmingham Ice Arena,
645-0730. St. Clair Shores Civic Arena, 774-
7530. Westland Sports Arena, 729-4560.
Wyandotte's Yack Arena, 281-7813.

Maple's Sweet Story

Area metroparks offer maple sugar demonstrations and walks through sugar bush country, with hands-on tastes. Weekends, throughout March. Kensington Farm Center, 685-
1561; or Indian Springs Nature Center, 685-
1561 ext. 482; or call toll-free, 1-800-47-
PARKS.

Maple Syrup Festival

Step up close to the big maples and snitch
a taste of the running sap, then walk over to
the Sugar House and watch the sap being processed into maple syrup. Cranbrook Institute
of Science offers children a look behind the

grocery store shelves. Several weekends in March. 645-3200.

The Matzah Factory

See how matzah (unleavened bread used during the Jewish holiday of Passover) is made. Kids wear baker's caps and are offered hands-on experience, plus a sample to take home. Jewish Community Center, West Bloomfield, 661-1000.

Purim Carnival

The ancient Jewish holiday is celebrated with a costume parade, food, carnival games, storytelling, and hamantaschen baking. Hamantaschen are traditional, sweet, fruit-filled pastries. Designed for kids preschool to early elementary. Jewish Community Center, West Bloomfield, 661-1000.

Royal Hanneford Circus

In addition to clowns, trapeze artists, and jugglers, this circus is famous for wonderful animal acts. See trained tigers, ponies, sea lions, dogs, and bears. The Palace, 377-0100.

St. Patrick's Day

One of Detroit's liveliest parades takes place the Sunday before St. Patrick's Day with lots of green hoopla and a stroll down Michigan Avenue in Corktown. Check newspaper listings for a full schedule of events, including Irish folksinging and ethnic dancing at local halls. Or call the Irish-American Club, 964-8700.

The Shrine Circus

Wild animals, cavorting clowns, prancing horses, daring trapeze artists—everything you always wanted in a circus and more. The kids can see from almost every seat in the State Fair Coliseum, 368-1000.

Spring Vacation Programs

A variety of community institutions, parks and recreation programs, and area libraries offer programs for children during spring break. A sampling: "Children's Easter Vacation

Festival" — free movies, mime, puppets, magic, and stories at the Detroit Public Library, 833-4029. "Spring Banner Days" — free movies at the Southfield Public Library, 354-5342. "Spring Vacation Program" — daily swim, field trip, games, and crafts at the Farmington YMCA, 553-4020.

April

Baby Animal Day
Upland Hills Farms brings the farm animals to the city, at the Birmingham Community House. 644-5832.

Celebration of Spring
A lumberjack festival, Arbor Day ceremony, and youth bike safety skills clinic. Cobblestone Farm and Buhr Park, Ann Arbor, 994-2928.

Detroit Public Schools Student Exhibition
Detroit school children share their dreams and visions in this joyous annual show (now over half a century old), which fills the Detroit Institute of Arts with puppets, drawings, sculpture, paintings, textiles, mixed media, and photography. Your kids will become inspired to run home and create. 833-7900.

Downriver Schools Art Festival
Downriver students celebrate the arts and showcase their talents. Folk dancing, drama, and jazz band are some of the special performances. 283-8933.

Ice Shows — An April Sampling
Melvindale Ice Arena, 928-1200. Southfield Ice Arena, 354-9357. Dearborn's Adray Arena, 582-7470.

Kitefest
Join kite enthusiasts at Kalamazoo's River Oaks Park for a special weekend full of kite flying demonstrations, kite making workshops, and a celebration of the balmy winds of spring. The last weekend in April. 616-383-8778.

Law Day
The police and fire departments of Allen Park and Melvindale team up to demonstrate their wares and their capabilities. Kids are encouraged to touch and try. 928-0535.

Muppet Babies
The plot is not very sophisticated, but kids will enjoy singing and clapping along with their favorite cartoon characters. The Fox Theatre hosts Muppet babies Kermit, Miss Piggy, and their friends. To charge tickets by phone, Ticketmaster 645-6666.

Sheepshearing Day
It's a Scottish Spring Festival at the Rochester Hills Museum complete with sheepshearing, old-fashioned craft demonstrations, bagpipes, highland dancing, and authentic food. 656-4663.

May

Children's Flea Market and Carnival
Collectibles of all kinds, plus a carnival. Children's Museum, 494-1210.

Civil War Days
Historic Fort Wayne opens for the season with a Civil War re-enactment. Usually the first weekend of May. 297-9360.

Eastern Market Flower Day
Pile the kids in the little red wagon, stroll around Eastern Market, and buy your spring flowers at bargain prices. Be prepared for crowds. Usually mid-May and again in mid-June. 833-1560.

Good Old Summertime Family Day
Celebrate Memorial Day with an old-fashioned family picnic, complete with clowns, pony rides, fireworks, petting farm, plus park facilities. Independence Oaks County Park, 858-0906.

Heritage Day
The Troy Historical Museum sponsors a day of old-fashioned craft demonstrations, musical entertainment, and speech making in the style of Abe Lincoln. Usually the first weekend in May. 524-3570.

Heritage Festival
Rochester Municipal Park is the site of old-fashioned family fun, including a pioneer homestead, petting farm, craft booths, demonstrations, and pony rides. Usually the end of May. 656-0999.

Ice Shows — A May Sampling
Fraser Hockeyland, 294-2400. Berkley Ice Arena, 546-2460. Garden City Ice Arena, 261-3491.

International Kite Fly-In
Twenty-two acres of kite flyers demonstrate the beauty, grace, and just plain fun of this pastime. Historic Fort Wayne, 297-9360.

It's All Happening at the Zoo
Belle Isle Zoo, Detroit Zoo Train, and Log Cabin Learning Center open for the season May 1. 398-0900.

Memorial Day Parades
Check your local city office for Memorial Day parade activities. These parades are very spirited, noisy, and full of local color.

Michigan Student Film and Video Festival
Continuous showing of winning films by students in kindergarten through 12th grade. Detroit Public Library. 285-7906.

Michigan Taste Fest
Celebrate Memorial Day weekend in Detroit's New Center Area with continuous children's entertainment, hands-on crafts and activities, samples of made-in-Michigan products and specialties of Michigan chefs, plus evening concerts by nationally known musicians. 872-0188.

Renaissance City Storyfest
A Wayne State University conference that offers evening storytelling concerts, perfect for family entertainment. 577-6296.

Spring Festival
Spring has sprung at the Kensington Farm and Nature Centers. There are lots of baby animals, sheep-shearing and wood-carving demonstrations, hayrides, and wildflower walks. 685-1561.

√
flyer
Tulip Time
Holland is ablaze with tulips, costumed dancers, musical shows, and parades, all celebrating the city's Dutch heritage. Usually the second week of May. Holland Chamber of Commerce, 616-396-4221.

WDET Music Festival
Children's Hospital of Michigan hosts a children's activity area as well as children's stage with a full schedule of performers, musicians, and clowns as part of WDET's Music Festival, held at Meadow Brook Music Festival. Proceeds benefit Children's Hospital. 745-5373 or 577-4146.

June

Belleville Strawberry Festival
call
Strawberry lovers, rejoice! Belleville, one of the Detroit area's biggest strawberry producers, celebrates the crop with a weekend of games, parades, and children's entertainment. 697-3137.

Carrousel of Nations
call
Windsor's many ethnic and cultural communities sponsor two weekends of multi-cultural experiences. Experience foods, sights, dances, and sounds of many cultures. 519-255-1127.

Children's Grove at the Frankenmuth Bavarian Festival
call
The Children's Grove includes a petting

farm, kinder haus with hands-on craft activities, and theater tent with hourly puppet, clown, and musical show. Usually held mid-June. 517-652-8155.

A Fort Night Celebration

Watch the International Freedom Festival's culminating fireworks spectacular from Historic Fort Wayne. Refreshments and music add to the excitement. 297-9360. *For more information on Historic Fort Wayne, see* Historic Sites.

Henry Ford Day

Celebrate the anniversary of Henry Ford's birth with a day of old-fashioned family fun, including storytellers, clowns, jugglers, magicians, games, and food. Held early June on the grounds of Henry Ford Estate–Fairlane, Dearborn, 593-5590.

International Freedom Festival

Beginning mid-June through July 4, there are over 100 events celebrating the friendship between Canada and the United States, including parades, music, fireworks, boat races, and of particular note, two Children's Days. Windsor's Children's Day is held along the riverfront mid-June with a big wheel grand prix and a teddy bear picnic. Detroit's Children's Day is held in the University Cultural Center usually the last Wednesday in June. It's a "don't miss" potpourri of entertainment and hands-on activities sponsored by all Cultural Center institutions. 259-5400 (Detroit), 519-252-7264 (Windsor).

Muzzle Loaders Festival

Hundreds of costumed participants colorfully depict Civil War life. This is the first of many theme weekends held throughout the summer and fall at Greenfield Village. 271-1620. *For more information on Greenfield Village, see* Historic Sites.

Oak Park Funfest

Ten days of special activities celebrating Independence Day, including a parade, fireworks, and children's fun day. 545-6400.

July

Ann Arbor Art Fair

Besides the displays by fine artists, there's enough food, street musicians (have you ever seen a grown man playing a piano in the middle of the street?), and stage entertainers to turn any child on to art. Be sure to take your budding artists over to Liberty Plaza on Liberty Street for the great Chalk Art-a-Thon. Usually held the third week in July. 994-5260.

Battle Creek International Balloon Championship

During the middle of this eight-day festival is children's day, when children meet Tony the Tiger, Ronald McDonald, and McGruff, and enjoy balloon launches, special entertainment, and games. 616-962-0592.

Children's Celebration

Flint's Cultural Center sets the stage for a day of hands-on activities and children's shows. Usually held mid-July. 762-1169.

Children's Days at the Ann Arbor Summer Festival

Free children's entertainment, dance, and gymnastic demonstrations precede the special headlining children's show. Usually several consecutive Sundays in early July. 747-2278.

July Fourth Festivities and Parades

Check you local city for parade and fireworks schedules. Area historic villages also offer special July Fourth activities. A sampling: Cobblestone Farm, Ann Arbor, 994-2928; Greenfield Village, Dearborn, 271-1620; Crossroads Village, Flint, 736-7100.

Port Huron's Blue Water Festival

Port Huron comes to life with family fun, including a carnival, midway, parade, and entertainment. 985-9623.

August

Abbott's Magic Get-Together
Magicians from all over the world meet in Colon, Michigan, to swap ideas, buy and sell magic paraphernalia, and practice their art. The public is invited to several shows during the four-day convention, held early August. 616-432-3235.

Medieval Festival
Wandering minstrels, musicians, and many other costumed participants — beggars, mimes, wenches, courtly ladies, jugglers, buffoons, smiths, fools, and monks — recreate a medieval village on University of Michigan's North Campus, in Ann Arbor. Craftspeople demonstrate their wares; players perform. The atmosphere is rowdy and fun. Another advantage — it's free. Usually held the first weekend in August. 995-7281.

Michigan Festival
Say Yes! to Michigan and celebrate Michigan's homegrown culture, ethnic diversity, folk crafts, and performers. Ten days of continuous performances on ten different stages, held all over the Michigan State University Campus, in East Lansing. The Children's Stage and Creation Station feature children's entertainers and hands-on science and art projects. The Main Stage offers nationally known entertainers. Usually held mid-August. 517-351-6620.

Michigan State Fair
The Michigan farmer is still at the heart of this granddaddy of all Michigan fairs. Kids will love viewing the award-winning animals, collecting free made-in-Michigan samples in the coliseum, feeding the animals at the petting farm, and cheering for the little porkers in the Kowalski Pig Races. Every day offers a full variety of specialty acts (demolition derby, monster trucks, wrestling) and nationally known entertainers. I recommend taking advantage of all the fair freebies; midway rides are very ex-

pensive. Held the last weekend in August through the first weekend in September. 368-1000.

Oakland County 4-H Fair
Springfield Oaks in Davisburg hosts livestock exhibits, demolition derby, pro-wrestling, a truck pull, and carnival rides. Usually opens the fifth Monday, prior to Labor Day. 634-8830.

Renaissance Festival
The sixteenth century comes to vivid life with authentically costumed roving players, jugglers and jousters, wenches and knaves, a village marketplace, plus Renaissance-flavored games and rides. The kids will enjoy the continuous merriment and ribald entertainment. Held weekends in the Holly area from mid-August through the end of September. "Childhood's Quest," a weekend with special children's activities, is usually held the first weekend. 645-9640.

Ypsilanti Heritage Festival
Parades, concerts, living history encampment, old-fashioned circus, and antique car shows highlight Ypsilanti's historical past. Usually held at the end of August. 482-4920.

September

Art in the Park
While Mom and Dad browse through the art fair, children can create at the art station and have their faces painted. Usually held the second weekend in September. Shaine Park, Birmingham. 645-1173.

Autumn Fest
Watch apple cider and honey being made, jump into a haystack, and play old-fashioned harvest games at Cranbrook Institute of Science, Bloomfield Hills. Several consecutive weekends at the end of September. 645-3220.

Autumnfest
The city of Southfield celebrates its pioneer history with a day full of butter churning, rug weaving, farm animals, dancing, singing, and touring the old Mary Thompson home, built in 1831. Usually the second Sunday of the month. 354-9603.

Autumn Harvest Festival
It's autumn at Greenfield Village in Dearborn. Celebrate the changing season with harvest activities, cider making, and entertainment. Held the last weekend in September. 271-1620

Channel 2's Great Balloon Festival
Green Oak Township's Huron Meadows Recreational Area hosts a day of hot-air ballooning plus acrobatic air shows, skydivers, arts and crafts, clowns, jugglers, mimes, and magicians. 557-2000.

**Children's Fair at the Detroit
Festival of Arts**
Join Detroit's biggest street party and celebrate the arts. More than 70 free activities for children, including face painting, puppet making, chalk drawing, musical performances, and storytelling, plus a chance to act as TV anchors in Channel 2's model television studio. Held on the Wayne State University Campus, mid-September. 577-5088.

Detroit Mini Grand Prix
The New Center Area hosts a mini grand prix for the entire family. While 50 three-horsepower go-carts race in seven heats, Kids Korner offers children's activities: clowns, jugglers, balloon animals, free ice cream, storytelling, crafts, video games, and more. Usually a mid-September Saturday. West Grand Boulevard and Second, Detroit, 875-MINI.

Fall Festival
Ann Arbor's Cobblestone Farm sponors a traditional nineteenth-century harvest festival featuring cooking, crafts, hayrides, and a corn husking bee. 994-2928.

Fall Festival

Kensington Metropark celebrates the season with family activities: hay rides, puppet shows, woodcraft demonstrations, nature crafts, clowns, candle dipping, and apple cider making. Usually a mid-September weekend. 685-1561.

Royal Oak Grand National

Kids thrill to the sights and sounds of over 30 remote control, quarter-scale cars vrooming around a 150-lap race course. Music, mimes, clowns, food, and face painting turn downtown Royal Oak into a large street fair. Usually held on a mid-September Saturday. 547-4000.

Stroh's Montreux/Detroit Jazz Festival

Just for kids — listen as Michigan high school and college bands jazz it up and get into the action. Held the first week in September. 259-5400.

Wiard's Orchards Country Fair

It's a country fair every September and October weekend, at Wiard's Orchards in Ypsilanti. You can pick apples and pumpkins, take a pony or miniature train ride, play games, watch craft demonstrations, listen to country music, and eat harvest foods. 482-7744.

October

Civil War Fall Lantern Tours

Authentically uniformed narrators conduct guided tours through lantern-lit sally-ports, tunnels, and bastions of Detroit's Historic Fort Wayne. Two evenings in October. 297-9360.

Detroit Youtheatre

The Youtheatre kicks off its season at the beginning of October offering performances of puppetry, mime, music, drama, and children's entertainers. Every Saturday through May. 833-2323.

Fall Fun Days at Symanzik's Berry Farm

Walk through a corn stock forest into a pumpkin patch bathed in sunlight. Children can pick their own pumpkins and gourds, play in a mock barn, visit farm animals, and take a ride on "space trollies." Weekends during October. 636-7714, 636-2775.

Halloween Parties

During the last two weeks of October, little ghosts and goblins are invited to costume parties and haunting nature walks at area institutions. A Sampling: "Zoo Boo," at the Detroit Zoo, 398-0900. Belle Isle Zoo's "Halloween Zoobilee," 267-7160. "Sir Pumpkin's Pumpkin Junction" at Freedom Hill in Mount Clemens, 979-8750.   Rochester's   Dinosaur   Hill "Halloween Hoot," a walk through a haunted forest, 656-0999. Independence Oaks' "Nature Fears and Halloween Fables," a story walk through the woods, 625-6473. "Halloween Haunt" at Cranbrook Institute of Science, 645-3200. "Bloomer Haunted Forest" in West Bloomfield, 334-5660. "Spooky Saturday" at Flint's Sloan Museum, 762-1169. "Ghosts and Goblins" at Detroit's Historical Museum, 833-1805.

Harvest Home Festival

The Troy Historical Museum sponsors nineteenth-century fall harvest activities for the entire family. Bob for apples, design your own scarecrow, participate in a hay bale toss or corn husk and shelling contest. Usually early October. 524-3570.

Harvest Jubilee

All aboard! Enjoy a fall color tour on the Huckleberry Railroad, near Flint. Then walk around historic Crossroads Village and enjoy country bands, cider making, kite flying exhibitions, and craft demonstrations. Usually mid-October. 736-7100.

Old World Market

The International Institute houses Detroit's largest ethnic festival, full of food, music, and crafts of over 25 nationalities. Usually mid-October. 871-8600.

Pioneer Days
The Waterloo Farm in Stockbridge comes to life with demonstrations of nineteenth-century fall harvest crafts, food, and music. Usually the first Sunday in October. 517-851-8247.

Ringling Brothers and Barnum & Bailey Circus
The circus comes to town with ferocious tigers, majestic elephants, silly clowns, and daring trapeze artists. Did you expect anything less? Usually early October. 567-6000 or for charging tickets by phone, Ticketmaster 645-6666.

Southern Michigan Railroad Fall Color Tours
The fall color tour leaves Tecumseh and Clinton each weekend in October for a one-hour-and-twenty-minute ride. 517-456-7677.

Upland Hills Pumpkin Festival
Upland Hills Farms in Oxford turns your pumpkin picking into a Halloween experience. On hand are the Great Pumpkin, Hildegard the Witch, and Farmer Webster, plus hay and pony rides, a petting farm, country fiddler, play area, haunted house, and harvest foods. Weekends during October. 628-1611.

November

Detroit A Glow/Community Sing-a-long
Crowds gather after work on the Monday before Thanksgiving to watch as the Hart Plaza Christmas tree lights are turned on. A community sing-a-long is held in Cobo Arena following the lighting ceremony. 961-1403

Detroit Thanksgiving Festival
Floating bumblebees, the seven dwarfs, dinosaurs, and Santa himself. Detroit's answer to the Macy's Parade takes place along Woodward Avenue on Thanksgiving Day morning.

Dress warmly and arrive early for a good view. The parade kicks off a week-long Thanksgiving celebration including a Children's Parade at the Detroit Zoo (the Sunday before the big parade), Little Gobbler's Race (the morning of the parade), and other special events. Don't miss Santa's Studio Tour (the Saturday and Sunday after the parade). You'll be able to take a behind-the-scenes peek at parade construction and see up close the giant inflatables and papier-mache head collection. 923-7400.

Festival of Trees

Cobo Hall is transformed by 100 profesionally decorated trees, a gingerbread village, and an aisle of wreaths. Children can visit with Santa in Santaland. Begins just before Thanksgiving and runs through Thanksgiving weekend. 224-1010.

Kidstuff

Henry Ford believed in "learning by doing," so the folks at the Henry Ford Museum offer a Thanksgiving weekend full of creative, hands-on activities for families, including live performances, storytelling, treasure hunts, invention stations, games, and toys. 271-1976.

Moscow Circus

Lions, tigers and bears, plus dazzling high wire acts and zany clowns, all with a touch of Russian humor. Early November. The Palace of Auburn Hills, 377-0100. For charging tickets by phone, Ticketmaster 645-6666.

Science Toys Weekend

Make your own discoveries and learn something about science while exploring with toys and games. Special planetarium, laser, and auditorium shows round off the Thanksgiving weekend's special activities. Cranbrook Institute of Science, 645-3200.

Walt Disney's Magic Kingdom on Ice

Mickey Mouse and his friends fill the ice at Joe Louis Arena with color and movement as they act out a favorite Disney story. Usually early November. 567-6000. Ticketmaster 645-6666.

December

Detroit's holiday season officially opens with Santa's grand arrival during the Thanksgiving Parade. From November 24 through December 31, the city is a child's paradise, decorated in tinsel and lights, full of jolly St. Nicks at every mall. Families have their pick of puppets, plays, concerts, caroling, parades, festivals, workshops, and breakfasts with Santa. Here is a sampling of the city's very special holiday events. Keep an eye on your newspaper calendars for specific times and dates.

Puppets, Plays, Shows, and Concerts

Children's Classics
The following theaters and troupes have fine productions of children's classics during December: Detroit Youtheatre, Detroit, 833-2323. Marquis Theatre, Northville, 349-8110. Greenfield Village Theatre Company, Dearborn, 271-1620. Macomb Center for the Performing Arts, Mount Clemens, 286-2222. Flint Youtheatre, Flint, 239-6772. Bonstelle Theatre, Detroit, 577-2960 (every other year they perform "A Christmas Carol"). Peanut Butter Players, Detroit, 559-6-PBP. Grosse Pointe Children's Theatre, Grosse Pointe, 881-7511.

A Christmas Carol
Don't forget to treat the kids to their annual dose of Scrooge and Bob Cratchit. Two theaters annually perform the classic tale: Macomb Center for the Performing Arts, Mount Clemens, 286-2222. Meadow Brook Theater, Rochester, 377-3300.

Harlem Globetrotters
With their famous theme song "Sweet Georgia Brown" playing in the background, the Globetrotters skip around the Joe Louis Arena and The Palace, showing off fancy footwork and basketball tricks. Kids love the teasing

banter and the surprises. If you sit up close, you might get a free treat . . . or quite wet. Usually early December. 567-6000 (Joe Louis), 377-0100 (The Palace).

Holiday Planetarium and Lasera Shows

Cranbrook Institute of Science offers the holiday lasera show, "Ornaments," and two holiday planetarium shows, "The Christmas Star" and "Wonderful Rocket," 645-3200. The Children's Museum in Detroit offers two holiday planetarium shows, 494-1210. University of Michigan Exhibit Museum Planetarium, offers two holiday planetarium shows, 764-0478. Holiday planetarium shows are also offered at Flint's Longway Planetarium, 762-1181, and MSU's Abrams Planetarium, 517-355-4672.

Nutcracker Suite

There will be many performances of the Nutcracker this month. Each triumphs the season with vibrant and magical costumes, scenery, music, and dance. The Detroit Symphony Orchestra with Marygrove Dancers at the Fox Theatre, Detroit, 833-3700. The Birmingham-Bloomfield Symphony with the Michigan Ballet Theater at West Bloomfield High School, West Bloomfield, 643-7288. The Ann Arbor Chamber Music Orchestra and the Ann Arbor Civic Ballet at Michigan Theater, Ann Arbor, 668-8397.

Snoopy's World of Magic

Snoopy becomes the "Great Snoopini" and takes the Peanuts gang on a magic carpet ride full of magic tricks and illusions. Usually early December. The Palace, 377-0100. For charging tickets by phone, Ticketmaster 645-6666.

Old-Fashioned Villages and Out-of-the-Ordinary Visits with Santa

Brunch with Santa

After a child-pleasing brunch, Santa arrives by helicopter and visits with the children. The day ends with gifts and caroling. Grosse Pointe War Memorial, Grosse Pointe Farms. Several Saturdays in December. Call for reservations. 881-7511.

A Child's World at Christmas

Dearborn's Henry Ford Museum relives Christmas traditions from past generations. There's a towering tree decorated with cookies, candy, and small toys; an animated Lionel train layout; and holiday puppet show. Santa presides over all the merriment. Early December through early January. 271-1620.

Christmas at Crossroads

Flint's Victorian village is decked out in holiday cheer, with special Christmas shows, traditional crafts, and rides in horse-drawn wagons, sleighs, or on the Huckleberry Railroad. From Thanksgiving weekend through the end of December. 736-7100.

Christmas at the Detroit Historical Museum

Don't miss the annual old-fashioned holiday fun: the decorated Old Detroit Streets, the miniature Lionel train chugging around an antique village, and the exhibit of antique children's toys. 833-1805.

Christmas Carnival

Cobo Hall becomes a large indoor playground, decorated for the holidays with animated displays. Wait in line to see Santa. Daily, the first two weeks of December. 224-1109.

Christmas Festival of Lights

Ann Arbor's Domino's Farms lights up with decorated trees, caroling and family entertainment. Three weekends in December. 995-4500.

Christmas Past In Greenfield Village

The village is decked out in holiday finery. Costumed staff demonstrate old-fashioned crafts, food preparation, and decorating. Plus holiday music, sleigh rides, shopping, and an 1850s holiday meal in the Eagle Tavern. Early December through early January. 271-1620.

Detroit Zoo Winter Wonderland
Holiday lights, treats, a special holiday show, and a visit with Santa. Evenings throughout December. Detroit Zoo, Royal Oak, 398-0903.

Hanging of the Greens
Create holiday ornaments, listen to holiday music, and stroll through the decorated historic village at the Troy Historical Museum. First Sunday in December. 524-3570.

Holiday in Lights
The Detroit Visitor Information Center offers maps for a self-guided driving tour of Detroit and Windsor's holiday decorations. 567-1170.

Holly's Olde-Fashioned Christmas Festival
Quaint shops, seasonal decorations, entertainment, and strolling characters from *A Christmas Carol* create a festive mood in Holly's Battle Alley. Weekends throughout December. 634-9331.

Noel Night
The University Cultural Center is aglow with lights, music, choirs, plus activities and entertainment for children inside and outside all the institutions. Early December. 577-5088.

Santa's at the Detroit Institute of Arts
Santa holds court on weekends in the Kresge Court Cafe. Breakfast with Santa during the week requires an advance reservation. Thanksgiving weekend through mid-December. 833-2323.

Santa's Workshop
Take a trail through the snowy woods to Santa's workshop, meet with him, enjoy a bowl of oyster stew, and receive a small present. Henry Ford Estate-Fairlane, Dearborn. Early December. Call for reservations: 593-5590.

Storytime with Santa and the Animals

Enjoy a puppet show, chat with Santa, make a bird feeder, and take a trail walk. Dinosaur Hill Nature Preserve, Rochester. Second Sunday in December. Call for reservations. 656-0999.

A Wondrous Christmas at
Meadow Brook Hall

Knole Cottage, a six-room children's playhouse on the grounds of Meadow Brook Hall, becomes Santa's home for 12 days after Thanksgiving. Older children will appreciate the decorations and floral displays in Meadow Brook Hall, the 120-room mansion. 370-3140.

4
MUSEUMS

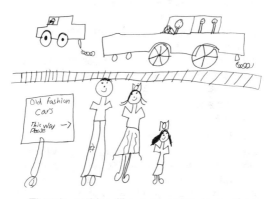

There's nothing like a museum to awaken children's creativity and curiosity about the world. Yet, even a museum full of dinosaur bones, space suits, African masks, or Van Goghs can be a formidable place for a young child. Try to make the museum outing match your child's temperament and interests. Never try to see everything. Just spend a brief time (no more than two hours at a time) visiting several exhibits. Take a break to have a snack — kids will remember giant cookies, space ice cream, or peppermint sticks — and be sure to visit the gift shop. Most area museums have a wide variety of children's toys, books, and trinkets, many for under $3. Leave before everyone is exhausted, let your children take home a special gift, and they'll be eager to return.

Abbreviations: SP — site offers school programs; T — site offers group tours; H — wheelchair accessible.

SP T H	Natural History

Alfred P. Sloan Museum
1221 East Kearsley Street, Flint
313-762-1169

Location: Flint's Cultural Center, off of I-475 and I-69 in downtown Flint

Hours: 10 a.m.-5 p.m. Tuesday-Friday. Noon-5 p.m., Saturday and Sunday. Open 10 a.m.-5 p.m., Monday during July and August. Closed major holidays.

Admission: $3 adults, $2.50 seniors, $2 children 5 to 12, under 5 free. Group rates and family memberships available.

Ages: 3 and up

Plan: Half day visit

Parking: Free on site

Lunch: Picnic area on front lawn. Windmill Place and Water Street Pavilion, two indoor festival marketplaces, are located nearby and offer a wide variety of food booths. Or try Halo Burger, Flint's fast-food burger.

Facilities: Bathrooms, drinking fountain. The museum store has a large collection of dinosaur gifts.

The Sloan is primarily known for its large collection of antique and experimental cars tracing the city's love affair with the automobile. The museum is also full of engaging exhibits covering the spectrum of natural history. Peek into a large, well-furnished dollhouse, meet Sheriff Tuffy Tooth, play hands-on games in a Health Education gallery, and step back into Genessee County history in the recreated fur trader's cabin, lumber camp, and pioneer log cabin. Small children will marvel at the mastodon skeleton; older children will be interested in the Pierson's Children's Gallery, which features finely crafted dolls resembling famous people in world history.

NEARBY SITES:

Cultural Center: Flint Institute of Arts, Longway Planetarium

In town: AC Spark Plug Tour, Buick City Tour, Michigan Humane Society, Children's Museum

During the summer: Penny Whistle Place, Crossroads Village/Huckleberry Railroad, Mott Farm

SP T H   Hands-On Science

Ann Arbor Hands-On Museum
219 East Huron Street, Ann Arbor
313-995-5439

Location: Downtown Ann Arbor, across from City Hall, at the corner of Fifth and Huron Streets.

Hours: 10 a.m.-5:30 p.m., Tuesday-Friday, 10 a.m.-5 p.m., Saturday. 1-5 p.m., Sunday. Groups can make special arrangements for morning visits. Children's classes are held on Saturday mornings.

Admission: $7.50 family, $3 adults, $2 children and seniors, 3 and under free. Family memberships available.

Ages: All ages

Plan: Half day visit. Once the kids get busy, they won't want to leave.

Parking: Structures on adjacent streets, or use metered street parking

Lunch: There are many restaurants on the U of M campus. For fast food close by: Burger King on Liberty Street, McDonald's on Maynard.

Facilities: Bathrooms, elevator, and imaginatively stocked gift shop

Become enveloped in a bubble; make waves; fly a mini hot air balloon; command a robotic arm; play tic-tac-toe with soft foam balls; create a rainbow; climb into a structure of reflecting mirrors. The Ann Arbor Hands-On Museum is one of the area's most ambitious and successful "please-touch" museums. Four floors of exhibits offer would-be scientists a variety of sensory experiences and just plain fun.

On your first visit, it takes a few minutes to get accustomed to the activity. If you're visiting with preschoolers, start on the second floor with the bubbles and Discovery Room. Older elementary children enjoy the third floor's darkened optics and light gallery and the fourth floor's computers and games.

NEARBY SITES:
On or near campus: Ann Arbor Farmers' Market, Kerrytown Plaza, Museum of Art, UofM Exhibit Museum and Planetarium, Ecology Center of Ann Arbor
North Campus: Phoenix Memorial Laboratory, UofM Matthaei Botanical Gardens, Domino's Farms, Leslie Science Center, Stearns Collection of Musical Instruments
South of campus: Cobblestone Farm, Scrap Box

`SP T`   `Ethnic`

Arab-American Folk Museum
Arab Community Center
2651 Saulino Court, Dearborn
313-842-7010

Location: Between Vernor and Dix Roads
Hours: 9 a.m.-5 p.m., Monday-Friday
Admission: Free
Ages: All ages
Plan: Under one hour
Parking: Use lot in front of the center
Lunch: Many ethnic eateries nearby
Facilities: Bathrooms, library, lounge

Winding through the hallways of the community center are wall-mounted display cases of Arab heirlooms and treasures as well as artifacts demonstrating Arab culture, history and lifestyle. Included are Saudi Arabian rugs, pots and baskets, and scale models of Middle Eastern architecture.

NEARBY SITES:
Detroit Water Department-Springwells Water Plant

SP T H   Art

Art Gallery of Windsor
445 Riverside Drive, Windsor
Ontario, Canada
519-258-7111

Location: Riverside Drive and Bruce Street

Hours: 11 a.m.-5 p.m., Tuesday, Wednesday, Saturday. 11 a.m.-9 p.m., Thursday and Friday. 1-5 p.m., Sunday

Admission: Free

Ages: 6 and up

Plan: Short visit

Parking: Use lot on the corner of Bruce and Pitt Streets

Lunch: Third floor Gallery Cafe restaurant is a cafeteria with a great view of the Detroit River and skyline

Facilities: Bathrooms. Gift shop offers children's items.

The Art Gallery of Windsor is a spacious, attractive building whose collection represents two centuries of Canadian art. The gallery is small enough that children are able to walk through without becoming tired and they will find lots of visually exciting objects — especially the outdoor and Inuit sculpture. A children's gallery on the second floor also offers changing exhibits. Hands-on workshops, films, and multi-cultural events are offered throughout the year.

NEARBY SITES:
Hiram Walker Historical Museum, city parks, Windsor City Market

SP H   Culture & Arts

Children's Museum
67 East Kirby, Detroit
313-494-1210

Location: In the Cultural Center, just north of the Detroit Institute of Arts. A prancing silver horse sculpture made of chrome car bumpers sits on the front lawn.

Hours: 1-4 p.m., Monday-Friday. 9 a.m.-4 p.m., Saturday. Workshops 10 a.m. and 2 p.m. every Saturday during the school year and 2 p.m., Monday-Friday during the summer. Planetarium shows, 11 a.m and 1 p.m., Saturdays; afternoons only during the summer.

Admission: Free for museum. $1 for workshops

Ages: Geared to elemetary school age children

Plan: Half day, including workshop and planetarium show

Parking: Use metered parking along Kirby or park in the Science Center lot on John R ($2) and walk a block to the museum

Lunch: The DIA Kresge Court Cafe is across the street

Facilities: Bathrooms, drinking fountain. Gift shop with lots of handmade and educational toys and gifts.

The Children's Museum is one of Detroit's best kept secrets. Its Saturday morning and summer afternoon workshops are consistently well-organized, creative explorations of the arts, taught by Detroit Public School teachers. Throughout the house are displays of stuffed and live animals, musical instruments, puppets, old-fashioned toys, boats and ethnic crafts. Be sure to notice the large, elaborately furnished Jeremiah Hudson dollhouse.

The Planetarium shows, held in a small, intimate room, and offered with a sense of humor and wonder, are wonderful first-time stargazing experiences for young children.

NEARBY SITES:
Cultural Center: Detroit Institute of Arts, Detroit Historical Museum, Museum of African American History, International Institute, Detroit Public Library, Detroit Science Center, Your Heritage House

SP T H   Hands-On Creative Play

Children's Museum
432 North Saginaw Street, Flint
313-238-6900

Location: On basement level of the Northbank Center building, downtown Flint, North Saginaw and Second Avenue

Hours: 10 a.m.-5 p.m., Monday-Saturday. Noon-5 p.m., Sunday. Special workshops held on Saturdays throughout the year.

Admission: $9 family, $2 general. Group rates and family memberships available.

Ages: 2 to 13 years

Plan: Half day

Parking: Free parking on Second Avenue and Harrison

Lunch: Juice machine. Picnic areas on south side of building. Water Street Pavilion, an indoor food emporium, is several blocks away.

Facilities: Bathroom, drinking fountains, elevator. Small gift shop with lots of inexpensive items.

With carefully planned true-to-life displays, Flint's Children's Museum invites children to role-play various occupations and hobbies, providing them with the props and costumes for pretending. Children become firefighters, dentists, doctors, judges, clowns, and musicians. There's a bank vault, a jail, and a child-sized TV studio, where a child can become a weather forecaster or talk-show host. There's a Cinderella Coach and a Red Baron airplane, plus an atrium full of bones, stones, and insects. Children also like to play with "Stuffee," a five-foot-tall stuffed character, who comes complete with removeable lungs, heart, appendix, stomach and other organs. Your kids won't want to leave.

NEARBY SITES:
In town: AC Spark Plug Tour, Buick City Tour, Michigan Humane Society
Cultural Center: Flint Institute of Arts, Alfred P. Sloan Museum, Longway Planetarium
During the summer: Penny Whistle Place, Crossroads Village/Huckleberry Railroad, Mott Farm

---

SP T H   Art

Cranbrook Academy of Art Museum
500 Lone Pine Road, Bloomfield Hills
313-645-3312, 313-645-3323
(group tour information)

Location: Use the entrance to the Cranbrook Educational Community, the farthest east off Lone Pine Road between Lahser and Cranbrook Roads

Hours: 1-5 p.m., Tuesday-Sunday. Tours for school groups are available.

Admission: $1.50 adults, 75 cents children and seniors. Family membership available.

Ages: 5 and up. The guards are very wary of young children. Please be sure to hold onto your children since many of the exhibits are three-dimensional and easy to bump into.

Plan: Under one hour

Parking: Park along the semi-circle in front or in the lot on the east side of the museum

Lunch: The Cranbrook Institute of Science, just down the road, has several vending machines and a lunch room. Picnicking on Cranbrook grounds is strictly forbidden.

Facilities: Bathrooms on lower level. Gift shop has a small selection of children's art books and beautifully illustrated picture books.

If you think this museum is off limits to children, you are missing one of the finest visual art experiences the city has to offer your children. The museum is connected to the Cranbrook Art Academy and is a haven for the avant-garde and contemporary. Most of the exhibits show the unusual and witty. Kids love this kind of art. We once saw a drawing of a nose and a colorful doghouse sculpture, and my kids' sense of art has never been the same. Try to visit during the spring Student Show.

NEARBY SITES:
Cranbrook Institute of Science, Cranbrook House and Garden

SP T H   Hands-On Science

Cranbrook Institute of Science
500 Lone Pine Road, Bloomfield Hills
313-645-3200

Location: Use the entrance to the Cranbrook Educational Community, the farthest east off Lone Pine Road between Lahser and Cranbrook Roads. You'll know you're there when you see the stegosaurus.

Hours: 10 a.m.-5 p.m., Monday-Friday. Also 7-10 p.m., Friday. 10 a.m.-10 p.m., Saturday. 1-5 p.m., Sunday. Closed on major holidays. Lasera Shows: 7:30, 8:30, 9:30 p.m., Friday. 3:45, 8:30, 9:30 p.m., Saturday. 3:45 p.m. Sunday. Planetarium Shows: 3, 3:45, 7:30 p.m., Saturday. 3, 3:45 p.m., Sunday.
Discovery Room/Nature Place: 1-5 p.m., Saturday and Sunday.

Admission: $4 adults, $3 children ages 3-17 and seniors, under 3 free. Family membership and group rates available. Planetarium: $1 additional, members free. Lasera: $1.50 additional.

Ages: All ages for the museum. 5 and up for most lasera and planetarium shows.

Plan: Half day visit

Parking: Lot adjacent to and in front of building

Lunch: A lunch room with vending machines

Facilities: Bathrooms, drinking fountain on lower level. Two gift shops offer a wonderful selection of science toys. The Dino Shop specializes in dinosaur gifts; the lobby shop has everything else.

Cranbrook Institute of Science is the all-purpose science museum for children of all ages. Hands-on exhibits, a Discovery Room full of touch-me displays, lasera and planetarium shows, science demonstrations, and seasonal family events encourage science creativity and exploration.

Family membership is well worth its price. The membership allows you free entrance into Detroit's Science Center and Lansing's Impression 5 Museum as well as the Institute's spring Maple Syrup Festival and Autumn Fest, perfectly choreographed sensory events celebrating the seasons. For a fee, your children can also take classes at the Institute throughout the year.

NEARBY SITES:
Cranbrook Academy of Art Museum, Cranbrook House and Garden

SP T H   History

Dearborn Historical Museum: McFadden Ross House and Exhibit Annex
915 South Brady, Dearborn
313-565-3000

For full information, see Historic Sites

SP T   Fire-Fighting Equipment

Detroit Fire Department Historical Museum
2737 Gratiot Avenue, Detroit
313-224-2035

Location: One mile north of Fisher Freeway (I-75) on Gratiot. The museum is off the beaten track; be sure to call for exact directions.

Hours: Tours are offered 9 a.m.-5 p.m., Monday-Friday, by reservation only

Admission: Free

Ages: All ages

Plan: 1-1½ hour tour

Parking: On street, adjacent to building

Lunch: Hop back on the expressway and drive to Eastern Market or your favorite neighborhood restaurant

Facilities: Bathrooms upstairs

The red brick building with the large yellow doors, Detroit's oldest standing Engine House, is full of beautifully restored fire rigs, fire-fighting clothing, and artifacts. It offers children a glimpse into the exciting and dangerous history of Detroit Fire fighting.

Kids are allowed to play fire chief. They try on the clothes, sit up on the rigs, and ring the bells. Upstairs, there's an authentic brass firepole. Kids peek down 30 feet to the first floor and imagine hurried firefighters whooshing down the pole. School and civic groups are encouraged to reserve tour dates.

NEARBY SITES:
Eastern Market, Belle Isle

SP T H   History

Detroit Historical Museum
5401 Woodward Avenue, Detroit
313-833-1805

Location: In Cultural Center, across from the Detroit Institute of Arts, on Woodward Avenue

Hours: 9:30 a.m.-5 p.m., Wednesday-Sunday. Closed major holidays.

Admission: Free, donations accepted

Ages: All ages

Plan: Half day visit

Parking: Use street meters or free lot on west side of building

Lunch: Go across the street to the Detroit Institute of Art's Kresge Court Cafe

Facilities: Bathrooms on lower level. Beautifully appointed gift shop with many old-fashioned replicas and hand-made toys.

If you grew up in Detroit, you will hardly recognize the newly refurbished historical museum. Exhibits are fresh, creative, and well-lit. The old favorites are still as wonderful as ever. Introduce your children to the basement level's "Streets of Old Detroit," the hauntingly authentic cobblestone streets full of old shop windows and talking mannequins.

On the third floor, a Lionel train set winds its way through an elaborate old-fashioned village. There's a newly installed costume gallery and furnished doll houses. Older children will also enjoy the main floor exhibit of artifacts and curious objects that tell Detroit's history.

NEARBY SITES:

Cultural Center: Detroit Institute of Arts, Children's Museum, Museum of African American History, Your Heritage House, International Institute, Detroit Science Center, and Detroit Public Library

SP T H   Art

Detroit Institute of Arts (DIA)
5200 Woodward Avenue, Detroit
313-833-7900

Location: In the heart of the Cultural Center, on the east side of Woodward Avenue, just south of Kirby

Hours: 9:30 a.m.-5:30 p.m., Wednesday-Sunday. Closed Monday, Tuesday, and major holidays.

Admission: Free. Family membership available.

Ages: All ages

Plan: Half day

Parking: Use the Detroit Science Center lot east of the DIA on John R, $2 for all day parking. Available meter parking on street is difficult to find.

Lunch: The Kresge Court Cafe is a pleasant cafeteria offering a wide selection of hot and cold meals, plus snacks. Be sure to show your kids the faces and gargoyles in stone along the walls of the dining room. You could bring your lunch and augment it with a snack or drink. The dining room has open access; it isn't necessary to go through the food line. Hours: 11 a.m.-4 p.m., Wednesday-Saturday. 1-4 p.m., Sunday. Student Lunch Room, by appointment only. 833-7981.

Facilities: Bathrooms and drinking fountain near the cafe. The gift shop, located at the Farnsworth entrance, has a children's section full of beautifully illustrated picture books, books about artists, t-shirts, and art supplies.

The DIA has wonderful secrets and amazing visual delights for children of all ages. Begin your visit walking through the rainbow hallway to the Kresge Court Cafe and up the hidden, winding wrought iron staircase to the Great Hall's showcases of knights' armor and swords. The Rivera Court is straight ahead. Here are the famous Diego Rivera murals and the information desk for "The Mystery of the Five Fragments," a one-hour creative treasure hunt that will delight any youthful pirate. Suggested adult-child ratio is one adult for every child.

Don't forget the mummies, African masks, Indian clothing, impressionist and modern galleries. Get the kids involved by asking them to mimic a gesture or expression they see in a painting or sculpture. And be sure to turn on one modern sculpture that looks like a sunflower fan. (Ask a guard to help you find Jean Tinguely's *O Sole Mio.*)

"The Mystery of the Five Fragments" can be checked out at the Rivera Court Information Desk, 10 a.m.-2 p.m., Wednesday-Sunday. "The Thinker," a computer game about art, is located on the main level at the edge of the red-carpeted area near the restrooms and phone and is available during regular museum hours. The DIA is also the home of the Detroit Youtheatre and Brunch with Bach. (*See* That's Entertainment.)

NEARBY SITES:
Cultural Center: Detroit Historical Museum, Children's Museum, Your Heritage House, Museum of African American History, Detroit Public Library, International Institute, Detroit Science Center

---

SP T H   Hands-On Science

Detroit Science Center
5020 John R, Detroit
313-577-8400

Location: One block east of Woodward on the corner of Warren and John R, behind the DIA

Hours: 9:30 a.m.-4 p.m., Tuesday-Friday. 10 a.m.-6 p.m., Saturday. Noon-6 p.m. Sunday. Closed Mondays and major holidays. Space Theatre shows Omnimax movies every hour on the half hour. (Preschoolers might be uncomfortable with the Omnimax movie's motion and speed.)

Admission: $9 family rate (Saturday and Sunday evenings only). $5 adults and children 13 and up, $4 children 6 to 12 and seniors, $2 children 4 and 5, under 4 free. Family membership gives you free admission to Cranbrook Institute of Science and Lansing's Impression 5 Museum.

Ages: All ages

Plan: Half day visit

Parking: Lot adjacent to entrance, off John R, $2 all day parking

Lunch: Vending machines and several tables in basement

Facilities: Bathrooms and drinking fountain on basement level. Gift shop near entrance has great science, dino, and space items.

At the Detroit Science Center, children can peek into a space capsule, ride a rainbow escalator, meet Ozzie the Robot create giant bubbles, try a computer voice synthesizer, look in fun-house mirrors, ride a stationary bike, and become immersed in an Omnimax movie experience.

There are over 50 hands-on exhibits inviting children to touch, explore, and learn about computers, the human body, machines, physics and communications. Special demonstrations are held hourly, each weekend in the Demonstration Theater.

NEARBY SITES:
Cultural Center: Detroit Historical Museum, Children's Museum, Your Heritage House, Museum of African American History, Detroit Public Library, International Institute, Detroit Institute of Arts

---

SP T   History

Dexter Area Museum
3443 Inverness, Dexter
313-426-2475

Location: At Inverness and Fourth Street

Hours: 1-3 pm., Friday and Saturday, May 1-Christmas. Tours by appointment, only.

Admission: Free. Family membership available.

Ages: 5 and up

Plan: Under one hour

Parking: Free on site

Lunch: Many restaurants are located in Ann Arbor, 20 minutes east off I-94

Facilities: Bathrooms. Gift shop offers toys, craft, and hobby books.

This 1883 church built by early German settlers showcases local history items. Children will enjoy the early dentist's office, printing equipment, antique toys and dolls, telephone switch board, and old household appliances.

NEARBY SITES:
Spring Valley Trout Farm, cider mills

SP T H   Marine History

Dossin Great Lakes Museum
100 Strand
Belle Isle Park, Detroit
313-267-6440

Location: Cross the Belle Isle Bridge and go southeast to Strand Road on the south shore of Belle Isle

Hours: 10 a.m.-5:30 p.m., Wednesday-Sunday. Closed major holidays.

Admission: Free. Suggested donation $1 adults, 50 cents children 12 to 17.

Ages: All ages

Plan: Short visit

Parking: Free on site

Lunch: Belle Isle is full of picnic tables. During the summer, there are food concessions near the zoo and playground.

Facilities: Bathrooms, drinking fountain. Gift shop has nautical items.

You won't get seasick at the Dossin Museum, but you will come away with a better understanding of ships, their innards, and perils at sea. There's a large collection of scale-model Great Lakes ships, a spectacular carved oak Gothic Room, once a smoking lounge on a 1912 steamer, and a room full of shipwreck exhibits spanning two centuries of shipping tragedies. Kids can view Detroit and Windsor through the periscope that goes up through the roof, and pose next to the War of 1812 cannon on the museum lawn.

NEARBY SITES:
Belle Isle Aquarium, Anna Scripps Whitcomb Conservatory, Belle Isle Nature Center, Belle Isle Zoo, Playscape

`SP T H`   Hands-On Gallery

Ella Sharp Museum
3225 Fourth Street, Jackson
313-787-2320

For full information, see Historic Sites

`SP T H`   Art

Flint Institute of Arts
1120 East Kearsley Street, Flint
313-234-1695

Location: Flint's Cultural Center, off of I-475 and I-69 in downtown Flint

Hours: 10 a.m.-5 p.m., Tuesday-Saturday. 1-5 p.m., Sunday. Also 7-9 p.m., Tuesday, October-May.

Admission: Free

Ages: All ages

Plan: Short visit

Parking: Use lot adjacent to Sloan Museum

Lunch: Drive to nearby Windmill Place or Water Street Pavilion

Facilities: Bathrooms, drinking fountain, gift shop

Flint's art museum offers children a sampling of art from every period of history. Children will enjoy the collection of paperweights displayed in lighted tables, the modern sculpture gallery, and the exterior court sculpture that moves with the wind. During the Christmas season, the museum sets up a 14-foot Christmas tree decorated with children's artwork.

NEARBY SITES:
Cultural Center: Alfred P. Sloan Museum, Longway Planetarium
In town: AC Spark Plug Tour, Buick City Tour, Michigan Humane Society, Children's Museum

During the summer: Penny Whistle Place, Crossroads Village/Huckleberry Railroad, Mott Farm

SP T H   History, Ethnic

Great Lakes Indian Museum
Fort Wayne
6325 West Jefferson, Detroit
313-297-9360

Location: Within Historic Fort Wayne, Livernois and Jefferson, on the far west side of the fort

Hours: 9:30 a.m.-5 p.m., Wednesday-Sunday, May-October

Admission: $1 adults, 50 cents children and seniors

Ages: All ages

Plan: The museum takes under one hour, but plan on a half day to see the entire fort

Parking: Ample free visitor parking near entrance

Lunch: Drink and snack vending machines, picnic tables in front of the visitor center

Facilities: Bathrooms in the visitor center, outhouses near the Indian Museum

Photos of courageous-looking Indian chiefs, intricately carved wooden peace pipes, colorful clothing, and historic weapons tell the story of the Great Lakes Indians. An Indian burial mound dating to 750 A.D., the last surviving burial mound in the Detroit area, is adjacent to the museum.

NEARBY SITES:
Fort Wayne also houses the National Museum of Tuskegee Airmen, the restored 1880 Commanding Officer's House, and the restored Spanish-American Guardhouse. Boblo Island's Detroit dock is a few blocks from the Fort.

SP T H   History

Greenmead Museum and
Historical Village
38125 Eight Mile Road, Livonia
313-477-7375

For full information, see Historic Sites

SP T H   ·   Transportation and History

Henry Ford Museum
20900 Oakwood Boulevard, Dearborn
313-271-1620

Location: Michigan Avenue and Southfield
Freeway

Hours: 9 a.m.-5 p.m., daily. Closed Thanksgiving Day and Christmas Day.

Admission: $10.50 adults, $9.50 seniors,
$5.25 children 4 to 12, under 5 free. Group
rates, family membership, annual pass, and
two-day pass available.

Ages: All ages

Plan: Half day or full day. With small children,
it's impossible to comfortably visit both the
museum and adjacent Greenfield Village in one
day.

Parking: Use free lots adjacent to the museum
and village

Lunch: American Cafe or Corner Cupboard

Facilities: Bathrooms and drinking fountains in
several locations. The Greenfield Village Theatre Company, located in the museum, often
performs children's theater during December.
The two gift shops near the museum entrance
are well stocked with old fashioned coloring
books, model cars and trains, books, candies,
and toys.

Henry Ford Museum is the repository of automobile and aviation history, American furnishings, social history, and other collections begun by its founder, Henry Ford. Its 12 acres of memorabilia and artifacts bear a strong resemblance to the vastness of a Smithsonian Institution, and for children, there is far too much to see in one visit.

Try to visit the highlights. Children enjoy the new permanent exhibit, "The Automobile in American Life," plus the early airplanes, a hands-on section of early machines, and the Abraham Lincoln assasination artifacts — his shawl, theater program, and rocking chair.

One recommended strategy for enjoying the museum and village — become a family member or buy a seasonal pass. Then you will feel comfortable making many short visits throughout the year.

NEARBY SITES:
Greenfield Village, Dearborn Historical Museum

SP T H-main floor   History

Hiram Walker Historical Museum
254 Pitt Street West,
Windsor, Ontario, Canada
519-253-1812

Location: Pitt Street West and Ferry Street

Hours: 10 a.m.-5 p.m., Tuesday-Saturday. 2-5 p.m., Sunday. Closed Monday.

Admission: Free

Ages: 6 and up

Plan: Less than an hour

Parking: Use metered lot, 25 cents an hour

Lunch: Restaurants and riverside picnic areas nearby

Facilities: Bathrooms

There are Indian artifacts, pioneer objects, firearms, furniture, and tools on display in this very small museum, once the home of Francoise Baby. Kids enjoy calling the house the "BAH-bee" house and playing with hands-on activities in the "Discovery Island" exhibit.

NEARBY SITES:
Art Galley of Windsor, city parks

SP T H   History

Holocaust Memorial Museum
6602 West Maple Road, West Bloomfield
313-661-0840

Location: On the Jewish Community Center Campus, west of Drake Road. Connected to the Jewish Community Center.

Hours: 10 a.m.-4 p.m., Sunday-Thursday. 10 a.m.-8 p.m., Wednesday. School group tours are encouraged; educational materials are available for pre-visit preparation.

Admission: Free

Ages: Not recommended for children under sixth grade

Plan: Short visit

Parking: Two lots adjacent to building

Lunch: Cafeteria on main floor of Jewish Community Center

Facilities: Bathrooms. Archives and library.

Children need preparation before visiting the Holocaust Memorial Museum. The museum's explicit displays, videos, and photos offer an insightful and emotional look at the destruction of European Jewry during the Holocaust. Guided group tours are highly recommended.

NEARBY SITES:
Plaster Playhouse

SP T H   Hands-On Science

Impression 5 Museum
200 Museum Drive, Lansing
517-485-8116

Location: Between Grand and Cedar Avenues, three blocks east of the Capitol

Hours: 10 a.m.-5 p.m., Tuesday-Saturday. Noon-5 p.m., Sunday. Closed Monday and holidays.

Admission: $3 adults, $2.50 children 4 to 12, $2 seniors, 3 and under free. Group rates and family memberships available.

Ages: All ages

Plan: Half day. The kids won't want to leave.

Parking: Lot behind building

Lunch: A cafe on the first level closes one hour before museum closing

Facilities: Bathrooms, drinking fountain, coat check at museum entrance. Gift shop with extensive selection of science items.

Children and adults skip from exhibit to exhibit, playing, touching, building, and experimenting in this giant science playground. There's something for every age. Break into a jazzy tune on a giant cello in the Music Room; climb in darkness through the Touch Tunnel; play with shadows and rainbows in the Light Room; create undulating bubbles at the Bubble Table. Learn scientific principles while having fun.

NEARBY SITES:

Lansing sites: R.E. Olds Transportation Museum, Michigan Women's Historical Center, Michigan Historical Museum, State Capitol, Potter Park Zoo

MSU Campus sites: Abrams Planetarium, Horticultural Gardens, MSU Museum of Natural History

SP T H   Ethnic

International Institute
111 Kirby, Detroit
313-871-8600

Location: Just east of the Children's Museum, north of the DIA

Hours: 9 a.m.-5 p.m., Monday-Saturday. Call to arrange school or group tours.

Admission: Free

Ages: Elementary school children and up

Plan: Under one hour

Parking: Meters across the street or use Science Center Parking Lot on John R

Lunch: Melting Pot Cafe, featuring ethnic food, 11 a.m.-2 p.m., Monday-Friday

Facilities: Bathrooms. Gift shop with international toys and greeting cards in many languages, plus UNICEF gift shop with cards and books.

The "Hall of Nations" exhibit showcases objects, clothing, and musical instruments from countries around the world. Since school programs are held in this room, call ahead to be sure the exhibit room will be free during your visit.

NEARBY SITES:

Cultural Center: Detroit Historical Museum, Children's Museum, Your Heritage House, Museum of African American History, Detroit Public Library, Detroit Science Center, Detroit Institute of Arts.

`SP T H`   Art

Kresge Art Museum
Michigan State University, East Lansing
517-355-7631

Location: On Auditorium Road, MSU campus

Hours: 9:30 a.m.-4:30 p.m., Monday, Tuesday, Wednesday, Friday. Noon-8 p.m., Thursday. 1-4 p.m., Saturday and Sunday. Closed August 20-September 18, between Christmas and New Year's Day, and holidays.

Admission: Free. Family memberships available.

Ages: All ages

Plan: Short visit

Parking: Meters in front of building. 50 cent parking tokens are available at the front desk.

Lunch: Burger King and vending machines are located in the Michigan Union, corner of Abbott and Grand River. Many other restaurants are located on Grand River, across from campus.

Facilities: Bathrooms. Small gift cart with inexpensive items.

Small museums of art are always fun for children; they can digest the art experience. The Kresge Art Museum offers changing exhibits of art spanning art history, from prehistoric to contemporary, in an uncluttered, relaxing environment.

NEARBY SITES:

MSU Campus: Abrams Planetarium, Horticultural Gardens, MSU Museum of Natural History

Lansing: R.E. Olds Transportation Museum, Michigan Women's Historical Center, Michigan Historical Museum, State Capitol, Potter Park Zoo, Impression 5 Museum

SP T H   Michigan History

Michigan Historical Museum
717 West Allegan, Lansing
517-373-3559, 517-335-9165 (tours)

Location: Several blocks west of the Capitol, on Allegan between Butler and Sycamore Streets

Hours: 9 a.m.-4:30 p.m., Monday-Friday. 10 a.m.-4 p.m., Saturday. 1-5 p.m., Sunday. Call to arrange group or school tours. Special summer weekend activities include craft demonstrations and family workshops.

Admission: Free

Ages: All ages

Plan: Half day

Parking: Large parking lot adjacent to the museum charges 25 cents per hour

Lunch: Vending machines

Facilities: Bathrooms. Gift shop with Michigan souvenirs, history books, Made-in-Michigan products.

This brand new, 315,000-square-foot facility offers both children and adults a multi-sensory vision of Michigan's past, from prehistoric times to the nineteenth century, told through the eyes of Michigan's people. Hands-on audio-visual exhibits present Michigan's Indians, Michigan's role in the anti-slavery movement, pioneer life, coal mining days, and the lumber era. Kids will enjoy walking into a mine shaft and entering the facade of a lumber baron's home.

NEARBY SITES:
Lansing: R.E. Olds Transportation Museum, Michigan Women's Historical Center, Impression 5 Museum, State Capitol, Potter Park Zoo
MSU Campus: Abrams Planetarium, Horticultural Gardens, MSU Museum of Natural History

---

`SP T H`   `Space`

Michigan Space Center
2111 Emmons Road, Jackson
517-787-4425

Location: Jackson Community College campus

Hours: May 26-Sept. 1: 10 a.m.-6 p.m., Monday-Friday. Noon-5 p.m. Sunday. March 31-May 25: 10 a.m.-5 p.m., Monday-Saturday. Noon-5 pm., Sunday. Rest of year: 10 a.m.-5 p.m. Tuesday-Saturday. Noon-5 p.m., Sunday. A 15-minute movie is shown throughout the day.

Admission: $9 family rate, $3 adults, $2 students and seniors, 5 and under free. Group rates available.

Ages: All ages

Plan: Short visit

Parking: Lot adjacent to museum

Lunch: Vending machines with pop, treats, and sandwiches, tables in lobby. Picnic tables on grounds.

Facilities: Outdoor play area, bathrooms, drinking fountain. Gift shop with a variety of low-cost items. Be sure to try the astronaut ice cream (for maximum enjoyment, let the freeze-dried bits melt in your mouth, don't chew them).

The Michigan Space Center brings space travel down to earth. Hands-on experiences, true-to-life diplays, and used National Aeronautics and Space Administration artifacts help kids understand life in space from the astronaut's point of view. The museum even attempts to answer those nitty-gritty questions kids always ask, such as: How do astronauts go to the bathoom? Take a shower? Eat? There are space suits worn by the first astronauts, a space shuttle shower, space food, and moon rocks. Be sure to check with the gift shop for the movie schedule.

NEARBY SITES:
Ella Sharpe Museum, Illuminated Cascades (summer)

H   Sports History

Michigan Sports Hall of Fame
Cobo Hall, One Washington Boulevard
Detroit
313-224-1010

Location: Washington Boulevard at Jefferson. Gallery is hanging on the walls, second floor, Cobo Hall.

Hours: 24 hours daily

Admission: Free

Ages: All ages

Plan: Less than an hour

Parking: Use Cobo Arena garage

Lunch: Several restaurants within Cobo Hall

Facilities: Bathrooms, drinking fountain on each floor of Cobo Hall

Children with a love of sports will enjoy a stroll through these hallways, where Michigan sports heroes have been immortalized.

NEARBY SITES:
Cobo Arena, Joe Louis Arena, Renaissance Center, Greektown, Detroit People Mover

SP T H   Michigan & Natural History

Michigan State University (MSU) Museum of Natural History
101 West Circle Drive
Michigan State University Campus
East Lansing
517-355-2370

Location: West Circle Drive, on the MSU campus

Hours: 9 a.m.-5 p.m., Monday, Tuesday, Wednesday, Friday. 9 a.m.-9 p.m., Thursday. 1-5 p.m., Saturday and Sunday. 9 a.m.-1 p.m., home football Saturdays. Group tours available.

Admission: Free

Ages: All ages

Plan: Short visit

Parking: Metered parking in front. 50 cent meter tokens can be purchased in museum office.

Lunch: Burger King and vending machines are located in the Michigan Union, corner of Abbott and Grand River. Many other restaurants are located on Grand River Avenue, across from campus.

Facilities: Bathrooms. General store-gift shop with a variety of inexpensive gifts.

The MSU museum is small enough for kids to comfortably see almost every display. There are dramatic dioramas of cave people, an old fashioned city street, a full-sized, hungry-looking bear, stuffed animals, dinosaur bones, and a lower level full of evocative African and Indonesian masks.

In the Family Room, a relaxing corner of the lower level set aside for hands-on exploration and quiet activity, kids can read, play a computer game, or draw.

NEARBY SITES:
MSU Campus: Abrams Planetarium, Horticultural Gardens, Kresge Art Museum
Lansing: R.E. Olds Museum, Michigan Women's Historical Center, Michigan Historical Museum, State Capitol, Potter Park Zoo, Impression 5 Museum

SP T H   Women's History

Michigan Women's Historical Center and Hall of Fame
213 West Main Street, Lansing
517-484-1880

Location: Off I-96, Main Street exit, six blocks south of the State Capitol building, adjacent to Cooley Gardens

Hours: Noon-4 p.m., Wednesday-Friday. 2-4 p.m., Sunday.

Admission: $2.50 adults, $1 students 5 to 18. Group rates available.

Ages: Third grade to adult

Plan: Short visit

Parking: Free parking at Cooley Garden entrance off Capitol Avenue

Lunch: Picnic area in Cooley Garden

Facilities: Bathrooms. Gift shop selling books, notecards, posters, and American women paper doll cutouts.

From abolitionist Sojourner Truth to former First Lady Betty Ford, the Women's Center offers a picture of the lives, achievements, and history of Michigan women. Children old enough to appeciate historical exhibits will enjoy learning about famous Michigan women. The center also features original artwork by Michigan women.

NEARBY SITES:

Lansing: R.E. Olds Transportation Museum, Michigan Historical Museum, State Capitol, Potter Park Zoo, Impression 5 Museum

MSU Campus: Abrams Planetarium, Horticultural Gardens, MSU Museum of Natural History, Kresge Art Museum

---

SP T H   History

Monroe County Historical Museum
126 South Monroe Street, Monroe
313-243-7137

Location: South Monroe Street (M-125) and Second Street

Hours: 10 a.m.-5 p.m., Tuesday-Sunday, May1-September 30. 10 a.m.-5 p.m., Wednesday-Sunday, October 1-April 30.

Admission: Free, donations accepted

Ages: All ages

Plan: Under one hour

Parking: Free on site

Lunch: Restaurants available in town

Facilities: Bathrooms. Gift shop with early history, Woodland Indian, and General Custer items.

"Remember the Raisin!" Monroe's fiery role in the War of 1812 comes to life in this museum. Woodland Indian displays, military items, and General George Custer memorabilia make up the exhibits. Be sure to pick up a walking tour map of the nearby River Raisin Battlefield.

NEARBY SITES:

Navarre-Anderson Trading Post and Country Store Museum

`SP T H`   Music, Ethnic

Motown Museum
2648 West Grand Boulevard, Detroit
313-867-0991

Location: Off Lodge Freeway, West Grand Boulevard exit, west one block

Hours: 10 a.m.-5 p.m., Monday-Saturday. 2-5 p.m. Sunday.

Admission: $2 adults, $1 children

Ages: 6 and up

Plan: Short visit

Parking: Free parking on street

Lunch: Eat in the nearby New Center Area's Fisher Building, GM Building, or New Center One

Facilities: Bathrooms, gift shop

Enter the modest white stucco house with its "Hitsville, USA" sign and be transported back to the 1960s. Motown hits play softly in the background and bring to life the displays of Motown memorabilia: gold and platinum records, sequin-covered costumes worn by the stars, colorful album covers, and priceless photos. Enter Studio A and see where the Motown sound was created. This is Detroit's answer to Nashville, Tennessee.

NEARBY SITES:
Fisher Building, Detroit Police Horse Stables

`SP T H`   African American History

Museum of African American History
301 Frederick Douglass, Detroit
313-833-9800

Location: In the Cultural Center, two blocks east of the DIA. Turn onto Frederick Douglass off Mack.

Hours: 9:30 a.m.-5 p.m., Wednesday-Saturday. 1-5 p.m., Sunday. Closed Monday and Tuesday.

Admission: Free, donations welcome

Ages: All ages

Plan: Short visit

Parking: Free parking lot in front of museum

Lunch: Drive over to the DIA Kresge Court Cafe

Facilities: Bathrooms, drinking fountain in lobby. Gift shop with many African American heritage gifts: greeting cards, commemorative stamps, coloring books, and books.

Enter through intricately carved wooden portals and become immersed in tracing a people from their homeland in Africa through voyage to America, slavery, and heroic actions during the Abolitionist period. Photographs, maps, paintings, artifacts, sculptures, and audio phones tell the compelling story. Children of all ages will come away with important lessons in courage and humanity.

NEARBY SITES:

Cultural Center: Detroit Institute of Arts, Detroit Historical Museum, Children's Museum, International Institute, Detroit Public Library, Your Heritage House, Detroit Science Center

SP T H   Art

Museum of Art
525 State Street, Ann Arbor
313-763-1231

Location: In the heart of The University of Michigan's Central Campus, across from the Michigan Union

Hours: 10 a.m.-4 p.m., Tuesday-Friday. 1-5 p.m., Saturday and Sunday

Admission: Free

Ages: Older children, or young children who enjoy art

Plan: Less than an hour

Parking: Use metered parking on the street

Lunch: Many restaurants nearby

Facilities: Bathrooms, drinking fountain, gift shop with a variety of art-inspired items

The Museum of Art is a small building with just enough art for a quick visit and introduction to art. The museum gift shop sells an inexpensive treasure-hunt coloring book that offers families a self-guided tour of the art collection.

NEARBY SITES:

On or near campus: Ann Arbor Farmers' Market, Kerrytown Plaza, Ann Arbor Hands-On Museum, UofM Exhibit Museum and Planetarium, Ecology Center of Ann Arbor

North Campus: Phoenix Memorial Laboratory, UofM Matthaei Botanical Garden, Domino's Farms, Leslie Science Center, Stearns Collection of Musical Instruments

South of campus: Cobblestone Farm, Scrap Box

SP T   Michigan & Natural History

Museum of Art and History
1115 Sixth Street, Port Huron
313-982-0891

Location: ½ mile off US-25, corner of Wall and Sixth Streets

Hours: 1-4:30 p.m., Wednesday-Sunday

Admission: Donations

Ages: All ages

Plan: Short visit

Parking: Adjacent to museum on street

Lunch: Drive into town

Facilities: Bathrooms, gift shop

Three hundred years of local history are displayed in a restored, three-story home. Of interest to children are Indian artifacts, a pioneer log home, and artifacts from Thomas Edison's boyhood home.

NEARBY SITES:
Mary Maxim, Inc., Ruby Farms, Lexington Marina, Croswell Swinging Bridge

SP T H   African American History

National Museum of
Tuskegee Airmen
Historic Fort Wayne
6325 West Jefferson, Detroit
313-297-9360

Location: Within Fort Wayne, Livernois and Jefferson, near the entrance to the fort

Hours: 9:30 a.m.-5 p.m., Wednesday-Sunday, May-October. Groups can schedule special tours during the off-season.

Admission: $1 adults, 50 cents children and seniors

Ages: All ages

Plan: The museum takes under one hour, but plan on a half day to see the entire fort

Parking: Ample visitor parking lots near entrance

Lunch: Drink and snack vending machines, picnic tables in front of the visitor center

Facilities: Bathrooms in the visitor center, outhouses near the Indian Museum

Photographs, uniforms, and memorabilia tell the story of the Tuskegee Airmen, the country's first Black Army Air Force Battalion.

NEARBY SITES:
Fort Wayne also houses the Great Lakes Indian Museum, the restored 1880 Victorian commanding officer's house, and the restored Spanish-American guardhouse. Boblo Island's Detroit dock is a few blocks from the fort.

SP T H   History

Navarre-Anderson Trading Post and Country Store Museum
North Custer Road at Raisinville Road
Monroe
313-243-7137

For full information, see Historic Sites

SP T H   African American History

North American Black Historical Museum
277 King Street
Amherstburg, Ontario, Canada
519-736-7353

Location: From the tunnel, take Riverside Drive (Highway 18) into Amherstburg

Hours: 10 a.m.-5 p.m., Wednesday-Friday. 1-5 p.m. Saturday and Sunday.

Admission: Free. Donations welcome.

Ages: All ages

Plan: Short visit

Parking: Adjacent to museum

Lunch: Eat in Amherstburg or nearby city of Sandwich

Facilities: Bathrooms, gift shop

The Windsor area meant freedom for runaway slaves on the Underground Railroad as they moved through Detroit. The North American Black Historical Museum preserves the heritage of Essex County's Black community, which had its beginnings during this turbulent era. The museum, 1855 log house, and Nazarene A.M.E. Church depict Black origins from Africa through slavery, followed by freedom and development.

NEARBY SITES:
Fort Malden National Historic Park, Park House Museum, Amherstburg Boblo dock

SP T H   History

Park House Museum
214 Dalhousie Street
Amherstburg, Ontario, Canada
519-736-2511

For full information, see Historic Sites

SP T H   History

Pine Grove Historical Museum
405 Oakland, Pontiac
313-338-6732

For full information, see Historic Sites

SP T H   History

Plymouth Historical Museum
155 South Main Street, Plymouth
313-455-8940

Location: Main and Church Streets, two blocks north of downtown Plymouth

Hours: 1-4 p.m., Thursday, Saturday, Sunday. Open any time by appointment for groups of 20 or more.

Admission: $1 adults, 50 cents children 11 to 17, 25 cents children 5 to 10, under 5 free. Family membership available.

Ages: 5 and up

Plan: Short visit

Parking: Use lot on south side of building

Lunch: Drive back to downtown Plymouth

Facilities: Bathrooms. Gift shop with many folk toys, Indian items, and handcrafted dolls.

This is an engaging historical museum set up with kids in mind. On "Main Street Plymouth," kids can peek into storefronts representing trades and professions of the early

1900s. Downstairs is a hands-on area that helps children understand the olden days through make-believe. They can try on clothes from grandma's trunk, play with old-fashioned foods from a general store bin, and use Mc-Guffey's Primers and slates to play school.

NEARBY SITES:
Plymouth Farmers' Market, Ice Sculpture Fesitval in January (*see* Monthly Calendar of Special Events)

SP T H   Transportation History

R.E. Olds Transportation Museum
240 Museum Drive, Lansing
571-372-0422

Location: Off Michigan Avenue, two blocks east of the Capitol

Hours: 9:30 a.m.-5 p.m., Tuesday-Friday. Noon-5 p.m. Saturday, Sunday. Closed Monday.

Admission: $3 adults, $2 seniors and children, under 5 free. Group rates and family membership available.

Ages: 5 and up

Plan: Under one hour

Parking: Free lot on site

Lunch: Picnic area, cafe across the parking lot in Lansing's Impression 5 Museum

Facilities: Bathrooms. Gift shop with model car kits, car posters, pictures.

R.E. Olds Transportation Museum, with its extensive collection of antique cars, posters, pictures, advertisements, and old motoring clothing, is a must for children with a passion for cars. Special event: Riverfest on Labor Day weekend showcases antique cars.

NEARBY SITES:
Lansing: Impression 5 Museum, Michigan Women's Historical Center, Michigan Historical Museum, State Capitol, Potter Park Zoo

MSU Campus: Abrams Planetarium, Horticultural Gardens, MSU Museum of Natural History

---

`SP T`   History

Rochester Hills Museum
at Van Hoosen Farm
1005 Van Hoosen Road, Rochester
313-656-4663

For full information, see Historic Sites

`T`   Military History

Selfridge Military Air Museum
Selfridge Air Base, Mount Clemens
313-466-5035

Location: Take I-94 east to exit 240 (Hall Road), then two miles east on Hall Road to the Air Base

Hours: 1-5 p.m., Sunday, April 1-November 1

Admission: Donations

Ages: 5 and up

Plan: Under one hour

Parking: Free, on site

Lunch: Picnic tables

Facilities: Bathrooms. Small gift counter with model airplanes and aviation toys.

Most children will be able to see the Air Force and National Guard exhibits in the low-slung building in several minutes, but they will want to spend a lot of time outdoors playing in the field of once-heroic, now-grounded Navy and Air Force planes. Sunday airplane maneuvers will also keep the kids entertained. They will hear and see the planes zooming across the sky.

NEARBY SITES:
C.J. Barrymore's Sport Center, Macomb Center for the Performing Arts, Marino Sports

Center, Inc., Mount Clemens Train Ride, Mount Clemens Farmers' Market, WhirlyBall of Michigan

SP T H   Music

Stearns Collection of Musical Instruments
1100 Baits Drive, Ann Arbor
313-763-4389

Location: School of Music Galleries, University of Michigan North Campus

Hours: 10 a.m.-5 p.m., Thursday and Friday. 1-8 p.m. Saturday and Sunday. Guided tours are available by appointment at these and other times.

Admission: Free. Tours are $1 per person.

Ages: 5 and older

Plan: Under one hour

Parking: Metered lot in back of building

Lunch: Snack bar open daily. For lots of restaurants, drive onto the main UofM campus.

Facilities: Bathrooms

For children fascinated by music and instruments, here's an opportunity to see unusual instruments both old and new. Among the many fascinating examples, kids are sure to notice the Damaru, a Tibetan drum made from a human skull, African thumb pianos, and the very modern Moog synthesizer.

NEARBY SITES:

On or near campus: Ann Arbor Farmers' Market, Kerrytown Plaza, Museum of Art, UofM Exhibit Museum and Planetarium, Ecology Center of Ann Arbor, Ann Arbor Hands-On Museum

North Campus: Phoenix Memorial Laboratory, UofM Matthaei Botanical Gardens, Domino's Farms, Leslie Science Center

South of campus: Cobblestone Farm, Scrap Box

SP T   History

Troy Museum and
Historic Village Green
60 West Wattles, Troy
313-524-3570

For full information, see Historic Sites

SP T H   Natural History

University of Michigan
Exhibit Museum
1109 Geddes Avenue, Ann Arbor
313-764-0478

Location: Geddes Avenue near Washtenaw Avenue, on the UofM Central Campus

Hours: 9 a.m.-5 p.m., Tuesday-Saturday. 1-5 p.m., Sunday. Planetarium shows: 10:30 and 11:30 a.m., 2, 3, and 4 p.m., Saturday. 2, 3, and 4 p.m. Sunday.

Admission: Museum, free. Planetarium show, $1.25 on Saturday mornings, $1.50 all other shows.

Ages: All ages. Planetarium shows: 5 and older except for Saturday morning shows.

Plan: Half day including planetarium show

Parking: Use the public structure on Fletcher Street

Lunch: Walk into campus

Facilities: Bathrooms and drinking fountain. Gift shop with variety of inexpensive dinosaur and science items.

The University of Michigan Exhibit Museum is the best Michigan has to offer the dinophile in your family. Its second floor is full of dinosaur fossils. There is a fully mounted allosaurus skeleton and a duck-billed anatosaurus skeleton, the giant leg of a brontosaurus, and the extinct elephant bird's tremendous egg.

Kids walk through and can't believe their eyes. For a bird's eye view, walk up to the third floor and peek over the balcony onto the backs of the prehistoric monsters. The museum's extensive stuffed wildlife collection will also delight younger chilren.

NEARBY SITES:
On or near campus: Ann Arbor Farmers' Market, Kerrytown Plaza, Ann Arbor Hands-On Museum, UofM Exhibit Museum and Planetarium, Ecology Center of Ann Arbor
North Campus: Phoenix Memorial Laboratory, UofM Matthaei Botanical Garden, Domino's Farms, Leslie Science Center
South of campus: Cobblestone Farm, Scrap Box

SP T   History

Waterloo Area Farm Museum
9998 Waterloo-Munith Road, Stockbridge
517-851-7636, 313-769-2219

For full information, see Historic Sites

SP T   Military History

Yankee Air Force Museum
Willow Run Airport, Ypsilanti
313-483-4030

Location: Willow Run Airport, Hangar 2041, east side of field
Hours: 10 a.m.-4 p.m., Tuesday-Sunday
Admission: $2
Ages: 6 and up
Plan: Under one hour
Parking: Free, on site
Lunch: Drive into Ypsilanti or Belleville
Facilities: Bathrooms. Gift shop with aviation pins, patches, books, models and posters.

For children with a passion for airplanes, a visit to the Yankee Air Force Museum is a must. Housed in a tremendous hangar are colorful examples of World War II and Korean War era airplanes. Aviation history exhibits are on the second level. Feel free to engage the volunteers in discussion; they will gladly give you an informal tour of the aircraft. An air show is performed each year in May.

NEARBY SITES:
Depot Town Caboose, Ypsilanti Farmers' Market, Wiard's Orchards (fall), Rowe's Produce Farm (spring)

SP T H   Ethnic, Art

Your Heritage House
110 East Ferry, Detroit
313-871-1667

Location: One block north of DIA, corner of Ferry and John R
Hours: Call to schedule an appointment or tour
Admission: Fee for classes
Ages: Preschool and up
Plan: Under one hour
Parking: Metered parking along John R
Lunch: Go to the DIA Kresge Court Cafe
Facilities: Bathrooms

Your Heritage House offers children programs in fine arts instruction throughout the year. The beautifully restored pre-World War I home also offers a wide selection of Black heritage materials including folk tales, field recordings, and African and rural South handcrafts and household implements. Children are allowed to play with the doll, puppet, and musical instrument collection. There are also changing fine arts exhibits. If you know you'll be in the Cultural Center, call to make an appointment.

NEARBY SITES:
Detroit Institute of Arts, Detroit Historical Museum, Children's Museum, Museum of African American History, Detroit Public Library, Detroit Science Center, International Institute

SP T   History

Ypsilanti Historical Society
and Museum
8220 North Huron Street, Ypsilanti
313-482-4990

Location: Off I-94, exit 183, follow Huron Street to Cross Street. On the east side of Huron Street.

Hours: 2-4 p.m., Friday-Sunday

Admission: Free

Ages: 6 and up

Plan: Under one hour

Parking: Metered parking on street. City lots nearby

Lunch: Depot Town offers several restaurants

Facilities: Bathrooms, drinking fountain. Gift shop has old-fashioned toys.

The restored Victorian home offers authentic furnishings, period clothing, home and farm tools and implements, plus changing exhibits from the 1800s. Children who are interested in history and old enough to understand "look but don't touch," will especially enjoy the winding staircase, Scottish Drum and Bugle Corps uniform, dollhouse, and old toys.

NEARBY SITES:
Depot Town Caboose, Ypsilanti Farmers' Market, Wiard's Orchards (fall), Rowe's Produce Farm (spring), Yankee Air Force Museum

5
HISTORIC SITES

Listed in this chapter are a diverse assortment of nineteenth-century restored homes, villages and farmsteads, forts, auto baron mansions, lighthouses, and Detroit landmarks. Michigan's historic sites often reveal its communal pioneer history and the important role it played in the automobile industry. Many sites have a commitment to living history, offering demonstrations and costumed guides that are quite appealing to children five and older. While the auto baron homes tours are not geared specifically to children, each home has aspects that children will find interesting. After accompanying me on many homes tours, my children are quite adept at staying near the guide and asking questions. They now see history as an accumulation of many personal stories.

Abbreviations: SP — site offers school programs; T — site offers group tours; H — wheelchair accessible.

U.S.-Canada Bridge

Ambassador Bridge
Juncture of I-75 and I-96, Detroit
313-226-3157

For children, a drive across this bridge is high adventure. Peeking out the window, they can see both the Detroit and Windsor skylines, as well as the Detroit River and its barge traffic. When we visit Windsor, we always try to use both the bridge and tunnel in our coming and going. Open 24 hours, daily. A toll fee ($1.25 American, $1.50 Canadian) is collected before entering on both sides of the Detroit River.

U.S.-Canada Bridge

Blue Water International Bridge
At end of I-94 going east, Port Huron
313-985-9541

We like to take this less-trafficked bridge into Canada when we are going to Eastern Ontario. On the way back to the U.S., we always stop for an ice cream cone at the London Farm Dairy Bar (2136 Pine Grove Avenue, 984-5111), just south of the foot of the bridge. Above the dairy sign, a giant cow with horns looks out at the traffic.

SP T   Carillon Tower

Burton Memorial Tower
230 South Ingalls Street, Ann Arbor
313-764-2539

Visitors can climb to the top floor of the carillon tower, one of the landmarks on the University of Michigan campus, during concerts from 12-12:30 p.m. weekdays when school is in session. Way up there you'll have a bird's-eye view of Ann Arbor and will also see and hear 55 bells, the world's third largest carillon instrument. Carillon concerts are also held at 7 p.m. once a month.

SP T H-main floor   Farmhouse

Cobblestone Farm
2781 Packard, Ann Arbor
313-994-2928

Location: On Packard Road, between Platt and Stone School Roads

Hours: 1-4 p.m., Thursday-Sunday, May-October

Admission: $5 family rate, $1.50 adults, 75 cents children 3 to 17 and seniors, under 3 free

Ages: 5 and up

Plan: Short visit

Parking: Free, behind the barn

Lunch: Picnic area near playground. Many restaurants in nearby Briarwood Mall or on UofM campus.

Facilities: Bathrooms. Gift shop with handcrafted toys in farmhouse. Playground on site.

Cobblestone Farm is a living farm museum that tells the story of nineteeth-century Michigan farm life through a variety of restored, authentically furnished buildings: the elegant Ticknor-Campbell house, a pioneer log cabin, and a replica of an 1880s barn, full of animals. Costumed guides lead public tours through the house; the other buildings are open for browsing. A playground is on the grounds. Children will benefit most from a pre-arranged group tour. Seasonal festivals are held once a month from May to October.

NEARBY SITES:
South of Campus: Scrap Box
Near campus: Ann Arbor Farmers' Market, Kerrytown Plaza, Little Dipper Candle Shop, Museum of Art, UofM Exhibit Museum and Planetarium, Ecology Center of Ann Arbor
North Campus: Phoenix Memorial Laboratory Tour, UofM Matthaei Botanical Gardens, Domino's Farms, Leslie Science Center

SP T H   Historic Home

Cranbrook House and Gardens
380 Lone Pine Road, Bloomfield Hills
313-645-3149

Location: Enter off Lone Pine Road, just west of Cranbrook Road

Hours: Home tour: 2-4 p.m.; fourth Sunday of the month, April-October and selected Sundays in July and August.

Garden: 10 a.m.-5 p.m., Monday-Saturday. 1-5 p.m., Sunday, June-August. Daily 1-5 p.m., May and September. Pre-arranged group tours are given weekdays.

Admission: Home tour: $2 adults, $1.50 children 6 to 14, 5 and under free.

Gardens: $2 adults, $1.50 children and seniors, under 5 free.

Ages: Home tour: older children. Garden walk: all ages.

Plans: Short visit for each

Parking: Along Lone Pine Road or across the street in Christ Church parking lot

Lunch: Vending machines in the Cranbrook Institute of Science, or find restaurants in nearby Birmingham or along Woodward Avenue or Telegraph Road.

Facilities: Bathrooms in house

Cranbrook House is an English manor house designed by Albert Kahn and built in the early 1900s for *Detroit News* publisher and Cranbrook founders, George Booth and his wife, Ellen Scripps Booth. Older children will enjoy learning about the life of these two influential people. The gardens surrounding the home offer 40 acres of formal plantings, woods, pine forest walks, and two lakes. The gardens are a perfect way to experience seasonal changes. Kids love scampering along the paths and ducking into the pine forest.

NEARBY SITES:
Cranbrook Academy of Art Museum, Cranbrook Institute of Science

SP   Historic Home

Crocker House
15 Union Street, Mount Clemens
313-465-2488

Location: Cass Avenue and Gratiot

Hours: 10 a.m.-4 p.m., Tuesday-Friday and first Sunday of each month. Closed in January. Increased hours during December. Group tours available.

Admission: $1 adults, 50 cents children

Ages: 8 and up

Plan: Under one hour

Parking: On street

Lunch: Restaurants in town

Facilities: Bathrooms. Small gift shop with Victorian replica toys and other inexpensive items.

Older children with an interest in the Victorian age will enjoy Crocker House's authentically furnished rooms and costumed mannequins. They will also enjoy the home's special Christmas exhibits and decorations during December.

NEARBY SITES:
C.J. Barrymore's Sport Center, Macomb Center for the Performing Arts, Marino Sports Center, Inc., Mount Clemens Train Ride, Mount Clemens Farmers' Market, Selfridge Military Air Museum, WhirlyBall of Michigan

SP T H   Historic Village & Train

Crossroads Village/Huckleberry Railroad
G-5055 Branch Road, Flint
313-736-7100

Location: Just north of Flint. Follow I-475 off either I-75 or I-69 to Carpenter Road (exit 11).

Hours: 10 a.m.-5:30 p.m., Monday-Friday. 11 a.m.-6:30 p.m., weekends and holidays. Train departs hourly 11 a.m.-4p.m., weekdays. Noon-5 p.m., weekends and holidays. Christmas at Crossroads: 3:30-9:30 p.m., Fridays, Saturdays, Sundays, November 25-December 30.

Admission: $6.95 adult, $4.95 children 4 to 12, $5.95 seniors, 3 and under free. Group rates and family membership available.

Ages: 3 and up

Plan: Half day visit

Parking: Free lot adjacent to village

Lunch: Small cafe, ice cream parlor, picnic area, cider mill

Facilities: Bathrooms. General store features country and handcrafted items, dolls and candy. Depot Souvenir Shop offers train memorabilia and novelty items.

   Crossroads Village and Huckleberry Railroad offer families a perfect summer outing. Take a 45-minute ride on the full-size steam train and witness a melodramatic scene involving a damsel in distress and snide villain. Walk the nineteeth-century village streets and explore 26 beautifully restored buildings, including three working mills, a toy maker's barn, one-room schoolhouse, and general store. Keep your eyes open for the staged bank robbery and duck into the Opera House for a half-hour magic show. Costumed guides, hands-on experiences, and craft demonstrations add to children's enjoyment. Christmas at Crossroads Village is a festive time with over 70,000 sparkling lights, Santa's workshop, and sleigh rides.

NEARBY SITES:
In town: AC Spark Plug Tour, Buick City Tour, Michigan Humane Society
Cultural Center: Flint Institute of Arts, Alfred P. Sloan Museum, Longway Planetarium

During the summer: Penny Whistle Place, Mott Farm

SP T   Historic Home

Curwood Castle
224 Curwood Castle Drive, Owosso
517-723-8844

Location: One block east and two blocks north of M-52 and M-21 intersection

Hours: 1-5 p.m., daily

Admission: Free. Donations accepted.

Ages: All ages

Plan: Short visit

Parking: Free on site

Lunch: Drive into downtown Owosso

Facilities: Bathrooms inside castle. Surrounding the castle is a park that includes an old log cabin and a footbridge over the Shiawassee River.

Curwood Castle is the former work studio of James Oliver Curwood, a famous writer of adventure books. He built the castle in 1922, based on a romantic reproduction of a Norman chateau. Children will love climbing up to the top of the towering turret and looking out the windows at the rushing Shiawassee River below.

NEARBY SITES:
Owosso is located west of Flint and northeast of Lansing

SP T H   Historic Buildings

Dearborn Historical Museum:
McFadden Ross House
and Exhibit Annex
915 South Brady, Dearborn
313-565-3000

Location: Just north of Michigan Avenue

Hours: 9 a.m.-5 p.m., Monday-Saturday, May-October. 1-5 p.m., Monday-Saturday, November-April.

Admission: Free

Ages: All ages

Plan: Short visit

Parking: Use lot adjacent to buildings

Lunch: Nearby Fairlane Town Center has a wide variety of restaurants both inside the mall and on the grounds

Facilities: Bathrooms, gift shop

The 1800s come to life in three buildings. The first two are located on Brady Street. The McFadden-Ross House contains domestic and period exhibits; the Exhibit Annex has craft shops, wagons, and buggies. The Commandant's Quarters, located at the corner of Michigan and Monroe, houses military exhibits and period rooms.

NEARBY SITES:
Henry Ford Museum and Greenfield Village, Henry Ford Estate-Fairlane, Dearborn Trolley Company

Caboose

Depot Town Caboose
23½ Cross Street, Ypsilanti
313-483-4256

While shopping or browsing in Ypsilanti's restored Depot Town shops, be sure to let the kids climb on board the shiny red caboose and play "engineer."

SP T   Detroit-Windsor Tunnel

Detroit-Windsor Tunnel
100 East Jefferson, Detroit
313-567-4422

Young children won't believe you at first

when you tell them they are driving under the Detroit River. Older children will be amazed that such a tunnel could ever be built. It's a Detroit landmark that makes your trip to Windsor begin as an adventure. The tunnel is located at the foot of Randolph and Jefferson. Open 24 hours, daily. A toll fee ($1.25 American, $1.50 Canadian) is collected before entering on both sides of the Detroit River. *For a closer look at the tunnel, see* Detroit At Work.

SP T   One-Room Schoolhouse

Dewey School
11501 Territorial Road, Stockbridge
517-851-8247

Location: Mayer and Territorial Roads, just off M-106, south of Stockbridge

Hours: 1-4 p.m., Sunday, June-August. 1-4 p.m., Saturday and Sunday, September-first weekend in October. Special "Rural Schooldays" tour available during May and September.

Admission: Donation. 75 cents per child for group tours.

Ages: 8 and up

Plan: Under one hour

Parking: Free lots adjacent to schoolhouse

Lunch: Picnic area in nearby Waterloo Recreation Area

Facilities: Gift shop with old-fashioned school supplies

Children can become nineteenth-century schoolchildren in this one-room historic schoolhouse.

NEARBY SITES:
Waterloo Area Farm Museum

SP T H   Auto Baron Home

Edsel and Eleanor Ford House
100 Lake Shore Road
Grosse Pointe Shores
313-884-4222
313-884-3400 (group tours)

Location: Off I-94, Vernier Road Exit. Go east to Lake Shore Drive (Jefferson).

Hours: One-hour tours are offered noon, 1, 2, 3 and 4 p.m., Wednesday-Sunday. Group tours by appointment. Grounds are open 11:30 a.m.-5 p.m., May-October.

Admission: $4 adults, $3 seniors, $2 children. $1 per person, grounds only, May-October

Ages: 7 and up

Plan: Short visit

Parking: Free, on site

Lunch: A tea tent on the grounds, selling drinks, sandwiches, and snacks is available May-October. Picnicking on the grounds is allowed.

Facilities: Bathrooms in guard house. Books and postcards are on sale in home's main lobby.

Friendly, engaging tour guides help children find many things of interest in the Edsel and Eleanor Ford home, such as the ever-present view of Lake St. Clair, curious and beautiful decorative pieces, and a many-sided mirror in the Art Deco study that gives off infinite images. Best of all, the tour offers an inside look into one of Detroit's first families. After the 50-minute tour, walk or drive over to the Play House. For most children, this will be the highlight of the visit. Built to resemble the mansion, this playhouse is created in three-quarter size with furnishings to match. Adults will feel like Alice in Wonderland.

NEARBY SITES:
Grosse Pointe War Memorial, Arts and Scraps, Belle Isle

SP T   Railcar

Eisenhower Presidential Car
7203 US-12, Onsted (Irish Hills)
517-467-2300

Location: In front of Stagecoach Stop, U.S.A., off US-12

Hours: 10:30 a.m.-6:30 p.m., Tuesday-Sunday, June-August. Closed Monday. Self-guided tours. Group tours available.

Admission: $1.25 adults, 75 cents children. Group rates available.

Ages: 5 and up

Plan: Under one hour. With Stagecoach Stop, plan on a half day visit.

Parking: Free on site

Lunch: Restaurant in Stagecoach Stop, fudge shop adjacent to railroad car, picnic areas

Facilities: Bathrooms. Gift Shop in Stage-coach Stop.

Once known as the "White House on Wheels," this railroad car was used by President Eisenhower from 1952 to 1960. Today it houses Eisenhower memorabilia and offers children a look at the conditions of coach travel. Kids will especially enjoy seeing where Eisenhower slept and ate.

NEARBY SITES:
Stagecoach Stop, U.S.A., Prehistoric Forest

SP T H   Historic Farmstead

Ella Sharp Museum
3225 Fourth Street, Jackson
313-787-2320

Location: 4½ miles south of I-94 and US-127 intersection

Hours: 10 a.m.-5 p.m., Tuesday-Friday. Noon-5 p.m., Saturday and Sunday. Closed Mondays and holidays. Planetarium shows: 3 p.m., Sunday.

Admission: $5 family, $2.50 adults, $2 seniors, $1 children under 12. Family membership available.

Ages: 2 and up

Plan: Half day visit

Parking: Free on site

Lunch: Granary Restaurant: 10 a.m.-4 p.m., Tuesday-Friday. Noon-4 p.m., Saturday and Sunday. Ice cream parlor: 10 a.m.-4 p.m., Tuesday-Friday. Noon-4 p.m., Saturday and Sunday. Adjacent Ella Sharp Park has picnic area and playground.

Facilities: Bathrooms, drinking fountain. Gift shop full of kids' toys, games, books, tapes, jewelry, and science items.

The Ella Sharp Museum is a historic complex with a vision of the future. The cornerstone of the complex is the beautifully restored nineteenth-century Merriman-Sharp family farmhouse. Self-guided tours are scheduled on the hour and half hour, daily until 4:30 p.m. Children will enjoy learning about the life of Jackson's most famous lady, seeing the toys and dolls in the children's room, and walking up to the rooftop cupola. There are many other authentically furnished, restored buildings along Farm Lane: the Eli Stilson log house, country store, print shop, schoolhouse, barn, woodworking and broom-making shops.

The modern galleries include the Hurst Planetarium, Art Gallery, Heritage Hall's Native American exhibits, and the Discovery Gallery with hands-on exhibits that will delight children.

NEARBY SITES:
Michigan Space Center, Illuminated Cascades (summer)

H   Detroit Landmark

Fisher Building
3011 West Grand Boulevard, Detroit
313-874-4444

Point out the Fisher Building's green tiled roof to the kids, and it will always be a point of reference for them. Once in the lobby, crane your necks upwards to see the impressive mosaic, marble, and tiled ceiling; shop and browse, but don't forget the fun stuff. Take the kids through the skywalks and tunnels (the Fisher Building is connected to the GM Building, New Center One, and Hotel St. Regis) and up and down New Center One's glass elevators. Park in Crowley's lot.

T   Auto Baron Home

Fisher Mansion/Bhaktivedanta Center
383 Lenox, Detroit
313-331-6740

Location: This site is off the beaten track. Take I-94 east to Cadieux exit. Go south to East Jefferson, then west to Dickerson. Follow Dickerson south. Dickerson becomes Lenox Avenue at Essex Street. After one block on Lenox, look for the Fisher Mansion on your right.

Hours: Noon-9 p.m., Friday-Sunday. One-hour tours: 12:30, 2, 3:30, and 6 p.m., Friday and Saturday. Noon, 1:30, 3, and 6 p.m., Sunday. Group tours available during the week.

Admission: $4 adults, $3 children, children 10 and under free when accompanied by adult

Ages: 8 and older

Plan: Short visit

Parking: Free, use second gate

Lunch: Govinda's, located in the elegant dining room, offers gourmet vegetarian cuisine as well as kid-pleasing desserts.

Facilities: Bathrooms. East Indian grocery and gift shop with made-in-India items, books, snacks, and incense.

Children with a vivid imagination will love this home, built by Auto Baron Lawrence Fisher in the 1920s, in a highly opulent and decorative style. Everywhere there are carved wooden faces, painted ceilings, gold inlaid patterns, and detailed tiles. Children will enjoy the indoor boatwells, the secret doors, and haunting mirrors.

The mansion, now cultural center for Krishna Consciousness followers, also has a remarkable collection of Indian paintings, tapestries, masks and sculptures. Children are welcomed on the tours and encouraged to ask questions. There are two audio-visual presentations, one 10 minutes, the other 20 minutes, both with Krishna religious content. The theme and message of both go over the heads of children, but they might enjoy the colorful costumes and images.

NEARBY SITES:
Belle Isle

SP T   Lighthouse

Fort Gratiot Lighthouse
2800 Omar Street, Port Huron
313-984-2602

Location: I-94 and Hancock Street

Hours: 8 a.m.-4 p.m. Tours by appointment only, April 1-October 30.

Admission: Free

Ages: 6 and up

Plan: Under one hour

Parking: Free lot to the right of lighthouse

Lunch: Picnic area behind lighthouse

Facilities: Bathrooms

Kids will enjoy climbing up the spiral staircase and romping around the outside picnic
area of this oldest lighthouse in operation in
the United States.

NEARBY SITES:
Mary Maxim, Inc., Museum of Art and History,
Ruby Farms

SP T H   Fort

Fort Malden National Historic Park
100 Laird Avenue
Amherstburg, Ontario, Canada
519-736-5416

Location: From tunnel, take Riverside Drive
(Highway 18) to Amherstburg. Turn right at
Alma Street, left at Laird Street. Approximately
25 minutes from tunnel.

Hours: 10 a.m.-6 p.m., daily, June-Labor Day

Admission: Free

Ages: All ages

Plan: Short visit

Parking: Free lot in front of fort

Lunch: Picnic areas along fort's grassy avenues

Facilities: Visitor center, bathrooms, benches
along Detroit River

Built in 1796 by the British, Fort Malden saw
action during the War of 1812. Today, her four
remaining buildings sit among rolling hills and
grassy avenues. Kids will enjoy almost everything about this fort. The slide history is only
six minutes long; costumed guides demonstrate musket firing and other nineteenth-century military routines. Children are allowed to
try on military costumes. Best of all, the hills
and avenues are perfect for running and rolling. After your visit, drive down a block to Austin "Toddy" Jones Park, located at the corner
of Laird Avenue South and North Street. Here

you'll find creative slides and swings, plus a wooden fort climber.

NEARBY SITES:
Amherstburg Boblo dock, Park House Museum, North American Black Historical Museum

H   Detroit Landmark

Fox Theatre
2211 Woodward, Detroit
313-567-6000

Golden ornaments, red marble pillars, sculptured animals with jeweled eyes, glittering chandeliers — these are only a few of the details which make the Fox a majestically exotic former movie palace. Try to catch a family show, which will have more modestly priced tickets than the major attractions.

H   Detroit Landmark

GM Building
3044 West Grand Boulevard, Detroit
313-556-6200

Take the skywalk from the Fisher Building into this landmark building, and you'll be surrounded by cars. The kids will enjoy eating at an old-fashioned cafeteria with old-fashioned prices, located on the basement level of the building, and open to the public only after 1 p.m. Take the tunnel back to the Fisher Building for Stroh's ice cream.

H   Detroit Landmark

Greektown
Monroe Street near Beaubien, Detroit
313-965-3800 (Hot line)

Come to Greektown hungry and sample

baklava, shish kabob, and flaming cheese. Monroe Street is lined with Greek bakeries, Greek restaurants, ice cream parlors, fudge shops, and gourmet bakeries. Trappers Alley, a festival marketplace opening onto Monroe Street, has a People Mover station on the third level.

SP T H   Historic Village

Greenfield Village
20900 Oakwood Boulevard, Dearborn
313-271-1976 (24-hour information)
313-271-1620

Location: Michigan Avenue and Southfield Freeway

Hours: 9 a.m.-5 p.m., daily, mid-March-first week in January. Closed Thanksgiving Day and Christmas Day.

Admission: $10.50 adults, $9.50 seniors, $5.25 children 5 to 12, under 5 free. Family memberships and annual passes available. Additional fees for Steam Train Ride, Suwanee Steamboat, Carousel and Carriage Tours

Ages: All ages

Plan: Full day

Parking: Free, adjacent to museum and village

Lunch: The Eagle Tavern for full dinners, Suwanee Restaurant at Suwanee Park for cafetria selection, Main Street Lunch Stand for light refreshments, Covered Bridge Lunch Stand for snacks. Picnicking is allowed throughout the village. I recommend bringing a picnic lunch and adding snacks as the day wears on.

Facilities: Bathrooms, drinking fountains, stroller rental. Three gift shops. The well-stocked Great American Emporium, located at the entrance, has many reproductions of old-fashioned children's toys, books, and craft items.

Greenfield Village is one of the Detroit area's best-known sites. Its restored homes, workshops, and stores offer a glimpse into America's past and a look at inventors Thomas Edison, the Wright Brothers, and Henry Ford, men who revolutionized our world. The village is too large to see everything on one visit with small children. Your best bet is to concentrate on the sure-fire childpleasers. Take the 30-minute round-trip train ride and visit the Firestone Farm, a working farm where costumed interpretive guides live and work according to a nineteenth-century schedule. The nearby demonstration barns, particularly glass blowing and printing, appeal to children and offer vivid memories. Ride the Suwanee Steamboat and the restored carousel, then buy an ice cream, and call it a day. You can always come again. There are many theme weekends throughout the summer and fall and Christmas festivities in December.

NEARBY SITES:
Henry Ford Museum, Dearborn Historical Museum, Henry Ford Estate-Fairlane

SP T H   Historic Village

Greenmead Museum and Historical Village
38125 Eight Mile Road, Livonia
313-477-7375

Location: Newburgh and Eight Mile Roads

Hours: 1-4 p.m., Sunday, May-December. The grounds are open daily during daylight hours. Group tours available by appointment.

Admission: $1 adults, 25 cents children 10 and under. Grounds free.

Ages: 5 and up

Plan: Short visit

Parking: Free on site

Lunch: Picnic tables in park

Facilities: Outhouses available during spring. Gift shop with variety of old-fashioned toys and trinkets.

This small historic nineteenth-century village includes Hill House, 2 other houses, a church, general store, and interpretive center. Kids will enjoy the interpretive center's ten-minute slide show, the general store's penny candy, and the restored buildings' furnishings and costumed mannequins. The on-site park has a small playground. There are special programs and decorations at Christmas.

NEARBY SITES:
Ladbroke Detroit Race Course

SP T   Auto Baron Home

Henry Ford Estate-Fairlane
4901 Evergreen
University of Michigan-Dearborn
313-593-5590

Location: Michigan Avenue and Evergreen Road

Hours: Home tours begin on the half hour 1-4:30 p.m., Sunday. On the hour 10 a.m.-3 p.m., except at noon, Monday-Saturday, April-December. Sundays only, January-March. Guided nature tour of grounds: year-round, call for reservations. Self-guided nature tour: year-round, maps available from parking lot vending machine.
"The Grand Experience," a hands-on, nineteenth-century experience for children, held in the Children's Farmhouse, noon-3 p.m., each Sunday, June-August.
Breakfast with Santa and Santa's Workshop are held in December.

Admission: Home tour: $5 adults, $4 children and seniors. The Grand Experience: Free. Santa's Workshop: $3. Breakfast with Santa: $6. Guided nature tour: Free.

Ages: 8 and up for home tour. 2 to 10 years for The Grand Experience, Breakfast with Santa and Santa's Workshop.

Plan: Home tour: 1½ hours. Add an hour each for Grand Experience and nature walk

Parking: Free lot across from estate

Lunch: Pool restaurant: 11 a.m.-2 p.m., Monday-Friday, year-round; picnic areas

Facilities: Bathrooms. Gift shop with Ford-related items, old-fashioned toys, and books.

For children, the main attraction on this estate is the white clapboard miniature farmhouse, full of hands-on, nineteenth-century clothes, games, toys, and miniature farm and household implements. Parents need to duck while entering the farmhouse; children fit perfectly.

The 1½ hour tour of the Ford mansion might be too much for little children, but older children will enjoy walking single file through a 16-foot deep underground tunnel connecting the main house with the electric power house, peeking into the indoor bowling alley, and being allowed to sit on the unauthentic furniture as the tour guide speaks.

NEARBY SITES:
Henry Ford Museum, Greenfield Village, Dearborn Historical Museum, Dearborn Trolley Company

SP T   Fort

Historic Fort Wayne
6325 West Jefferson, Detroit
313-297-9360

Location: Take I-75 to Livernois exit, go south. Livernois deadends at the fort

Hours: 9:30 a.m.-5 p.m., Wednesday-Sunday, May-October

Admission: $1 adults, 50 cents children and seniors

Ages: All ages

Plan: Half day

Parking: Free lot near visitor center

Lunch: Vending machines and tables inside, picnic tables outside visitor center

Facilities: Bathrooms in visitor center, outhouses near Commanding Officer's House. Gift shop with lots of under-$1 items in visitor center.

Visit Fort Wayne on a sunny summer day and pass through the sally port, back 140 years. The kids will love the sally port — the fort's original stone and brick gate, now several damp, secret, tunnel-like rooms. They will also enjoy running up and down the 20-step metal stairway to the ramparts where the Detroit River comes into glorious view. Take time to watch costumed guides in Civil War uniforms demonstrate military maneuvers and tour the several on-site museums. The 83-acre fort includes the National Museum of Tuskegee Airmen (*see* Museums), Great Lakes Indian Museum (*see* Museums), a restored 1880 Victorian Commanding Officer's House, visitor center, and the Spanish-American War Guardhouse.

NEARBY SITES:

Detroit's Boblo dock is several blocks away

SP T   Historic Farmstead

John Freeman Walls Historic Site
Puce Road, Maidstone Township
Ontario, Canada
519-258-6253 (office, not site)

Location: Take Highway 401 east, exit Puce Road north. The site is approximately two miles north on Puce Road, 20 minutes from Windsor-Detroit border.

Hours: 9 a.m.-5 p.m., daily, May 15-early October. School and group tours available by appointment.

Admission: $3 adults, $2 seniors, $1 children

Ages: All ages
Plan: Short visit
Parking: Free on site
Lunch: Picnic area
Facilities: Bathrooms. Gift shop with Canadian and Underground Railroad crafts and souvenirs.

Former slave John Freeman Walls and his wife escaped to freedom and settled in Maidstone Township in 1846. Their farmstead became an important terminal on the Underground Railroad. This historic site features a train caboose museum of Underground Railroad history and African art, a 1798 log cabin, and 1846 log cabin. A movie about Underground Railroad history is also shown. The site makes history vividly come to life.

NEARBY SITES:
Windsor: Hiram Walker Historical Museum, city parks, Windsor City Market

SP T H   Historic Village

John R. Park Homestead
360 Fairview Avenue, Essex
Ontario, Canada
519-738-2029

Location: Essex County Road 50 between Kingsville and Colchester. From Windsor, take Highway 18 southeast to Road 50 (45 minutes southeast of Windsor).
Hours: 10 a.m.-4 p.m., Monday-Friday, all year, also weekends in July and August. Group tours available, call at least two weeks in advance.
Admission: $6 family, $2 adults, $1.50 children 6 to 16, 5 and under free
Ages: 5 and up
Plan: Short visit
Parking: Free, on site

Lunch: Picnic area, cold drinks and snack foods for sale

Facilities: Bathrooms. Gift shop with wooden toys and candy sticks.

The John R. Park Homestead, including Park's home and several restored buildings — shed, smoke house, ice house, outhouse, blacksmith shop, sawmill, and livestock stable — offer children a hands-on look into nineteenth-century life. Costumed guides demonstrate and involve children in seasonal crafts such as candle dipping, spinning, butter churning, and nineteenth-century games. Children will also enjoy the short introductory slide show presentation. Many special seasonal events celebrate maple syrup, fall harvest, and Christmas.

NEARBY SITES:
Southwestern Ontario Heritage Village, Colasanti's Tropical Gardens
Amherstburg: Amherstburg Boblo dock, Fort Malden National Historic Park, North American Black Historical Museum

H	Restored Shopping Plaza

Kerrytown Plaza
407 North Fifth Avenue, Ann Arbor
313-662-4221

Thirty-five specialty shops and restaurants are located in this charming setting of restored nineteenth-century buildings. Kids will love the aromas coming from the specialty foods shops and market. Little Dipper Candle Shop lets children dip their own candles. On Saturday mornings, the adjacent Farmers' Market is bustling with activity.

SP T H   Auto Baron Home

Meadow Brook Hall
and Knole Cottage
Oakland University, Rochester
313-370-3140

Location: On Adams Road, five miles north of I-75

Hours: July and August: 10 a.m.-5 p.m., Monday-Saturday and 1-5 p.m., Sunday. Rest of year: 1-5 p.m., Sunday only. Last tour is at 4 p.m.
Christmas walk: 10 a.m.-4 p.m. or 10 a.m.-8 p.m., depending on the day, late November-early December.

Admission: $4 adults, $3 seniors, $2 children 12 and younger. Christmas walk: $6 adults, Monday-Friday. $8 adults, Saturday and Sunday. $5 seniors, $4 children 12 and younger.

Ages: 8 and up

Plan: Short visit (indoor tour takes approximately two hours)

Parking: Free lot adjacent to mansion

Lunch: Dining room facilities are open to the public for formal Sunday buffet dinners. Available for groups at other times by prior reservations.

Facilities: Bathrooms. Small gift counter with Meadow Brook Hall stationery.

Matilda Dodge Wilson, widow of auto baron John Dodge, built her 100-room Tudor mansion in the 1920's for approximately $4 million. Meadow Brook Hall is Michigan's Biltmore, a magnificent tribute to a bygone era, decorated richly with authentic furnishings. The two-hour tour is not appropriate for small children, but patient older children will be rewarded with visual architectural delights and interesting anecdotes. Meadow Brook Hall's grounds are lovely at every season, and children will want to walk into the woods to explore the Knole

Cottage, a six-room playhouse built to three-quarter size for Matilda and John Wilson's daughter. During the Christmas walk, Santa presides over Knole Cottage, and children are encouraged to visit during daylight hours.

NEARBY SITES:
Leader Dog for the Blind, Dinosaur Hill Nature Preserve and Den, Wright and Filippis, Inc., cider mills

---

SP T	Historic Village

Mill Race Historical Village
Griswold, north of Main Street, Northville
313-348-1845

Location: Just west of Haggerty Road, between Eight Mile Road and Main Street

Hours: 1-4 p.m., Sundays, June-October. Grounds always open. Pre-arranged tours available all year. School groups can spend a day in the Wash Oak School, October-November or April-May.

Admission: $1 adults, 50 cents children

Ages: 8 and up

Plan: Short visit

Parking: Free on site

Lunch: Picnic sites on grounds

Facilities: Bathrooms in main house, small gift shop

This historic village includes a restored nineteenth-century home with exhibits of local history, plus several other restored homes and buildings — church, inn, school, and blacksmith shop — all on a seven-acre site along Mill Pond. Children will enjoy the one-room schoolhouse and gazebo.

NEARBY SITES:
Marquis Theatre, Alfonse Jacques Farm, cider mills and u-pick farms, Maybury State Park Petting Farm

SP T H   Historic Buildings

Navarre-Anderson Trading Post and Country Store Museum
North Custer Road at Raisinville Road
Monroe
313-243-7137

Location: Four miles west of Monroe on North Custer at the Raisinville Bridge

Hours: 1-5 p.m., Saturday and Sunday, Memorial Day-Labor Day. Group tours available.

Admission: Free

Ages: All ages

Plan: Under one hour

Parking: Free adjacent to Country Store Museum

Lunch: Restaurants in town

Facilities: Bathrooms. Country store offers penny candy and souvenirs.

The restored and furnished trading post, built in 1789, is the oldest residence in Michigan. The Country store is typical of the early 1900s general store. Children will enjoy choosing penny candy.

NEARBY SITES:
Monroe County Historical Museum

SP T H   Historic Home

Park House Museum
214 Dalhousie Street, Amherstburg
Ontario, Canada
519-736-2511

Location: Highway 18 and Rankin Avenue

Hours: Summer: 9 a.m.-5 p.m., daily. Winter: 11 a.m.-5 p.m., Tuesday-Friday, and Sunday. Closed Monday and Saturday.

Admission: $1 adults, 50 cents children 6 to 16, under 6 free. Family membership available.

Ages: 7 and up

Plan: Short visit

Parking: Free on street

Lunch: Picnic area, restaurants, bakery, and ice cream parlor on Dalhousie Street

Facilities: Bathrooms. Gift shop with books and tinware.

Park House, the oldest house within a 250 mile radius, was built in Detroit in 1796 and later moved across the river. The first floor has been restored to show what life was like in the 1850s. Costumed guides demonstrate early domestic life, including tinsmithing and printing. Children will be interested in the doctor's and ship captain's offices, the children's nursery full of toys, and the sewing room. Upstairs, there are pioneer and local history exhibits. Best of all, Park House is located in the Navy Yard, along the Detroit River, a wonderful place to picnic and boat watch in the summer.

NEARBY SITES:
Amherstburg Boblo dock, Fort Malden National Historic Park, North American Black Historical Museum

SP T H   Historic Home

Pine Grove Historical Museum
405 Oakland, Pontiac
313-338-6732

Location: ½ mile north of Y-Track Drive

Hours: 9 a.m.-4 p.m., Monday-Friday. 1-4 p.m., first Sunday of each month. Group tours available.

Admission: $3 adults, $1.50 children and seniors

Ages: 6 and up

Plan: Short visit

Parking: Free on site

Lunch: Carriage house doubles as a lunchroom. Picnicking is allowed on the museum's four acres.

Facilities: Bathrooms. Gift shop with old-fashioned, hand-made toys and items, ranging in price from 25 cents to $20.

At Pine Grove, the home of Michigan Governor Moses Wisner, children are encouraged to step back into the past. The Greek Revival home is chock full of authentic furnishings, clothing, and home implements. The four-acre estate also includes a fully equipped summer kitchen, smoke house, root cellar, and one-room schoolhouse. Costumed guides lead group tours and offer children hands-on experiences.

NEARBY SITES:
Bald Mountain Riding Stables, Pontiac Farmers' Market

H   Detroit Landmark

Renaissance Center
Jefferson Avenue, Detroit
313-568-5600

Kids will love walking through the three futuristic silver towers that have come to symbolize Detroit. Park in the structure off Beaubien (three hours validated parking for $1), ride the People Mover in a circle, and disembark at the RenCen station. Stores and restaurants are located on Levels 1 and 2. Visit the Westin's eight-story atrium lobby filled with plants, observation lookouts, and reflecting pools. Don't leave without viewing "The World of Ford," a display of the newest in Ford and Lincoln-Mercury cars (Tower 300, Level 2. 10 a.m.-6 p.m., Monday-Friday. Noon-6 p.m., Saturday).

SP T   Historic Farmhouse

Rochester Hills Museum at Van Hoosen Farm
1005 Van Hoosen Road, Rochester
313-656-4663

Location: One mile east of Rochester Road off Tienken Road, five miles north of M-59

Hours: 1-4 p.m., Wednesday-Saturday

Admission: $2 adults, $1 seniors, 50 cents children

Ages: 8 and up

Plan: Short visit, includes driving tour of Stoney Creek Village

Parking: Free on site

Lunch: Picnic area along Stoney Creek

Facilities: Bathrooms. Gift shop with local history books, stationery, craft items.

The Sarah Van Hoosen Jones homestead is a low, rambling estate nestled in the middle of historic Stoney Creek Village. Authentic furnishings and household implements make nineteenth-century rural Michigan come to life. Children will especially enjoy the doctor's office and farm office, the kitchen with its 1902 washing machine and old-fashioned ice box, and the child's bedroom, furnished with toys, games, clothes, and child-sized furniture. The grounds and gazebo are ideal for an afternoon romp. There are special annual events, including Christmas activities and summer camp. Archaeological digs are in progress on the site.

NEARBY SITES:
Dinosaur Hill Nature Preserve and Den, Leader Dog for the Blind, Meadow Brook Hall, Wright and Filippis, Inc., cider mills

SP T H   Historic Village & Car Museum

Southwestern Ontario Heritage Village
Essex County Road 23, Essex
Ontario, Canada
519-776-6909

Location: From Detroit-Windsor bridge, take Highway 3 east to 23 south. The village is just south of the Highway 19 and 23 junction.

Hours: 11 a.m.-5 p.m., Wednesday-Sunday, April-November. 11 a.m.-5 p.m., daily, July-August. Group tours available. Special times available for school groups.

Admission: $2.50 adults, $1.50 seniors and children 13 to 18, $1 children 5 to 12. Group rates are available.

Ages: All ages

Plan: Short visit

Parking: Free on site

Lunch: Picnic tables in village park. Refreshment stand available during special events.

Facilities: Bathrooms in car museum. Souvenirs and candy in general store.

Southwestern Ontario Heritage Village's ten turn-of-the-century buildings—a railway station, schoolhouse, church, general store, shoe repair/barber shop, home, three log cabins, and barnyard buildings—are located in the midst of 54 wooded acres. A transportation museum documents the early settlers' travel from snowshoes and wagons to modern automobiles. The buildings, artifacts, and museum make history come to life for children. Special events are the Teddy Bear Reunion and Steam Engine Show.

NEARBY SITES:
Colasanti's Tropical Gardens, John R. Park Homestead
Amherstburg: Amherstburg Boblo dock, Fort

Malden National Historic Park, North American
Black Historical Museum

T H	Restored Shopping Plaza

Trappers Alley Festival Marketplace
Monroe and Beaubien, Greektown, Detroit
313-963-5445

Location: Corner of Monroe and Beaubien,
five blocks north of the Renaissance Center, in
the heart of Greektown

Hours: 10 a.m.-9 p.m., Monday-Thursday. 10
a.m.-midnight, Friday and Saturday. Noon-9
p.m., Sunday. Fifteen-minute historic tours
available; call ahead.

Admission: Free

Ages: All ages

Plan: Short visit

Parking: Street parking is very difficult to find.
Use the rear parking lot on Lafayette. $1 first
½ hour, $1 second ½ hour, 50 cents each ad-
ditional hour.

Lunch: Seven fast-food booths with tables and
chairs, six sit-down restaurants

Facilities: Bathrooms. Many gift and clothing
stores. People Mover Station located on third
level.

A fur tannery in the 1850s, Trapper's Alley is
now three levels of aromatic food booths, colorful gift shops, and hanging sculpture. Children will enjoy the carnival atmosphere. It is
also a convenient People Mover station.

NEARBY SITES:
Greektown, Underground Railroad-Second
Baptist Church, Renaissance Center, Hart
Plaza

SP T   Historic Village

Troy Museum and Historic Village Green
60 West Wattles, Troy
313-524-3570

Location: Corner of Wattles (Seventeen Mile Road) and Livernois

Hours: 9 a.m.-5:30 p.m., Tuesday-Saturday. 1-5 p.m., Sunday.

Admission: Free

Ages: 6 and up

Plan: Under one hour

Parking: Lot west of the museum

Lunch: Lots of restaurants in the area

Facilities: Bathrooms. Gift shop with old-fashioned toys, candy sticks, coloring books.

The Troy Museum offers several special exhibits each year of curious local artifacts. While young children might find these static exhibits boring, they will enjoy the village green's restored and furnished buildings. Buy each of the little historians a candy stick and roam around out back. You'll find a gazebo, pioneer log cabin, one-room school house, wagon shop, print shop, and the Greek Revival home of early pioneer Solomon Casewell. Be sure to climb upstairs in the Casewell house to see the authentically dressed mannequins ready for bed.

NEARBY SITES:
Lloyd A. Stage Outdoor Education Center

SP T   African American History

Underground Railroad - Second Baptist Church
441 Monroe Avenue, Detroit
313-961-0920

Location: Monroe at Beaubien in Greektown

Hours: Pre-arranged tours are offered 9:30 a.m.-3 p.m., Monday-Thursday

Admission: Free, donations accepted

Ages: 8 and older

Plan: Short visit. Tour lasts approximately one hour.

Parking: Use lots west and north of the church; the church will validate the parking ticket.

Lunch: Nearby Greektown

Facilities: Bathrooms, drinking fountain

The Second Baptist Church was one of several Detroit stations on the famous Underground Railroad. Between 1836 and 1865, more than 5,000 fugitive slaves passed through the 12-by-13-foot windowless cellar room. For many, it was their last stop on the road to Canada and to freedom. The tour begins with an introduction in the chapel and then continues down a narrow staircase into the once-barren room. Colorful murals depict freedom routes and famous abolitionists. Church historian/tour guide Nathaniel Leach makes the era come to life. Sitting in the actual hiding room is quite an emotional experience.

NEARBY SITES:
Greektown, Renaissance Center, Hart Plaza

SP H   Historic Inn & Barn

Walker Tavern Historic Complex
US-12, Brooklyn
313-467-4414

Location: Just north of US-12 on M-50, across the street from the Brick Walter Tavern, now an antique mart

Hours: 10 a.m.-5 p.m., daily, Memorial Day-Labor Day

Admission: Free

Ages: 8 and older

Plan: Under one hour

Parking: Free lot
Lunch: Picnic tables
Facilities: Outhouses

You can learn some interesting facts at the Walker Tavern Visitor Center. Built in the 1830s, the Walker Tavern was a regular stop on the Great Sauk Trail, the stagecoach route traveling between Detroit and Chicago. One hundred years ago, it took five days to get to Chicago from Detroit; it cost 25 cents a night and 25 cents for a meal at the tavern. Although the visitor center's exhibits are colorful and easy-to-read, they will only interest older children with a yen for history. There is also a barn with displays and a restored and furnished tavern.

NEARBY SITES:
Continue west on US-12 to antique store and flea market territory

SP T   Historic Farmstead

Waterloo Area Farm Museum
9998 Waterloo-Munith Road, Stockbridge
517-851-7636, 313-769-2219

Location: I-94 west to exit 153. Take Clear Lake Road to Waterloo, then follow signs three miles to farm.
Hours: 1-4 p.m., Tuesday-Sunday, June-August. 1-4 p.m., Saturday and Sunday, September-early October. Last tour at 3:30 p.m.
Admission: $2 adults, $1.50 seniors, 50 cents children 5 to 11, under 5 free. Family memberships available.
Ages: 6 and up
Plan: Short visit
Parking: Free lot adjacent to farmhouse
Lunch: Picnic area on grounds and in nearby Waterloo Recreation Area
Facilities: Outhouses. Gift shop with lots of craft and Made-in-Michigan items and toys.

The Waterloo Museum consists of an 1850s farmhouse, log cabin, and outbuildings—ice house, barn, bake house, windmill, milk cellar, and farm repair shop—that were once part of the homestead of German immigrant Jacob Ruehle. Like many families of the time, the Ruehles were industrious, thrifty, and imaginative. Their personalities live on in the homestead, furnished in detail with authentic clothing, furniture, tools, and implements. Kids will enjoy the 100-year-old gadgets, including a sausage stuffer, honey extractor, rug beater, and copper boiler. There's even a dog treadmill attached to a churn so the family pet could help make butter. Tour guides encourage young visitors to polish silver with white ash and try on the child-sized yoke with hanging buckets used to carry water up to the house from the stream. Special events are Pioneer Day in October and Christmas on the Farm in December.

NEARBY SITES:
Dewey School

T	Historic Home

Willistead Manor
1899 Niagara Street, Windsor
Ontario, Canada
519-255-6545

Location: Niagara Street at Kildare Road

Hours: 1-4 p.m., First and third Sunday of each month, January-June. 1-4 p.m., Sunday-Wednesday, July-August. 1-6 p.m., Sunday, and 7-9 p.m., Wednesday, December. No tours December 24-26, 31. Last tour begins at half hour before closing.

Admission: $1.75 adults, $1.25 seniors, 75 cents children

Ages: 6 and up

Plan: Short visit

Parking: Free on site

Lunch: Many restaurants along Riverside Drive in downtown Windsor.

Facilities: Bathrooms. Christmas Shoppe in the Coach House during Christmas touring schedule.

Willistead Manor will fuel imaginative children with the stuff of great stories. The elaborately furnished home of Edward Chandler Walker, son of distillery founder Hiram Walker, spares no expense in details and materials. There are elaborate hand-carved wooden mantels, colorful furnishings, draperies, and an impressive staircase. Children will love the home's secret doorways and walk-in safe. Fifteen acres of park land offer families a wonderful place to romp.

NEARBY SITES:
Hiram Walker Historical Museum, city parks, Windsor City Market

---

SP T H   Grist Mill

Wolcott Mill
Kunstman Road, Ray Township
313-749-5997 or 313-791-4621
(Stoney Creek Metropark)

Location: Kunstman Road, north of Twenty-Nine Mile Road, between Van Dyke and North Avenue in Ray Township, just outside of Romeo.

Hours: 10 a.m.-5 p.m., daily, May-October. Groups may also schedule tours by advance appointment.

Admission: Free

Ages: School age

Plan: Short visit; 1½ hour tour

Parking: Free on site

Lunch: Picnic tables

Facilities: Bathrooms

The restored 140-year-old Wolcott Mill offers imaginative displays on the milling industry, pioneer life, and farming.

NEARBY SITES:
Stoney Creek Nature Center, cider mills

6
SCIENCE AND NATURE

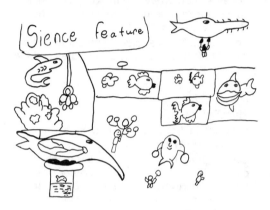

This chapter helps you cater to your children's innate curiosity about the world. Watch them soar through space at area planetariums and explore science and their environment with hands-on exhibits and activities at area science museums and nature centers. Take a family stroll through the seasons along marked trails; visit eternal summer in area conservatories lush with tropical ferns and arid cacti. Feed corn kernels to a hungry goat; watch a baby calf suckle; witness electric eels at feeding time. It's all happening at area zoos, nature centers, and petting farms.

Abbreviations: SP — site offers school programs; T — site offers group tours; H — wheelchair accessible.

SP T H	Planetarium

Abrams Planetarium
Michigan State University, East Lansing
517-355-4672, 517-355-4676
(ask the astronomer)

Location: Near Shaw and Farm Lanes, MSU campus

Hours: Building: 8:30 a.m.-Noon, 1-4:30 p.m., Monday-Friday. Planetarium shows: 8 p.m., Friday and Saturday, 4 p.m., Sunday. Weekday shows for groups by appointment. Christmas show during December.

Admission: $2.50 adults, $2 students and seniors, $1.50 12 and under. Group rates and family memberships available.

Ages: All ages. Some shows require minimum age.

Plan: Short visit

Parking: In front of building. Free on weekends. 50 cents weekdays.

Lunch: Burger King and vending machines located in the Michigan Union, corner of Abbott and Grand River. Many other restaurants on Grand River Avenue, across from campus.

Facilities: Bathrooms. Gift shop with astronomy-related novelties, books, star maps.

The Abrams Planetarium's 360-degree domed sky theater, post-show sky talks, and blacklight space art gallery will introduce children to the wonders of the universe.

NEARBY SITES:

MSU Campus sites: MSU Museum of Natural History, Horticultural Gardens, Kresge Art Museum

Lansing sites: R.E. Olds Transportation Museum, Michigan Women's Historical Center, Michigan Historical Museum, State Capitol, Potter Park Zoo, Impression 5 Museum

SP T H   Petting Farm

Alfonse Jacques Farm
Napier Road, Northville
313-349-0392

Location: I-696 west to I-275 south. Exit at Eight Mile Road. Go west to Napier Road. Turn right; farm is ½ mile north on Napier Road.

Hours: By appointment only; groups are welcome

Admission: $1 adults, $1 children

Ages: Preschool-early elementary

Plan: Short visit

Parking: Free on site

Lunch: Picnic tables

Facilities: Bathrooms

Come on down to the farm for a tour and a hay ride and, in early spring, baby animals.

NEARBY SITES:
Marquis Theatre, Mill Race Historical Village, cider mills and u-pick farms, Maybury State Park Petting Farm

---

SP T H   Hands-On Science Museum

Ann Arbor Hand-On Museum
219 East Huron Street, Ann Arbor
313-995-5439

For full information, see Museums

H   Greenhouses

Anna Scripps Whitcomb Conservatory
Belle Isle Park, Detroit
267-7133, 267-7134

Location: On Belle Isle

Hours: 9 a.m.-6 p.m., daily, May-September. 9 a.m.-5 p.m., daily, October-April.

Admission: Free, donations accepted

Ages: All ages

Plan: Under one hour

Parking: Free on site

Lunch: Picnic area, nearby concession stands (summer only)

Facilities: Bathrooms

Each room offers children a temperate climate with lush tropical flowers, greens, and unusual cacti. Point out the orange and banana trees; listen for chirping birds. The conservatory is a particulary nice place to visit during the winter. Kids can skip from room to room, soaking in the warmth.

NEARBY SITES:
Belle Isle Aquarium, Belle Isle Nature Center, Dossin Great Lakes Museum, Playscape, Belle Isle Zoo

SP T H   Aquarium

Belle Isle Aquarium
Belle Isle Park, Detroit
313-267-7159

Location: On Belle Isle

Hours: 10 a.m.-5 p.m., daily. Electric eel feeding shows: 10:30 a.m., 12:30 and 2:30 p.m.

Admission: Free

Ages: All ages

Plan: Short visit

Parking: Free on site

Lunch: Picnic areas and concessions during the summer

Facilities: Bathrooms located in nearby building. Gift shop with shells and other marine items.

The green-tiled, domed building is the nation's oldest aquarium, built in 1904. Murky and still, it echoes with an underwater sensation and houses more than 200 species of fish, reptiles, and amphibians. Kids become transfixed by the exotic and the frightening aquatic creatures gliding about in 50 well-labeled tanks. Electric eel feeding shows are worth seeing. As the eels are fed, their current turns on a lightbulb and sounds a horn.

NEARBY SITES:
Anna Scripps Whitcomb Conservatory, Belle Isle Nature Center, Dossin Great Lakes Museum, Playscape, Belle Isle Zoo

---

SP T H   Wildlife & Plants

Belle Isle Nature Center
Belle Isle Park, Detroit
313-267-7157

Location: On east end of Belle Isle
Hours: 10 a.m.-5 p.m., Tuesday-Sunday. Closed Mondays.
Admission: Free
Ages: 5 and up
Plan: Under one hour
Parking: Free, adjacent to center
Lunch: Picnic area across the street
Facilities: Bathrooms, nature trails

Nature Center displays, exhibits, films, slide programs, and live native animals, plus two nature trails, help children better understand their environment. Kids will also be interested in the Injured Animal Shelter, which houses injured native animals and is located adjacent to the center.

NEARBY SITES:
Anna Scripps Whitcomb Conservatory, Belle Isle Aquarium, Dossin Great Lakes Museum, Playscape, Belle Isle Zoo

---

SP T H   Zoo

Belle Isle Zoo
Belle Isle Park, Detroit
313-267-7160, 313-267-7161

Location: On Belle Isle
Hours: 10 a.m.-5 p.m., daily, May 1-October 31. Sea lion feedings at 4 p.m., daily.

Admission: $2 adults, $1 seniors, 50 cents 5 to 12, 4 and under free
Ages: All ages
Plan: Short visit
Parking: Free on site
Lunch: Snack stands
Facilities: Bathrooms, souvenir stand

Belle Isle Zoo's elevated boardwalk is ¾ mile long with a refreshment stand mid-way. It offers families with small children a wonderfully unique way to view over 130 animals, take a walk, and have a snack, all at the same time. Kids will love the exotic animals: pink flamingoes, kangaroos, sea lions, and the siamangs —unusual, hooting apes.

NEARBY SITES:
Anna Scripps Whitcomb Conservatory, Belle Isle Aquarium, Dossin Great Lakes Museum, Playscape, Belle Isle Nature Center

SP T H   Working Dairy Farm

Calder Brothers Dairy Farm
9334 Finzel Road, Carleton
313-654-2622

Location: South Stoney Creek and Finzel Roads. Carleton is about 70 minutes south of downtown Detroit, off I-75 south.
Hours: 10 a.m.-8 p.m., Monday-Saturday. 11 a.m.-8 p.m., Sunday. Closes at 9 p.m. during the summer. Call ahead to schedule tours.
Admission: Free for farm visit. $2 per person for pre-arranged tour.
Ages: All ages
Plan: Short visit
Parking: Free on site
Lunch: Picnic tables. A full-service ice cream parlor featuring Calder Brothers ice cream, plus a farm store selling Calder Brothers dairy products: milk bottled in glass, chocolate milk, buttermilk, sour cream, butter, eggs, and egg nog.

Facilities: Bathrooms. Farm store also sells jellies, jams, and hand-woven baskets.

Visit a true working dairy farm. The kids will enjoy petting and watching the animals—lots of cows, plus peacocks, dogs, burros, and geese. Buy milk in bottles and enjoy delicious handmade ice cream. Pre-arranged tours include milking a cow by hand, bottle feeding a calf, watching a cow being machine-milked, and watching how milk is stored for transport to the Calder Brothers processing plant. Each tour participant also receives a complimentary ice cream cone.

NEARBY SITES:
Monroe is farther south along I-75

SP T H   Nature Center, Trails

Carl F. Fenner Arboretum
2020 East Mt. Hope Avenue, Lansing
517-483-4224

Location: Trowbridge Road exit off I-496, south on Harrison Road, west on Mt. Hope Avenue

Hours: Grounds: 8 a.m.-dusk, daily. Nature Center Building: 9 a.m.-4 p.m., Monday-Friday. 10 a.m.-5 p.m., Saturday. 11 a.m.-5 p.m., Sunday

Admission: Free

Ages: All ages

Plan: Short visit

Parking: Free on site

Lunch: Picnic area

Facilities: Bathrooms. Nature center gift shop (open on the weekends) sells nature-oriented coloring books, story books, magnifying glasses, polished stones.

For a 5-cent donation, children can buy packets of crackers to throw to the birds, geese, and squirrels living within the Fenner Arboretum's 120 acres. Walking along the easy trails you'll also find an herb garden, waterfowl pond, replica of a pioneer cabin, and if you're lucky, you'll catch a glimpse of the arboretum's American bison. The nature center houses displays, touch-me exhibits, and live Michigan animals. Seasonal events are the Maple Syrup Festival in March and the Apple Butter Festival in October.

NEARBY SITES:
Lansing: R.E. Olds Transportation Museum, Michigan Women's Historical Center, Michigan Historical Museum, Impression 5 Museum, State Capitol, Potter Park Zoo
MSU Campus: Abrams Planetarium, Horticultural Gardens, MSU Museum of Natural History

SP T H   Petting Farm

Charles L. Bowers Farm
1219 East Square Lake Road
Bloomfield Hills
313-540-5269

Location: Off I-75 between Adams and Squirrel Roads

Hours: Pre-arranged tours available 10 a.m.-3 p.m., weekdays. Open Barn Days, free to the public two Saturdays in fall and spring.

Admission: $2 per person

Ages: Preschool to 12th grade

Plan: Short visit

Parking: Free on site

Lunch: Lots of restaurants located on Telegraph Road

Facilities: Bathrooms

Children will cherish the Charles L. Bowers School Farm experience, offered as part of a group tour or during the several Open Barn Days throughout the year. They can observe and participate in many rural activities—milking cows, churning butter, harvesting crops, spinning wool, feeding barnyard animals, preserving food, making cheese, and going on a hayride.

NEARBY SITES:
E.L. Johnson Nature Center, Cranbrook Academy of Art Museum, Cranbrook House and Garden, Cranbrook Institute of Science

SP T H   Planetarium

Children's Museum Planetarium
67 East Kirby, Detroit
313-494-1210

Location: In the Cultural Center, just north of the Detroit Institute of Arts. A prancing silver horse sculpture made of chrome car bumpers sits on the front lawn.

Hours: Planetarium demonstrations: 11 a.m. and 1 p.m., Saturday. Afternoons only during the summer.

Admission: $1

Ages: Geared to elementary school-age children

Plan: Under one hour

Parking: Use metered parking along Kirby or park in the Science Center lot on John R ($2) and walk a block to the museum

Lunch: Eat across the street in the DIA Kresge Court Cafe

Facilities: Bathrooms, drinking fountain. Gift shop with lots of handmade and unique toys and gifts.

Planetarium shows are held in a small intimate second-story room. With a sense of humor and wonder, they offer explanations of seasonal wonders, folk tales, and legends relating to the night sky. They are wonderful first-time experiences for young children.

NEARBY SITES:
Cultural Center: Detroit Institute of Arts, Detroit Historical Museum, Museum of African American History, International Institute, De-

troit Public Library, Detroit Science Center, Your Heritage House

---

Colasanti's Tropical Gardens
Ruthven, Ontario, Canada
519-326-3287

Location: Off Highway 3, approximately 25 miles from the Ambassador Bridge

Hours: 8 a.m.-5 p.m., Monday-Saturday. 8 a.m.-8 p.m., Thursday. 8 a.m.-6 p.m., Sunday.

Admission: Free

Ages: All ages

Plan: Short visit

Parking: Free on site

Lunch: Picnic table area and snack bar with hot dogs, soft drinks, ice cream, and snacks

Facilities: Bathrooms. Almost all of the hundreds of species of tropical plants and cacti are for sale (only bulbs and citrus can't be brought back through U.S. customs).

Enter a tropical rain forest or warming desert, and see 15 greenhouses full of brilliant tropical flowers and unusual cacti. Mixed in with these fragrant and colorful plants are exotic birds and a barnyard of animals to pet and play with, from sheep and goats to an ostrich and bison. On the weekends, pony rides for children are available for 25 cents.

NEARBY SITES:
Jack Miner's Bird Sanctuary, Point Pelee

Cook's Farm Dairy
2950 Seymour Lake Road, Ortonville
313-627-3329

Location: Take I-75 north to M-15 north. Go east on Seymour Lake Road one mile.

Hours: Summer: 9 a.m.-10 p.m., Monday-Saturday. 2-9 p.m., Sunday. Winter: 9 a.m.-8 p.m., Monday-Saturday. 2-8 p.m., Sunday. Call to schedule tours for groups of ten or more.

Admission: Free for grounds and farm store. $2 per person for tour, includes a complimentary ice cream cone and glass of Cook's chocolate milk.

Ages: All ages

Plan: Short visit. Tour takes approximately one hour.

Parking: Free on site

Lunch: Picnic tables. Ice cream parlor with Cook's ice cream, farm store with Cook's dairy products—all made on premises.

Facilities: Outhouses. Farm store also sells seasonal items such as honey and pumpkins.

After visiting Cook's Farm Dairy, toddlers will have no problem telling you what a cow says. Cows are everywhere, lounging on the grass, nosing up against the fence. You can visit the cows in the barn and treat the family to an ice cream cone, or call ahead for the tour and still enjoy an ice cream cone. The informal tours start in the cow barn. After meeting newborn calves, you are taken into the production plant for a dry run of the process that turns cows' milk into ice cream and chocolate milk. The tour ends in the ice cream parlor/farm store with a complimentary cone and glass of chocolate milk.

NEARBY SITES:
Cider mills

SP T H   Hands-On Science Museum

Cranbrook Institute of Science
500 Lone Pine Road, Bloomfield Hills
313-645-3200

For full information, see Museums

SP T H   Planetarium

Cranbrook Institute of
Science Planetarium
500 Lone Pine Road, Bloomfield Hills
313-645-3200

Location: Use the entrance to the Cranbrook Educational Community, the farthest east off Lone Pine Road between Lahser and Cranbrook Roads. You'll know you're there when you see the stegosaurus.

Hours: Lasera Shows: 7:30, 8:30, 9:30 p.m., Friday. 3:45, 8:30, 9:30 p.m., Saturday. 3:45 p.m., Sunday. Planetarium Shows: 3, 3:45, 7:30 p.m., Saturday. 3, 3:45 p.m., Sunday. Additional shows are added during holidays and school vacations.

Admission: $4 adults, $3 children ages 3 to 17 and seniors, children under 3 free. Family membership available. Group rates available on weekdays. Planetarium: $1 additional, members free. Lasera: $1.50 additional.

Ages: 5 and up for most lasera and planetarium shows. 3 and up are admitted to the holiday show, "Ornaments."

Plan: Shows are approximately one hour

Parking: Free on site

Lunch: A lunch room with vending machines

Facilities: Bathrooms, drinking fountain on lower level. Two gift shops offer a wonderful selection of science toys. The Dino Shop specializes in dinosaur gifts; the lobby shop has everything else.

Cranbrook Institute of Science offers creative, colorful, and educational stargazing shows, and sound and light lasera shows in a state-of-the-art planetarium. Older children and teens will especially enjoy the lasera shows set to rock music.

NEARBY SITES:
Cranbrook Academy of Art Museum, Cranbrook House and Garden

SP T H   Hands-On Science Museum

Detroit Science Center
5020 John R, Detroit
313-577-8400

For full information, see Museums

SP T H   Omnimax Theater

Detroit Science Center
Space Theater
5020 John R, Detroit
313-577-8400

Location: One mile east of Woodward on the corner of Warren and John R

Hours: The Space Theater shows Omnimax movies every hour on the half hour. 9:30 a.m.-3:30 p.m., Tuesday-Friday. 10:30 a.m.-5:30 p.m., Saturday. 12:30-5:30 p.m., Sunday. Closed Monday and major holidays.

Admission: Omnimax Theater is included in general admission: $9 family rate (Saturday and Sunday evenings only) $5 adults and children 13 and up, $4 children 6 to 12 and seniors, $2 children 4 and 5, under 4 free. Family membership gives you free admission to Cranbrook Institute of Science and Lansing's Impression 5 Museum.

Ages: All ages, but preschoolers might be uncomfortable with the Omnimax movie's motion and speed

Plan: Movies vary from 30 minutes to one hour

Parking: Lot adjacent to entrance, off John R, $2 all day parking

Lunch: Vending machines and several tables in basement

Facilities: Bathrooms and drinking fountain on basement level. Gift shop near entrance has great science, dino, and space items.

Omnimax's 360-degree domed screen will fill your senses and immerse you in the middle of the action. You might be soaring above the earth, caught in a windstorm, or rushing down a waterfall. Nature's most beautiful images are caught in vivid breadth and color.

NEARBY SITES:

Cultural Center: Detroit Historical Museum, International Institute, Children's Museum, Your Heritage House, Museum of African American History, Detroit Public Library, Detroit Institute of Arts

SP T H	Zoo

Detroit Zoological Park
8450 West Ten Mile Road, Royal Oak
313-398-0900

Location: Ten Mile and Woodward Avenue. Entrance off Woodward, north of Ten Mile.

Hours: 10 a.m.-5 p.m., daily, May-October. 10 a.m.-6 p.m., Sundays and holidays, mid-May-Labor Day. 10 a.m.-4 p.m., Wednesday-Sunday, November-April.

Feeding Schedule: Penquins: 10:30 and 11:30 a.m., daily. Polar Bears: 1:30 p.m., May-mid-October. Sea Lion demonstration: 11 a.m. and 2 p.m., Wednesday-Sunday, late May-mid-October. Lemurs: 2:30 p.m., early June-mid-October.

Admission: $5 adults, $3.50 seniors, $2.50 children 5 to 12, under 5 free. Includes parking and zoo train (trains operate daily May 1 through October 1, weekends through November 1, then shut down until May 1). Family membership and group rates available. Kids 6 to 14 can join the Lemur Club, an animal and nature club with several special events, $4/person, $7.50/two or more family members.

Ages: All ages

Plan: Half day visit

Parking: Free, use parking garage across from entrance

Lunch: Picnic areas, tables, food concessions

Facilities: Bathrooms, drinking fountains, gift concessions. Kids Kabs (strollers) $2+$1 deposit/day. Roller Chairs (fits an adult or 3 kids) $3/day+$1 deposit.

The Detroit Zoo offers families several attractions all rolled into one admission. There are wonderful outdoor exhibits of animals both exotic and exciting, including the brand new "Chimps of Harambee," a four-acre African rain forest environment. There are indoor exhibits—the bird house, reptile house, and penguinarium. For small children, there's a barnyard full of farm animals and the zoo train you can ride from one end of the zoo to the other as much as you want. The Log Cabin Learning Center (located near the train station on the far end of the zoo) offers lots of hands-on experiences for learning about animals up close. Special events occur throughout the year, including the Zoo Boo at Halloween and Winter Wonderland during December.

NEARBY SITES:
Captian's Cove Adventure Golf, Grand Slam Baseball Training Center, Royal Oak Putt Putt, Star-light Archery, Starr-Jaycee Park Train, Superior Fish Co., Inc.

SP T H	Nature Center, Trails

Dinosaur Hill Nature Preserve and Den
333 North Hill Circle, Rochester
313-656-0999

Location: Tienken and Rochester Roads

Hours: Nature den: 9 a.m.-5 p.m., Tuesday-Friday. Noon-3 p.m., Saturday and Sunday (when naturalist is available). Trails: dawn to dusk. There are trail maps in the light blue mailbox attached to the den.

Admission: Free. A fee is charged for group tours, classes, and special events.

Ages: All ages

Plan: Short visit

Parking: Free on street

Lunch: Picnic area

Facilities: Bathrooms. Squirrel Corner Gift Shop offers many inexpensive nature and dinosaur related items.

This gem of a city park sits quietly in the corner of a tidy neighborhood. In spite of its name, Dinosaur Hill is not a repository of dinosaur bones, but 16 heavily wooded acres full of trails and the Dinosaur Den, a combination nature center-library-classroom-gift shop. The den is full of nests, eggs, stuffed birds, small forest animals, butterflies, an aquarium, and fossils. There are lots of hands-on artifacts and small eye lenses to encourage a closer look. The den offers classes, summer camp, birthday parties, and special seasonal events.

NEARBY SITES:
Cider mills, Wright and Filippis, Inc., Meadow Brook Hall

SP T H	Petting Farm, Hayrides

Domino's Farm
24 Frank Lloyd Wright Drive, Ann Arbor
313-995-4258

Location: Off US-23, exit 41, at Earhart and Plymouth Roads.

Hours: Petting farm: 11 a.m.-1 p.m., Wednesday-Friday. Petting farm and hayrides: 1-4 p.m., Saturday and Sunday. Group hayrides available at other pre-arranged times. Animal shows: 1, 2, 3 p.m., Saturday and Sunday.

Admission: Free

Ages: All ages

Plan: Short visit

Parking: Free on site

Lunch: The world's only eat-on-the-premises Domino's Pizza restaurant in World Headquarter's building. Open 11 a.m.-7 p.m., Monday-Friday. Noon-4 p.m., Saturday and Sunday.

Facilities: Bathrooms. Small gift shop in World Headquarter's building.

Meet Duke the Wonderdog and Duchess the Wonder, Chuckie the Chicken and Shirley Curly the Pig, at one of the area's cleanest petting farms. Kids will enjoy wandering through the barn and peeking into the outdoor pens. The pace of the haywagon ride is just slow enough to allow a steady breeze and a good view of Domino's Farms' 300 acres.

NEARBY SITES:

On or near campus: Ann Arbor Farmers' Market, Kerrytown Plaza, Museum of Art, UofM Exhibit Museum and Planetarium, Ecology Center of Ann Arbor, Ann Arbor Hands-On Museum

North Campus: Phoenix Memorial Laboratory, U of M Matthaei Botanical Gardens, Leslie Science Center

South of campus: Cobblestone Farm, Scrap Box

SP T	Nature Center, Trails

Drayton Plains Nature Center
2125 Denby Drive, Drayton Plains
313-338-4496

Location: ¼ mile west off Dixie Highway, on Hatchery Road

Hours: Grounds only: sunrise to dusk, daily. Interpretive Center: 10 a.m.-4 p.m., Saturday. Noon-4 p.m., Sunday. Group tours are available at mutually convenient times and can be arranged by calling ahead.

Admission: Grounds and interpretive center free. Minimum fee for group tour.

Ages: School age children and up

Plan: Short visit. Tours are approximately 1½ hours.

Parking: Free on site

Lunch: Picnic tables on site

Facilities: Bathrooms. Nature store with field guides, books, and coloring books for children.

Once the old state fish hatchery, Drayton Plains Nature Center sits on 137 acres on the banks of the Clinton River. Prairie, woods, and wetland make up its varied topography. Families can enjoy the outdoors year round on 4½ miles of marked nature trails. There are a variety of touch-and-see nature exhibits inside the Interpretive Center, including large fish tanks displaying local fish, such as blue gill and bass. There are a variety of group tour programs; one of the most popular includes a brief visit to a pioneer log cabin on the grounds.

NEARBY SITES:
Hillside Farm, Independence Oaks, Ridgemere Berry Farm

SP T H   Trails

E.L. Johnson Nature Center
3325 Franklin Road, Bloomfield Hills
313-540-5291

Location: On Franklin Road, south of Hickory Grove, north of Long Lake Road

Hours: 8:30 a.m.-4:30 p.m., Monday-Friday. 10:30 a.m.-4:30 p.m., Saturday and Sunday the second weekend of each month. Children can sign up for classes run by the Bloomfield Hills Parks and Recreation. Special pre-arranged tours are also available.

Admission: Free

Ages: All ages

Plan: Under one hour

Parking: Free on site

Lunch: Telegraph Road offers a variety of fast-food restaurants

Facilities: Bathroom in visitor center

This 32-acre site offers families a quiet trail through wooded terrain, dappled with wild flowers and a meandering stream. There are also wild animals—foxes, ducks, deer, owls, and turkeys—that make their home in the woods.

NEARBY SITES:

Charles L. Bowers Farm, Cranbrook Academy of Art Museum, Cranbrook House and Garden, Cranbrook Institute of Science

---

SP T H   Hands-On Science Museum

Ella Sharp Museum — Discovery Gallery
3225 Fourth Street, Jackson
313-787-2320

For full information, see Historic Sites

T H   Conservatory and Trails

Hidden Lake Gardens
M-50, Tipton
517-431-2060

Location: On M-50, five miles west of junction of M-50 and M-52

Hours: 8 a.m.-dusk, daily April-October. 8 a.m.-4 p.m., daily November-March.

Admission: $2 weekends and holidays, $1 weekdays. Family memberships available.

Ages: All ages

Plan: Short visit

Parking: Free on site

Lunch: Picnic tables

Facilities: Bathrooms. Gift shop in visitor center has science items, "Hidden Lake" and Michigan State t-shirts and sweatshirts.

Walk the scented trails, feed swans, picnic amid tall pine trees, drive through six miles of winding roads, and wander through the conservatory's unique tropical and arid plants. Hidden Lake Gardens, owned by Michigan State University and full of Spartan spirit, is a peaceful spot to stop on your way west across the state.

NEARBY SITES:
Chocolate Vault, Walker Tavern Historic Complex

SP T H   Working Farm

Hillside Farm
8351 Big Lake Road, Clarkston
313-625-1181, 313-625-2665

Location: Dixie Highway and I-75
Hours: Noon-5 p.m., Tuesday-Saturday. Groups of six or more by appointment only.
Admission: Free
Ages: 5 and over
Plan: Short visit
Parking: Free, near farmhouse
Lunch: Picnic tables
Facilities: Bathrooms. Gift shop with wool and sheepskin clothing items, plus spinning and craft supplies.

Kids can pet the lambs, and watch sheep being sheared and goats milked at this family-run working farm. On special days there are also spinning demonstrations, plus samples of Scotch broth and summer sausage. The Bellairs family enjoys introducing children to sheep and their products. Sheepshearing Days are held in April and October. Lamb Walks are in March and at Easter. Christmas Shopping open house is in December.

NEARBY SITES:
Independence Oaks, Ridgemere Berry Farm, Drayton Plains Nature Center

H	Greenhouse, Gardens

Horticultural Gardens
Michigan State University, East Lansing
517-355-0348, 517-355-8362

Location: Bogue and Wilson Streets, across from the Veterinary Clinic, on the MSU campus

Hours: Greenhouse: 7:30 a.m.-5:30 p.m., Monday-Friday, year-round. Gardens: May 1-October 1.

Admission: Free

Ages: All ages

Plan: Under one hour

Parking: Lot adjacent to gardens

Lunch: Burger King and vending machines are located in the Michigan Union, corner of Abbott and Grand River. Many other restaurants are located on Grand River Avenue, across from campus.

Facilities: Bathrooms in greenhouse

The Horticultural Center includes a garden of beautiful annuals and perennials and a teaching greenhouse, full of seasonal flowers and greens.

NEARBY SITES:
MSU Campus: MSU Museum of Natural History, Kresge Art Museum, Abrams Planetarium
Lansing: R.E. Olds Transportation Museum, Michigan Women's Historical Center, Michigan Historical Museum, State Capitol, Potter Park Zoo, Impression 5 Museum

SP T H	Nature Interpretive Centers

Huron-Clinton Metroparks
Nature Centers
The following metroparks have nature cen-

ters with hands-on exhibits for children, live
Michigan animals, nature trails, and year-
round programs. Vehicle permits $2 daily, $10
annual. General hours: 10 a.m.-5 p.m., daily
during the summer. 1-5 p.m., Monday-Friday.
10 a.m.-5 p.m., weekends, during the school
year. 10 a.m.-noon, Monday-Friday is generally reserved for school groups. Call 1-800-47-
PARKS or the individual nature center for
more information. *See* Parks.

Indian Springs Nature Center
5200 Indian Trail, Clarkston
313-625-7280

**Kensington Nature Center
and Farm Center**
2240 West Buno Road, Milford
313-685-1561

Metro Beach Nature Center
Metropolitan Parkway, Mt. Clemens
313-463-4332

Oakwoods Nature Center
Huron River Drive, Flat Rock
313-782-3956

Stony Creek Nature Center
4300 Main Park Road, Washington
313-781-4621

SP T H   Hands-On Science Museum

Impression 5 Museum
200 Museum Drive, Lansing
517-485-8116

For full information, see Museums

SP T H   Nature Center

Independence Oaks Nature Center
9501 Sashabaw Road, Clarkston
313-625-6473

Location: 2½ miles north of I-75 on Sashabaw Road

Hours: 10 a.m.-6 p.m., daily, Memorial Day-Labor Day. 10 a.m.-5 p.m., Tuesday-Sunday, school year. Trail hours: 8 a.m.-dusk. Family classes and programs are offered year-round.

Admission: Park entry fee, free admission to nature center

Ages: All ages

Plan: Short visit

Parking: On site

Lunch: Picnic areas available on rental basis

Facilities: Bathrooms. Amphitheater located adjacent to nature center.

Children will enjoy the discovery area's miniaturized exhibits and life-sized dioramas designed especially for hands-on learning. They will also enjoy looking through the windows and observing wildlife in the center's outdoor feeding station. A 200-seat amphitheatre offers many year-round family programs.

NEARBY SITES:
Hillside Farm

SP T H   Bird Sanctuary

Jack Miner Bird Sanctuary
Kingsville, Ontario, Canada
519-733-4034

Location: Three miles north of Kingsville, off Division Road (Road #29)

Hours: 9 a.m.-5 p.m., Monday-Saturday, year-round. October and November are peak migration months. Grounds are open 8 a.m.-sundown.

Admission: Free

Ages: All ages

Plan: Short visit

Parking: Free on site

Lunch: Picnic area

Facilities: Bathrooms, playground

Thousands of Canadian geese stop off at the Jack Miner Sanctuary during October and November on their way south. Children are encouraged to feed the waterfowl with handfuls of grain from the barley bucket located near the sanctuary's pond. Try to plan your trip for early morning or late afternoon. The geese come in for breakfast between 7 and 8 a.m. At 3 and 4 p.m., the geese put on an "airshow." They take off and land when a three-wheeled, all-terrain vehicle drives through the flocks.

NEARBY SITES:
Colasanti's Tropical Gardens, Point Pelee National Park

SP T H   Petting Farm

Kiwanis Children's Farm
255 North Christian Street
Sarnia, Ontario, Canada
519-332-0330, ext. 207

Location: Christina Street and Cathcart Boulevard, north of Highway 402

Hours: 8 a.m.-9 p.m., daily, May 24-September 30. 8 a.m.-4 p.m., daily, rest of year.

Admission: Free

Ages: All ages

Plan: Short visit

Parking: Free on site

Lunch: Picnic areas, concessions

Facilities: Bathrooms, playground

Within Cantara Park along Lake Huron is the small petting farm, perfect for young children. The farm has both domestic animals and poultry. Adjacent to the farm are three historic buildings: a pioneer log cabin, smoke house, and carriage house.

NEARBY SITES:
Fort Gratiot Lighthouse, Mary Maxim, Inc., Ruby Farms, Museum of Art and History

SP T   Working Poultry Farm

Langerderfer Poultry Farm
11844 Strasburg Road, Erie
313-856-4283

Location: Take Telegraph Road six miles south of Monroe to Woods Road. Go west one mile to Strasburg Road. Go south ¼ mile to farm.

Hours: 9 a.m.-6 p.m., Monday-Saturday. 11 a.m.- 5 p.m., Sunday, March-June. Farm is open to the public. Call ahead for a tour.

Admission: $1.75 per person for tour

Ages: All ages

Plan: Short visit

Parking: Free on site

Lunch: Picnic area

Facilities: Bathrooms

What better way to celebrate spring? The Langerderfer Poultry Farm is a working farm full of baby chicks and ducks. Families and large groups should call for a pre-arranged tour in order to maximize their visit. The tour allows children to hand feed the animals, learn about the incubation process, and visit a nursery full of baby animals. A snack of hot chocolate and farm-fresh hard-boiled eggs are given to all tour participants. The farm also offers a "Rent-an-Animal" program. Families can take home baby chicks and ducks for Easter and then return them to the farm.

NEARBY SITES:
Monroe County Historical Museum, Navarre-Anderson Trading Post and Country Store

SP T H   Conservation, Nature Center

Leslie Science Center
and Project Grow
1831 Traver Road, Ann Arbor
313-662-7802

Location: Traver Road and Barton Drive, east of Plymouth Road

Hours: Grounds open 10 a.m.-5 p.m., daily. Call two weeks ahead for tours of display area.

Admission: Free

Ages: 3 and up

Plan: Under one hour

Parking: Free on site

Lunch: Restaurants are located nearby on UofM campus.

Facilities: Bathrooms in main residence. Project Grow office has t-shirts and homegrown honey.

Leslie Science Center is a site for conservation related experiences, training, and education. Children will enjoy the indoor observation beehive and worm box. The center holds spring and fall festivals and workshops. Project Grow sponsors area community gardens.

NEARBY SITES:

On or near campus: Ann Arbor Hands-On Museum, Ann Arbor Farmers' Market, Kerrytown Plaza, Museum of Art, UofM Exhibit Museum and Planetarium, Ecology Center of Ann Arbor

North Campus: Phoenix Memorial Laboratory, U of M Matthaei Botanical Gardens, Domino's Farms

South of campus: Cobblestone Farm, Scrap Box

SP T H   Nature Center, Trails

Lloyd A. Stage Outdoor
Education Center
6685 Coolidge Highway, Troy
313-524-3567

Location: ¾ mile north of Square Lake Road, on Coolidge Highway

Hours: 8:30 a.m.-4:30 p.m., Tuesday-Saturday. Noon-5 p.m., Sunday. Scout and school groups are encouraged to call to arrange programs and tours.

Admission: Free

Ages: All ages

Plan: Short visit. Tours are approximately 1½ hours.

Parking: Free on site

Lunch: Picnic area

Facilities: Bathrooms. Gift shop with bird books, feeders, t-shirts, and notecards.

Lloyd A. Stage Outdoor Education Center includes 99 acres of rolling meadow, forest, and stream, plus a farm site and Interpretive Center. The Interpretive Center houses exhibits, dioramas, hands-on displays, and a gift shop. The self-guided nature trails are well marked and maps are available. The center also offers year-round family classes and outings. A Junior Naturalist Club is available for children. Maple Sugar Festival in March.

NEARBY SITES:
Troy Museum and Historic Village Green

SP T H   Planetarium

Longway Planetarium
1310 East Kearsley Street, Flint
313-762-1181

Location: Flint's Cultural Center, exit Longway Boulevard off I-475

Hours: Office 8 a.m.-5 p.m., Monday-Friday. Call for Laser and Planetarium shows; their hours vary.

Admission: $3 adults, $2 children. Group rates available.

Ages: All ages, but age requirements varies with show; call ahead

Plan: Short visit

Parking: Free on site

Lunch: Picnicking on planetarium lawn is permitted in warm weather

Facilities: Bathrooms. Gift shop with space, hologram, and star gazing gifts—gyroscopes, prisms, star explorers.

The Longway Planetarium is a treat for children of all ages. Be sure to call ahead to time your visit to one of their planetarium shows or laser shows set to rock music. Kids will also like the two 55-foot space murals lining the circular outer wall of the planetarium. Created with luminescent paint on black canvas, the murals make you feel as if you are looking out into space.

NEARBY SITES:
Cultural Center: Alfred P. Sloan Museum, Flint Institute of Arts
In town: AC Spark Plug Tour, Buick City Tour, Michigan Humane Society, Children's Museum
During the summer: Penny Whistle Place, Crossroads Village/Huckleberry Railroad, Mott Farm

SP T H   Petting Farm

Maybury State Park Petting Farm
20145 Beck Road, Northville
313-349-8390

Location: Entrance off Eight Mile Road, six miles west of I-275

Hours: Park: 8 a.m.-10 p.m., year-round. Farm: 10 a.m.-5 p.m., year-round.

Admission: $2 vehicle entrance fee. $10 yearly permit fee.

Ages: Preschool to 11 years

Plan: Short visit

Parking: Free on site

Lunch: Picnic area

Facilities: Outhouses, nearby playground. Hayrides occasionally on weekends, bike rental in fall and spring, cross-country skiing in winter.

Super-sized bunnies, honking geese, and shy turkeys share the spacious two-story barn with cows, pigs, and goats. Visit during early spring and you'll be rewarded with a new crop of animal babies. You'll also meet Farmer Beemer, the Maybury Park ranger, who's usually on hand to answer questions. Maybury playground, with one the area's best wooded all-purpose climbers, is nearby—if you can pry your little ones away from the animals.

NEARBY SITES:
Marquis Theatre, Alfonse Jacques Farm, Cider mills and u-pick farms, Mill Race Historical Village

SP T H   Space Museum

Michigan Space Center
2111 Emmons Road, Jackson
517-787-4425

For full information, see Museums

SP T H   Natural History Museum

MSU Museum of Natural History
101 West Circle Drive
Michigan State University Campus
East Lansing
517-355-2370

For full information, see Museums

SP T H   Petting Farm

Mott Farm
6140 Bray Road, Flint
313-762-1795

Location: Just north of Flint. Follow I-475 off either I-75 or I-69 to Carpenter Road (exit 11). Same entrance as Crossroads Village/Huckleberry Railroad.

Hours: 10 a.m.-5 p.m., daily May 1-November 1

Admission: Free

Ages: Preschool to early elementary

Plan: Short visit

Parking: Free on site

Lunch: Picnic areas

Facilities: Port-a-johns

Mott Petting Farm's two barns are full to the brim with animals gentle enough to pet and feed. Children will enjoy a quick visit to the farm before or after a visit to Crossroads Village/Huckleberry Railroad.

NEARBY SITES:

During the summer: Penny Whistle Place, Crossroads Village/Huckleberry Railroad

In town: AC Spark Plug Tour, Buick City Tour, Michigan Humane Society

Cultural Center: Flint Institute of Arts, Alfred P. Sloan Museum, Longway Planetarium

SP   Zoo

Potter Park Zoo
1301 South Pennsylvania Avenue,
Lansing
517-483-4221

Location: Just south of I-496

Hours: Zoo buildings: 10 a.m.-5 p.m., daily, year-round. Park: 8 a.m.-dusk, daily, year-round.

Admission: Zoo is free. $1 vehicle admission during the summer.

Ages: All ages

Plan: Short visit

Parking: Free on site

Lunch: Picnic areas and food concessions (summer only)

Facilities: Bathrooms, gift concessions

Children will enjoy visiting this zoo located in hilly Potter Park. They'll find a variety of animals as well as activities. There are 400 animals, including large cats, primates, an elephant, and wallaby, a penguinarium, farmyard with farm animals, small children's petting zoo, playground, and in the summer, pony rides.

NEARBY SITES:
Lansing: R.E. Olds Transportation Museum, Michigan Women's Historical Center, Michigan Historical Museum, State Capitol, Impression 5 Museum
MSU Campus: Abrams Planetarium, Horticultural Gardens, MSU Museum of Natural History

SP T H	Zoo, Petting Farm

Ruby Farms
6567 Imlay City Road, Goodells
313-324-2662

Location: Just northwest of Port Huron

Hours: 11 a.m.-5 p.m., Wednesday-Sunday, August-Christmas

Admission: For zoo only: $2.50 adults, $2 children

Ages: Especially geared for preschool and early elementary

Plan: Short visit

Parking: Free on site

Lunch: Cider mill/restaurant

Facilities: Bathrooms, gift shop

Ruby Farms offers city children a chance to frolic in the country, pet and feed a variety of farm animals, as well as watch several exotic zoo-type animals. The farm offers fresh cider from its cider mill/restaurant, and in December, cut-your-own Christmas trees.

NEARBY SITES:
Mary Maxim, Inc., Museum of Art and History, Lexington Marina, Croswell Swinging Bridge, Seven Ponds Nature Center

SP T H   Nature Center, Trails

Seven Ponds Nature Center
3854 Crawford Road, Dryden
313-796-3419

Location: North of Pontiac, east off M-24 on Dryden Road

Hours: 9 a.m.-5 p.m., Tuesday-Sunday. Programs every other Sunday in fall and winter. Nature walk every Sunday in spring.

Admission: $2 family, $1 adults, 50 cents children

Ages: All ages

Plan: Short visit

Parking: Free on site

Lunch: Picnic area

Facilities: Bathrooms. Gift shop-bookstore with children's books and bird-feeding supplies.

Children are encouraged to touch and explore at the Seven Ponds Nature Center. Inside the Interpretive Building, there are natural history collections of skins, insects, and minerals, a touch table for handling items, and an observation beehive for close inspection of bee activity. Outside, there are trails and a waterfowl feeding area.

NEARBY SITES:
Pontiac: Bald Mountain Riding Stables, Pontiac Farmer's Market, Pine Grove Historical Museum

SP T H   Fishing

Spring Valley Trout Farm
12190 Island Lake Road, Dexter
313-426-4772

Location: I-94 west to exit 167 (Dexter), then four miles west of Dexter to Island Lake Road

Hours: Spring and fall: 9 a.m.-6 p.m., Saturday and Sunday. Memorial Day-Labor Day. 9 a.m.-6 p.m., Wednesday-Sunday.

Admission: $1 for 6 years and older, under 6 free. You pay per pound for all you catch; fish can't be thrown back into the pond. Fish are cleaned and packaged in ice free of charge.

Ages: 2 and up

Plan: Short visit

Parking: Free on site

Lunch: Vending machines, picnic areas with grills

Facilities: Bathroom

For a first fishing experience, you can't beat Spring Valley Trout Farm. With admission, you are given all the equipment you need—pail, poles, hooks, and worms. Helpful staff members show you how to cut off a section of worm, snag it on the hook, and toss your line into the spring-fed pond. The fact that you are guaranteed a catch is the most amazing part for children (and you'll notice adults get very excited, too). For little ones, there is a small children's pond. They can also feed the 20,000 or more trout fingerlings in the trout farm's rearing areas.

NEARBY SITES:
Cider mills

SP T H   Nature Center

Sterling Heights Nature Center
42700 Utica Road, Sterling Heights
313-739-6731

Location: Van Dyke and Utica Roads, one block east of Van Dyke

Hours: 1-5 p.m., Monday-Thursday. 10 a.m.-5 p.m., Saturday. 1-5 p.m., Sunday. Closed Friday. Tours may be pre-scheduled at convenient times.

Admission: Free

Ages: 3 and up

Plan: Short visit

Parking: Free on site

Lunch: Picnicking is permitted. Auditorium may be used as a lunchroom.

Facilities: Bathrooms

The Sterling Heights Nature Center, part of the city's parks and recreation department, sits on seven acres overlooking the Clinton River. The display room features hands-on natural science experiences. There are live snakes, turtles and fish, nature puzzles, mystery boxes, and animal skins. Family nature movies are shown 7:30 p.m., Tuesday and Wednesday. Nature classes are also offered for children and adults.

NEARBY SITES:
Freedom Hill, Metro Beach Metropark, Four Bears Water Park

SP T H   Nature Preserve, Trails

University of Michigan-Dearborn Environmental Study Area
News and Information, Dearborn
313-593-5338

Location: On the grounds of the Henry Ford Fairlane Estate, 4901 Evergeen Road, west of Fairlane Town Center

Hours: Dawn-Dusk

Admission: Free

Ages: All ages

Plan: Short visit

Parking: Lot adjacent to Fairlane mansion powerhouse

Lunch: Picnicking is not allowed. The Fairlane mansion's Pool Restaurant is open 11 a.m.-2 p.m., Monday-Friday, year-round. Many restaurants are available in Fairlane Town Center.

Facilities: Self-guided nature trails, maps available for small fee in parking lot boxes

Nature lovers are encouraged to visit the sprawling nature area on the Rouge River that was once part of Henry Ford's estate. Special seasonal nature hikes are held throughout the year: January—winter ecology, February—maple tree tapping, summer—bird, tree, and water ecology tours, fall—color tours.

NEARBY SITES:
Henry Ford Museum, Greenfield Village, Dearborn Historical Museum, Dearborn Trolley Company

---

SP T H	Natural History Museum

University of Michigan Exhibit Museum
1109 Geddes Avenue, Ann Arbor
313-764-0478

For full information, see Museums

SP T H	Planetarium

University of Michigan Exhibit Museum Planetarium
1109 Geddes, Ann Arbor
313-764-0478

Location: Fourth floor of the UofM Exhibit Museum, corner of Geddes and Washtenaw Avenues on the U of M campus

Hours: 10:30 and 11:30 a.m., Saturday; tickets go on sale at 9 a.m. 2, 3, and 4 p.m., Saturday and Sunday; tickets go on sale at 1 p.m. Special Christmas Shows are offered during December and at extra times during vacation week. Groups may pre-arrange shows at convenient times.

Admission: $1.50 for Saturday morning shows. $2 for Saturday and Sunday afternoon shows.

Ages: All ages for Saturday morning shows. Age 5 and up for Saturday and Sunday afternoon shows.

Plan: Shows are approximately 35 minutes

Parking: Use street meters or Fletcher Street parking lot

Lunch: Many restaurants on campus

Facilities: Bathrooms. Gift shop with many inexpensive dinosaur and natural history items.

While most families come to the Exhibit Museum to see dinosaurs, the planetarium offers another trip into the exciting realm of natural science and creates a realistic image of the night sky on its 360° dome. Shows are imaginative and most interesting for children 5 and up.

NEARBY SITES:

On or near campus: Ann Arbor Farmers' Market, Kerrytown Plaza, Museum of Art, Ecology Center of Ann Arbor, Ann Arbor Hands-On Museum.

North Campus: Phoenix Memorial Laboratory, Domino's Farms, Leslie Science Center, UofM Matthaei Botanical Gardens

South of campus: Cobblestone Farm, Scrap Box

SP T H   Greenhouse. Trails

University of Michigan
Matthaei Botanical Gardens
1800 North Dixboro Road, Ann Arbor
313-998-7061

Location: Take US-23 north, exit at Geddes Road, and turn right. At Dixboro Road, turn left. Gardens are 1½ miles on your right.

Hours: Conservatory: 10 a.m.-4 p.m., daily. Grounds: sunrise-sunset. Group tours available. Call three weeks in advance.

Admission: $1 adults, 75 cents seniors, 50 cents children 6 to 12, under 6 free

Ages: All ages

Plan: Short visit

Parking: Free on site

Lunch: You'll find restaurants going west on Geddes or driving into UofM's campus
Facilities: Bathrooms. Gift shop with t-shirts, mugs, and botanical items.

It's perpetual summer in the Matthaei Botanical Gardens Conservatory. Lush tropical plants with vivid reds and pinks, exotic banana and lemon trees, and huge exotic cacti capture children's attention. They will also enjoy peering into two ponds full of gliding goldfish and other larger species. Four outdoor trails are marked for a self-guided stroll revealing seasonal changes.

NEARBY SITES:
North Campus: Phoenix Memorial Laboratory, Domino's Farms, Leslie Science Center
On or near campus: Ann Arbor Farmers' Market, Kerrytown Plaza, Museum of Art, UofM Exhibit Museum and Planetarium, Ecology Center of Ann Arbor, Ann Arbor Hands-On Museum
South of campus: Cobblestone Farm, Scrap Box

SP T H   Nature Center

Waterloo Geology Center
Waterloo Recreation Area, McClure Road
Chelsea
313-475-8307

Location: Off McClure Road in the Waterloo Recreation Area
Hours: 10 a.m.-6 p.m., daily
Admission: $2 daily vehicle pass
Ages: All ages
Plan: Short visit. The nature trails have walking times of 20 minutes to one hour.
Parking: Free on site
Lunch: Picniking sites are located on the far east side of the recreation area
Facilities: Bathrooms, gift shop

While the emphasis is on rocks, the center also offers children a chance to see stuffed animals and birds and live turtles. There are several nature trails, plus a geology trail with many large examples of rocks found in the around the Waterloo Recreation Area.

NEARBY SITES:
Jackson: Ella Sharp Museum, Michigan Space Center, Illuminated Cascades (summer)

7
SEASONAL HARVEST
A Sampling of Sites

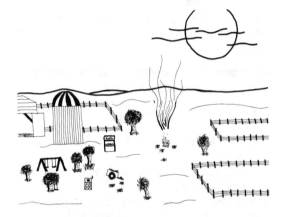

Here is a sampling of area farmers' markets, u-pick farms, and cider mills, enough sites to keep you out of doors and full of fresh foods all year long. Kids love bustling farmers' markets. Take your little red wagon to pull the kids and the crops, and be sure to peek under produce-laden tables; you just might find bunnies hidden in crates.

Or pick the produce yourself at Michigan's u-pick farms. Many offer a variety of activities during harvest season, from blue-grass music and hay rides to petting farms and candle dipping. How can you resist freshly picked strawberries in June, or apples, cider, and donuts in September? During October, many farms offer Halloween activities plus pumpkin and gourd picking. Beginning Thanksgiving weekend, tree farms offer Christmas activities—a visit with Santa, a sleigh ride, and a chance to choose your own Christmas tree.

Farmers' Markets

Ann Arbor Farmers' Market
407 North Fifth Street, Ann Arbor
313-662-4221

Location: Next door to Kerrytown, Catherine and Fifth Streets

Hours: 7 a.m.-3 p.m., Saturday, all year. 7 a.m.-3 p.m., Monday, Wednesday, and Saturday, summer only.

Eastern Market
2934 Russell, Detroit
313-833-1560

Location: 2 blocks east of I-75, take Mack Avenue exit

Hours: 5 a.m.-noon, Monday-Friday. Open until 6 p.m., Saturday.

The area's largest, most boisterous, and aromatic farmers' market. You'll find freshly baked goods, wonderful specialty stores, live animals, and a crush of colorful people. Arrive early Saturday morning to be sure of a parking space.

Monroe Farmers' Market
20 East Willow, Monroe
313-269-3275

Location: In back of Elias Brothers Big Boy on Monroe Street

Hours: 6 a.m.-noon, Tuesday and Saturday, spring-fall

Mount Clemens Farmers' Market
37685 South Gratiot, Mount Clemens
313-469-2525

Location: Downtown, on Pine and Macomb Streets

Hours: 9 a.m.-7 p.m., Monday-Thursday, and Saturday. 9 a.m.-8 p.m., Friday. 9 a.m.-5 p.m., Sunday

---

Plymouth Farmers' Market
Plymouth
313-453-1540 (Chamber of Commerce)

Location: At "The Gathering," across from Kellogg Park, on Penniman and Main Streets

Hours: 8 a.m.-1 p.m., Saturday, first week in June to mid-October

---

Pontiac Farmers' Market
Pontiac
313-858-9807

Location: Pontiac Lake Road, west of Telegraph

Hours: 6:30 a.m.-1 p.m., Tuesday, Thursday, Saturday, May 1-November 1. After November 1, Thursday and Saturday only.

Royal Oak Farmers' Market
316 East Eleven Mile Road, Royal Oak
313-548-8822

Location: One mile east of Woodward, three blocks east of Main Street

Hours: 7 a.m.-1 p.m., Tuesday, Thursday, Friday, and Saturday

---

Windsor City Market
Chatham Street East, Windsor
Ontario, Canada
519-255-6260

Location: On the corner of Pitt and McDougall

Streets, a few blocks from the tunnel exit in Windsor
Hours: 7 a.m.-4 p.m., Monday-Thursday. 7 a.m.-6 p.m., Friday. 5:30 a.m.-4 p.m., Saturday.

Ypsilanti Farmers' Market
Depot Town, Ypsilanti
313-483-1480

Location: In Depot Town, Cross Street just east of Huron River Drive
Hours: 7 a.m.-3 p.m., Wednesday and Saturday

U-Pick Farms and Cider Mills

Here is a sampling of the most popular farms and cider mills in the greater Detroit area. To help you find the site closest to your home, check the county in which each farm or cider mill is located. Also, be sure to call ahead for directions and hours. Hours vary depending on the season, the crop, and the weather.

Altermatt's Farm
16580 Twenty-Five Mile Road
Washington
313-781-3428

Location: Macomb County
Hours: Strawberries: 7 a.m.-dusk, June-July. Farm market: June-November.
Activities: U-pick strawberries, farm market with seasonal vegetables, pumpkins, and gourds

---

Blake's Big Apple Orchard
71485 North Avenue, Armada
313-784-9710

Location: Macomb County

Hours: 9 a.m.-6 p.m., daily

Activities: U-pick apples, pumpkins, raspberries, peaches. Group tours, produce store, fudge shop, bakery, animal petting farm, wagon rides, and train rides through the orchard on weekends.

Blake's Orchard and Cider Mill
17985 Center Road, Armada
313-784-5343

Location: Macomb County

Hours: 9 a.m.-6 p.m., daily, all year

Activities: U-pick apples and pears, wagon and pony rides, cider mill, Christmas trees, weekend activities, group tours

---

Crossroads Village Cider Mill
G-5055 Branch Road, Flint
313-736-7100

Location: Genesee County

Hours: 10 a.m.-5:30 p.m., Monday-Friday. 11 a.m.-6:30 p.m., Saturday and Sunday. Labor Day-Christmas.

Activities: Cider press demonstration. The mill is part of the Huckleberry Railroad/Crossroads Village complex

---

Degroot's Strawberries
4232 Bull Run Road, Gregory
517-223-9311

Location: Livingston County

Hours: 8 a.m.-8 p.m., June-July

Activities: U-pick strawberries

Denewith's Pick Your Own
Strawberry Farms

16125 Twenty-Two Mile Road, Utica
313-247-5533

Location: Macomb County
Hours: 7 a.m.-dusk, June-July
Activities: U-pick strawberries, wagon rides to and from field

---

Dexter Cider Mill
3685 Central Street, Dexter
313-426-8531

Location: Washtenaw County
Hours: 8 a.m.-5 p.m., daily, September-Thanksgiving
Activities: Cider press demonstrations, donuts for sale

Diehl's Orchard and Cider Mill
1478 Ranch, Holly
313-634-8981

Location: Oakland County
Hours: 9 a.m.-6 p.m. daily, August-October 30. 9 a.m.-5 p.m. daily, October 30-December 31. 9 a.m.-5 p.m., Monday-Saturday, 1-6 p.m., Sunday, January 1-August 1.
Activities: Country shop with cider, donuts, apples, jams, jellies, popcorn. Wagon rides and entertainment on weekends during fall; Ciderfest last weekend in September.

Erie Orchards
1235 Erie Road, Erie
313-848-4518

Location: Monroe County
Hours: July 1-December 31
Activities: U-pick blueberries, peaches, apples, pumpkins and Christmas trees. Cider press and donut-making demonstrations.

Weekend entertainment, pony rides, animal petting farm and hayrides. Group and school tours available.

Erwin Orchards
61019 Silver Lake, South Lyon
313-437-3132

Location: Oakland County
Hours: 9 a.m.-6 p.m., weekdays. 8 a.m.-7 p.m., weekends during picking season.
Activities: U-pick apples, raspberries, pumpkins. Group tours, wagon rides, country store. Erwin Orchards grows dwarf apple trees, just the right height for young pickers.

Foreman Orchards and Cider Mill
50050 West Seven Mile Road, Northville
313-349-1256

Location: Wayne County
Hours: 9 a.m.-6 p.m., weekdays. 9 a.m.-7 p.m., Sundays during the fall.
Activities: Large country store with apples, seasonal candies, baked goods, and gifts; cider-press demonstrations

---

Franklin Cider Mill
7450 Franklin Road, Franklin
313-626-2968

Location: Oakland County
Hours: 9 a.m.-6 p.m., daily, Labor Day-early December
Activities: Cider-press demonstrations, food stand selling apples, seasonal foods, donuts

---

Goodison Cider Mill
4295 Orion, Lake Orion
313-652-8450

Location: Oakland County

Hours: Noon-6 p.m., daily, August. 9 a.m.-6 p.m., weekdays, 8 a.m.-dark, weekends, September-November. 9 a.m.-6 p.m., Friday, Saturday, Sunday, December-July.

Activities: Cider-press demonstrations, donuts, jams & jellies, pony rides, and hayrides on Sundays during spring and fall

---

Hilltop Orchards and Cider Mill
11468 Hartland Road, Fenton
313-629-9292

Location: Livingston County
Hours: 10 a.m.-5:30 p.m., daily, September-Christmas
Activities: Cider, donuts, antique market

Hy's Cider Mill
6350 Thirty-Seven Mile Road, Romeo
313-798-8843

Location: Macomb County
Hours: 10 a.m.-6 p.m., daily, September-Thanksgiving
Activities: U-pick apples, cider, donuts, gift shops, chicken coops, and wagon rides

---

Johnny Appleseed Cider Mill
6001 Twenty-Six Mile Road, Washington
313-781-4288

Location: Macomb County
Hours: 10 a.m.-dusk, September-second week of November
Activities: Cider-press demonstrations, donuts, farm animals, picnic tables, and swings

---

Lakeview Farm and Cider Mill
12075 Island Lake, Dexter
313-426-2782

Location: Washtenaw County

Hours: 9 a.m.-6 p.m., Wednesday-Friday, 9 a.m.-5 p.m., Saturday and Sunday, September 15-November 15

Activities: Watch cider and donuts being made, fall harvest items, U-pick pumpkins in October

---

Leo Hellebuyck Farm
18850 Twenty-Five Mile Road, Washington
313-781-4031

Location: Macomb County

Hours: 7 a.m.-6 p.m., daily, June-July

Activities: U-pick strawberries and raspberries

Makielski Berry Farm
7130 Platt Road, Ypsilanti
313-487-9306

Location: Washtenaw County

Hours: 8 a.m.-8 p.m., daily during season

Activities: U-pick strawberries, raspberries, pumpkins

Martinsville Cider Mill
Greenfield Village, Dearborn
313-271-1620

Location: Wayne County

Hours: 9 a.m.-5 p.m., daily during the season

Activities: Cider-pressing demonstrations. The cider mill is one of Greenfield Village's historic buildings.

Meyer Berry Farm
48120 West Eight Mile Road, Northville
313-349-0289

Location: Oakland County

Hours: Strawberries in June, pumpkins in October

Activities: U-pick strawberries and pumpkins

Middleton Berry Farm
2120 Stoney Creek Road, Lake Orion
313-693-6018

Location: Oakland County

Hours: 10 a.m.-5 p.m., Saturday and Sunday, June-October

Activities: U-pick strawberries and pumpkins, petting farm, haystack climbers, wagon rides, fall gourds, and Indian corn. Group tours available.

Middleton Cider Mill
46462 Dequindre, Rochester
313-731-6699

Location: Oakland County

Hours: 9 a.m.-dark, daily September and October

Activities: Cider-press demonstrations, pony rides, wild geese and ducks, donuts, candy

---

Paint Creek Mill
4480 Orion Road, Rochester
313-651-8361

Location: Oakland County

Hours: Cider Mill: 9 a.m.-6 p.m., daily, September-March. Restaurant: 11:30 a.m.-2:30 p.m., 5-10 p.m., Tuesday-Saturday. 9 a.m.-2 p.m., Sunday, year-round.

Activities: Cider-press demonstrations, donuts, baked goods, candy, honey. Large mill water wheel and trails.

Parmeter Cider Mill
714 Baseline Road, Northville
313-349-3181

Location: Wayne County
Hours: 10 a.m.-8 p.m., daily, Saturday before Labor Day-Sunday before Thanksgiving
Activities: Cider-press demonstrations; country store with cider, donuts, caramel apples, honey, jam, candy

Peabody Orchards
12326 Foley Road, Fenton
313-629-6416

Location: Livingston County
Hours: 8 a.m.-7 p.m., June-July
Activities: U-pick strawberries, farm market with fresh produce

Plymouth Orchards and Cider Mill
10685 Warren Road, Plymouth
313-455-2290

Location: Washtenaw County
Hours: 9 a.m.-8 p.m., daily, September 1-October 31. 10 a.m.-6 p.m., November-December. 11 a.m.-10 p.m., daily; 10 a.m.-10 p.m., weekends, December-February
Activities: U-pick apples, pumpkins. Cider-press demonstrations, petting farm, wagon rides, country market, cross-country ski rental equipment and trails. Group tours available.

Pumpkin Factory
16421 Elwell Road, Belleville
313-697-9829

Location: Wayne County

Hours: 9 a.m.-9 p.m., daily, October
Activities: Halloween costumes, U-pick pumpkins, gift shop

Pumpkin Patch
32285 Sibley Road, New Boston
313-753-4586

Location: Monroe County
Hours: 9 a.m.-9 p.m., October
Activities: U-pick pumpkins, hayrides, pony rides, petting farm

---

Ray Schultz Farm
10090 Martz Road, Ypsilanti
313-483-1370

Location: Washtenaw County
Hours: 7 a.m.-7 p.m., June-July
Activities: U-pick strawberries

Ridgemere Berry Farm
2824 Clyde Road, Highland
313-887-5976

Location: Oakland County
Hours: 9 a.m.-dark, Monday-Saturday, June, September, October
Activities: Group tours available ("Raspberry Hayrides" include picking raspberries, a raspberry sundae, hayride, and pumpkin). Ten-minute slide show of Ridgemere Berry Farm, hayrides, u-pick raspberries and pumpkins, country store.

Rochester Cider Mill
5212 Rochester Road, Rochester
313-651-4224

Location: Oakland County

Hours: 9 a.m.-6 p.m., daily, September-October. 9 a.m.-5 p.m., daily except Wednesday, November-December.

Activities: Group tours available. Cider press and donut-making demonstrations, petting farm, antique tools and farm equipment on display, farm store with caramel apples, candy, apples, and other fall goodies.

Rowe's Produce Farm
10570 Martz Road, Ypsilanti
313-482-8538

Location: Washtenaw County

Hours: 8 a.m.-8 p.m., daily, June-October. 7 a.m.-8 p.m., during June.

Activities U-pick strawberries

Roy Schultz
7854 Lilley Road, Plymouth
313-453-6084

Location: Wayne County

Hours: June-July

Activities: U-pick strawberries

Ruby Farms
6567 Imlay City Road, Goodells
313-324-2662

For full information, see Science and Nature

Sherwood Forest
4981 Adams, Rochester
313-652-4920

Location: Oakland County

Hours: 10 a.m.-9 p.m., Monday-Saturday, 10 a.m.-8 p.m., Sunday, September-December

Activities: U-pick Christmas trees, Santa, petting farm, refreshments, large selection of Christmas decorations and gift items

---

Spezia's Strawberries
1220 Stoney Creek Road, Lake Orion
313-693-8434

Location: Oakland County
Hours: June-July
Activities: U-pick strawberries

Stoney Creek Orchard and Cider Mill
2961 West Thirty-Two Mile Road, Romeo
313-752-2453

Location: Macomb County
Hours: 9:30 a.m.-6 p.m., daily, September-Christmas. 9:30 a.m.-5:30 p.m., Thursday-Sunday, January-March.
Activities: U-pick apples, farm market with cider, donuts, jams. Christmas trees during December.

Stotz's Pumpkin Farm
3767 Lewis Avenue, Ida
313-269-2510

Location: Monroe County
Hours: 9 a.m.-6:30 p.m., Monday-Saturday; 11 a.m.-6:30 p.m., Sunday, October-November.
Activities: Group tours available. Halloween "Spook House," farm animals, pumpkin characters, gift shop.

Strawberry Patch
2375 Wixom, Milford
313-685-1393

Location: Oakland County

Hours: Daily, June-July
Activities: U-pick strawberries

Symanzik's Berry Farm
8146 East Baldwin Road, Goodrich
313-636-7714

Location: Genesee County
Hours: 9:30 a.m.-5 p.m., daily June, July, September, and October
Activities: Group tours available. U-pick strawberries, raspberries, and pumpkins, petting farm, play area, picnic tables, hayrides.

Thornhollow Berry Farms
16280 Martinsville Road, Belleville
313-699-9080

Location: Wayne County
Hours: 7 a.m.-8 p.m., daily, June-July
Activities: U-pick strawberries and raspberries

Uncle John's Cider Mill
8614 North US-27 Street, St. Johns
517-224-3686

Location: Clinton County (30 minutes north of Lansing)
Hours: 9 a.m.-8 p.m., daily, August-January 1
Activities: U-pick apples, cider-press demonstration, gift shop, baked goods, wagon ride, weekend bands and craft shows, Christmas trees and holiday gift items.

Upland Hills Farms
481 Lake George Road, Oxford
313-628-1611

Location: Oakland County

Hours: Pumpkin Festival: 11 a.m.-4 p.m., Saturday and Sunday, October

Activities: Pumpkin Festival: Hayride, u-pick pumpkins, playground, puppet show, haunted house, petting farm, pony rides, country store, fall goodies.

Wiard's Orchards
5565 Merritt Road, Ypsilanti
313-482-7744

Location: Washtenaw County

Hours: 9 a.m.-6 p.m., Saturday and Sunday, September-October

Activities: U-pick apples, pumpkins, petting farm, craft booths, entertainment, train, pony and wagon rides, country store with seasonal goodies, cider-press demonstrations

---

Wolcott Orchards
3284 West Coldwater Road, Mt. Morris
313-789-9561

Location: Genesee County

Hours: 9 a.m.-6 p.m., daily

Activities: U-pick apples, cider-press demonstration, bakery, gift shop, hayrides. Group tours available. Apple Festival last weekend in September.

Yates Cider Mill
1990 East Avon Road, Rochester
313-651-8301

Location: Oakland County

Hours: 9 a.m.-7 p.m., daily, September and October. 9 a.m.-5 p.m., daily, November. Noon-5 p.m., weekends, December-May.

Activities: Group tours available. Cider-press demonstration, donuts, apples and seasonal foods, fudge shop, picnic area, water wheel, trails.

Zabinsky Blueberry Farm
Beach Road, Dexter
313-426-2900

Location: Washtenaw County

Hours: 8 a.m.-8 p.m., late August-second week of September

Activities: Hook your bucket to the piece of rope around your waist and you're ready to pick blueberries. The farm supplies every picker with rope and bucket.

8
PARKS

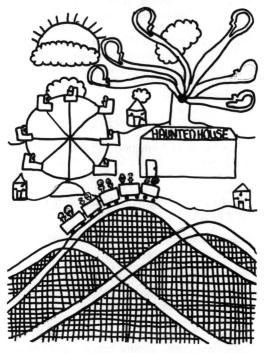

Beaches, picnic tables, creative playgrounds, and wild water slides—the map of southeastern lower Michigan is dotted with city, county, and state parks. The Detroit Parks and Recreation Department operates over 200 neighborhood parks and play lots, including Belle Isle and the newly developed riverfront parks. The Huron-Clinton Metropolitan Authority operates 13 popular metroparks offering a wide range of seasonal activities from nature centers and beaches to boat ramps and toboggan runs.

Macomb County's Freedom Hill is an outdoor concert site; Oakland County's eight developed parks offer wave-action pools, beaches, and cross-country skiing. Wayne

County's seven parks criss-cross the county, and the Michigan State Department of National Resources oversees parks offering family beaches, horseback riding, and a petting farm. There are also Windsor City Parks and Canadian National Parks within a short drive.

To make your park explorations even easier, I include a sampling of adventure parks and water parks. How can you resist these sure-fire kid pleasers?

Detroit Parks

For general information and location of city playgrounds and play lots, call 313-224-1180. For specific Detroit Parks and Recreation events and activities, call the "Leisure Line," 313-224-2-REC. Here is a sampling of Detroit's best family parks.

Belle Isle
313-267-7115

Location: East Jefferson at Grand Boulevard, 2½ miles east of the RenCen

Hours: Grounds are open 24 hours, daily. All buildings are open year-round. Food concessions, boat rental, and the zoo are open April-October. Check individual listings for specific hours of buildings.

Admission: All facilities are free to the public, except the zoo which charges a nominal fee.

Facilities: Playscape—a creative playground, Aquarium, Dossin Great Lakes Museum, Nature Center, Anna Scripps Whitcomb Conservatory, Zoo. *For full information, see* Museums *and* Science and Nature.

You'll see the giant slide as you drive across the bridge onto the island. It's part of Playscape, an imaginative playground made up of timbers of all sizes and shapes, a fireman's pole, tree house, suspended bridge, tire swings, and other play equipment. Visit Belle Isle just for this playground—open all year—

or be sure to leave time at the end of your visit to the other sites. Your kids won't want to leave unless you promise they'll be back soon.

Chene Park
313-224-1144

Location: Along the Detroit River between Chene and DuBois Streets, just east of the RenCen

Hours: Outdoor amphitheater offers a summer season of family and children's concerts and programs

Admission: Free

Facilities: Outdoor amphitheater hill in the summer, outdoor ice skating in the winter

---

Hart Plaza
313-224-1184

Location: Jefferson Avenue, along the Detroit River, just west of the RenCen

Hours: Always open

Admission: Free

Facilities: Outdoor plaza, Noguchi fountain, benches, walkway along the river, summertime food concessions, wintertime ice skating

Hart Plaza epitomizes summertime in the city. It's home to the ethnic festivals each summer weekend from April to Labor Day, Freedom Festival activities during the July Fourth weekend, and the Montreux Jazz Festival in early September. Even on a day without a festival, the plaza is busy and lively. Kids will enjoy running around the Noguchi fountain's "shower" and walking along the river, watching for barges. During the winter, families can ice-skate on a large outdoor rink.

Historic Fort Wayne
6325 West Jefferson, Detroit
313-297-9360

For full information, see Historic Sites

St. Aubin Park
313-224-1144

Location: Atwater and St. Aubin, along the Detroit River, just east of the RenCen

Hours: Year-round children's play area

Admission: Free

Facilities: Creative play area, marina, picnic areas, river overlooks, bicycle paths and walkways

This brand-new riverfront park has been designated a family park and will boast an imaginative, marine-inspired children's playground.

Huron-Clinton Metroparks

Thirteen metroparks, with over 23,346 acres of parkland, offer a wide variety of recreation for residents of Livingston, Oakland, Macomb and Wayne counties. The parks are open year-round, but call ahead; hours may vary from park to park and for different activities and seasons. Young children enjoy the "tot lots," fantasy playground villages located at the following metroparks: Lake Erie, Lower Huron, Metro Beach, and Willow. Families also enjoy visiting the well-staffed, hands-on nature centers located at Indian Springs, Kensington (which also has a farm center), Metro Beach, Oakwoods, and Stoney Creek. Of special interest is Wolcott Mill Metropark, site of a historic grist mill.

Vehicle permits are required ($2 daily, $10 annual, $5 senior citizen annual). Huron-Clinton Metropolitan Authority is located at 13000

High Ridge Drive, Brighton. For toll-free information, call 1-800-47-PARKS.

Delhi Metropark
East Delhi Road, Ann Arbor
Call Hudson Mills Metropark for information
313-426-8211

Fifty-acre park along the Huron River, five miles northwest of Ann Arbor. Picnic sites with shelters and stoves, playfields, fishing sites, swings, and slides. Canoe rentals available May-September. Call Skips's Canoe Livery, 313-769-8686.

Dexter-Huron Metropark
Huron River Drive, Dexter
Call Hudson Mills Metropark for information,
313-426-8211

A riverside park with 122 acres, 7½ miles northwest of Ann Arbor. Shady picnic sites with tables and stoves, swings, slides, playfields, and fishing sites.

Hudson Mills Metropark
8801 North Territorial Road, Dexter
313-426-8211

A multi-purpose park of 1,624 acres, located 12 miles northwest of Ann Arbor, on North Territorial Road at the crossing of the Huron River. Picnic sites, swings, slides, playing fields, hike-bike trail, nature trail, fishing. The Activity Center has food service, tennis, basketball and shuffleboard courts, softball diamond, and bicycle rental in summer. During the winter, the Activity Center offers ski rental, two ice rinks, indoor food service, and cross-country ski trails.

Huron Meadows Metropark
8765 Hammel Road, Brighton
313-685-1561, ext. 484

A 1,538-acre park, located six miles south of Brighton. Picnic sites and Golf Center building with food service, driving range, and 18-hole golf course. During the winter, there is cross-country skiing.

Indian Springs Metropark
5200 Indian Trail, Clarkston
313-685-1561, ext. 482

A 2,206-acre park located near Clarkston, nine miles northwest of Pontiac. A six-mile bike-hike trail, picnic sites, 18-hole golf course, nature trails, and nature center.

Kensington Metropark
2240 West Buno Road, Milford
313-685-1561

This 4,337-acre multi-purpose park, located near Milford and Brighton, offers summertime boat rental, 18-hole golf course, bike-hike trail, picnic sites, fishing sites, the Island Queen — a 66-passenger sternwheeler, two beaches with bathhouses, heated showers, playgrounds, and food service. The Farm Center (including hay/sleigh rides and food service) and Nature Center are open year-round. During the winter, the park offers cross-country ski trails and rentals, ice-skating, tobogganing, and sledding.

Lake Erie Metropark
32481 West Jefferson, Rockwood
313-379-5020

A 1,572-acre park located in Brownstown

Township between Gibraltar and Rockwood, along Lake Erie. During the summer, the park offers picnic sites, wooden playscape, nautical tot lot, marina, and entertainment. The "Great Wave," a large wave-action pool with bathhouse, food service building, and wet shop is open 9 a.m.-7 p.m., weekdays; 9:30 a.m.-8 p.m., weekends and holidays, Memorial Day-Labor Day. Cross-country skiing, rental, and ice-skating during the winter.

Lower Huron Metropark
17845 Savage Road, Belleville
313-697-9181

A 1,237-acre park located along the Huron River near Belleville, with shorefishing, picnic-playfield sites, 18-hole golf course, playscape, nature trails, tennis courts, basketball courts, volleyball, and horseshoe equipment. The swimming pool with water slide, bathhouse, and food service is open 9:30 a.m.-7 p.m., weekdays; 10:30 a.m.-8 p.m., weekends and holidays, Memorial Day-Labor Day. Winter facilities include cross-country ski trails and three ice rinks.

Metro Beach Metropark
Metropolitan Parkway, Mount Clemens
313-463-4581

A 770-acre park located along Lake St. Clair, five miles southeast of Mount Clemens. Summer facilities include Olympic-size swimming pool, putt-putt golf, 18-hole golf course, shuffleboard and horseshoe courts, beach, boat ramp, beach shop, food service, and trackless train. A nature center and tot lot village are open all year. Cross-country ski trails and rental, ice-skating and ice-fishing are available during winter.

Oakwoods Metropark
Willow Road, Flat Rock
313-697-9181, ext. 40

A 1,756-acre park located five miles north-east of Flat Rock and adjacent to Willow Met-ropark offers a nature center and interpretive trails.

Stony Creek Metropark
4300 Main Park Road, Washington
313-781-4242

A 4,461-acre park located six miles north of Utica and northeast of Rochester. Two beaches with bathhouses, heated showers, food service, picnic sites, swings and slides, bike-hike trails, bike rentals, 18-hole golf course, boat launching, nature trails, and na-ture center.

Willow Metropark
South Huron, Huron Township
313-697-9181 (Lower Huron Metropark)

A 1,531-acre park located between Flat Rock and New Boston offers shuffleboard, tennis and basketball courts, food service, playfields, 18-hole golf course, and picnic sites with tables and stoves. The large tot lot is open April-October. The Olympic-size swim-ming pool is open 9:30 a.m.-7 p.m., weekdays; 10:30 a.m.-8 p.m., weekdays and holidays, Memorial Day-Labor Day. Winter facilities in-clude cross-country ski trails and rental, snack bar, and sledding hill.

Wolcott Mill Metropark
Kunstman Road,
north of Twenty-Nine Mile Road
between Van Dyke and North Avenue
in Ray Township
313-749-5997

A 2,124-acre park located along the banks of the north branch of the Clinton River, between Twenty-Six and Thirty-One Mile Roads in Macomb County. The park includes a 140-year-old grist mill open to the public 10 a.m.-5 p.m., daily and for pre-arranged group tours, May-October.

Macomb County Parks and Recreation

See Freedom Hill *in* That's Entertainment

Michigan State Parks

Michigan State parks dot the map offering sandy beaches, forest trails, and recreation facilities. Parks are open 8 a.m.-10 p.m., daily, year-round. Vehicle permits are required ($2 daily, $1 daily for seniors, $10 annual). Administrative offices are located in Lansing. Department of Natural Resources: 517-373-1220. Michigan State Parks: 517-373-1270. Here is a sampling of popular parks in southeastern lower Michigan.

Bald Mountain Recreation Area
1350 Greenshield Road, Lake Orion
313-693-6767

This 4,637-acre park offers picnic sites, playground, beach, beach house and concession, boat rental, hiking and cross-country skiing trails.

Dodge No. 4 State Park
4250 Parkway, Waterford
313-682-0800

A 139-acre park located off Cass Elizabeth Lake Road offering picnic sites, playground, beach, beach house and concession, boat rental, cross-country skiing, ice-skating, and snowmobiling.

Highland Recreation Area
5200 East Highland Road, Milford
313-887-5135

This 5,524-acre park offers picnic sites, playground, beach, beach house and concession, bridle paths, riding stable, cross-country and downhill skiing and rental.

Island Lake Recreation Area
12950 East Grand River, Brighton
313-229-7067

This 3,466-acre park offers picnic sites, canoe rental, playground, beach, beach house, and concession.

Lakeport State Park
7605 Lakeshore Road, Port Huron
313-327-6765

A 565-acre park along Lake Huron offering picnic sites, playground, beach, beach house and concession.

Maybury State Park
20145 Beck Road, Northville
313-349-8390

This 944-acre park offers picnic sites, bike

and hiking trails, living farm, playscape, horse trails and riding stables.

Pontiac Lake Recreation Area
7800 Gale Road, Pontiac
313-666-1020

A 3,700-acre park with picnic sites, playground, beach, beach house and concession, archery range, horse trails and riding stables.

Proud Lake Recreation Area
3500 Wixom Road, Milford
313-685-2433

A 3,614-acre park offering hiking trails, picnic sites, playground, beach, beach house and concession.

Rochester-Utica Recreation Area
47511 Woodall, Utica
313-731-2110

This 1,334-acre park along the historic Clinton-Kalamazoo Canal offers picnic sites, playground, and across the street, the Yates Cider Mill.

Sterling State Park
2800 State Park Road, Monroe
313-289-2715

This 1,000-acre park offers picnic sites, playground, beach, beach house and concession.

Oakland County Parks

Eight developed parks in Oakland County offer family beaches, picnic sites, boat rental, wave-action pools and water slides, nature trails, and much more. Parks are open year-round. Summer hours are 8 a.m. to one hour after sunset, daily. Winter hours are 8 a.m.-sunset, 9 a.m.-4 p.m. for golf courses, weather permitting. But call ahead; hours may vary from park to park and for different activities and facilities.

Daily weekday vehicle pass is $3 for Oakland County residents, $5 for non-residents. Daily weekend and holiday vehicle pass is $4 for residents, $6 for non-residents. Annual vehicle pass is $16 for residents, $26 for non-residents.

Addison Oaks
1480 West Romeo Road, Oxford
313-693-2432

A 750-acre park located 13 miles north of Rochester that offers camping, swimming, picnicking, boat rental, fishing, hiking and nature study, plus winter snowmobile trails, sledding and tobogganing hills, ice-fishing, and ice-skating.

Glen Oaks
30500 Thirteen Mile Road, Farmington Hills
313-851-8356

This 18-hole golf course, located between Orchard Lake and Middlebelt Roads, offers cross-country skiing and equipment rental in the winter.

Groveland Oaks
5990 Grange Hall Road, Holly
313-634-9811

A 200-acre park located at Dixie Highway and Grange Hall Road that offers a sandy beach, swimming lake, plus a flume water slide that splashes into Stewart Lake. There are also camping, picnicking, and boat rental facilities.

Independence Oaks
9501 Sashabaw Road, Clarkston
313-625-0877

This 850-acre park located on Sashabaw Road, 2½ miles north of I-75, offers ten miles of marked nature and ski trails, a nature interpretive center, 200-seat amphitheater, boat rental, picnicking, fishing, swimming, and ice-skating.

Red Oaks
29600 John R, Madison Heights
313-541-5030

Keep cool bucking the waves and whoosing around the curves in Red Oak's large wave-action pool and two water slides. Food service and inner tube and raft rental are available.

Springfield Oaks
12451 Andersonville Road, Davisburg
313-625-8133

The Youth Activities Center and outdoor arenas host August's annual 4-H Fair; the golf course offers cross-country skiing in the winter.

Waterford Oaks
2800 Watkins Lake Road, Pontiac
313-858-0913
313-858-0918 (wave pool)
313-858-5433 (tennis complex)
313-963-8305 (food service)

This 145-acre park located between Watkins and Scott Lake Roads offers a wave-action pool; giant two-flume "Slidewinder" water slides; bicycle motorcross track; games complex with platform tennis, tennis, volleyball, shuffleboard, and horseshoe courts; activities center; picnicking; hiking trail.

White Lake Oaks
991 South Williams Lake Road, Pontiac
313-698-2700

An 18-hole golf course with cross-country skiing and rental during the winter.

Wayne County Parks

For exact location, activities, and hours of each park, call the main information number, 313-261-1990, 9 a.m.-5 p.m., weekdays. Administrative offices are at 33175 Ann Arbor Trail, Westland, open 8 a.m.-4:30 p.m., Monday-Friday. Park grounds are open dawn to dusk daily.

Bell Creek Park and Lola Valley Park
Redford

Neighboring parks along the Bell branch of the Rouge River, Bell Creek offers softball and baseball diamonds and tennis courts; Lola Valley offers natural beauty and picnic tables.

Elizabeth Park
Trenton
313-671-5220

The state's oldest county park offers softball and baseball diamonds, tennis courts, tourist lodge, speed-skating rink, pony and sleigh rides, concessions, and an entertainment pavilion.

Lower Rouge Parkway
Dearborn to Canton Township

This 12-mile parkway along three Rouge

River forks offers baseball and softball diamonds, football and soccer field, tennis courts, picnic tables, and nature trails.

Middle Rouge Parkway
(commonly known as Edward Hines Park)
Dearborn to Northville

This 17½-mile parkway along the scenic banks of the Middle Rouge River offers softball and baseball diamonds, bike, hike, and bridle paths, picnicking sites, tennis courts, football and soccer fields, fishing, a wooded arboretum, plus sledding and toboggan hills, ice-skating, and cross-country skiing in winter.

Veterans Memorial Park
Hamtramck

Tennis courts, baseball and softball diamonds, playground and baseball stadium.

Warren Valley Golf Course
Dearborn Heights
313-561-1040

A 36-hole course with cross-country skiing, rental, and lessons in winter.

William P. Holliday Forest
and Wildlife Preserve
Westland

Picnicking and 12 miles of marked nature trails.

Windsor City Parks and Canadian National Parks

Take a family walk through downtown Windsor's city parks and explore Canada's national parks located in Southern Ontario.

Coventry Garden and
Peace Fountain
Two miles east of downtown Windsor
on Riverside Drive East
at Pillette Road
519-255-6270

During the summer, the Peace Fountain is illuminated with ever-changing patterns of colored lights and water.

Fort Malden National Historic Park
100 Laird Avenue, Amherstburg
519-736-5416

For full information, see Historic Sites

Navy Yard Park
Dalhousie Street, Amherstburg

Behind the historic Park House Museum on Dalhousie Street in Amherstburg, just east of the Amherstburg Boblo Dock, overlooking the Detroit River. There are park benches for picnicking and old anchors for creative photos of the kids.

Point Pelee National Park
South of Leamington
519-322-2371 (recorded information)
519-322-2365 (visitor center)

Location: From Detroit, take the Ambassador Bridge to Windsor. From Windsor, follow Route 3 to Leamington. Prominent signs give directions to the park. About an hour's drive from the bridge.

Hours: Grounds and nature trails, 6 a.m.-10 p.m., daily. Visitor center, 10 a.m.-6 p.m., daily, May-Labor Day. 12:30-4:30 p.m., Monday-Friday; 10 a.m.-5 p.m., weekends, rest of year. Closed January 1 and December 25.

Admission: Daily vehicle permit, $4; Seasonal vehicle permit $20 (Canadian dollars)

Ages: All ages

Plan: Full day

Parking: On site

Lunch: Picnic sites

Facilities: Visitor center with exhibits and theater, boardwalk, observation tower, nature trails. Canoe and bicycle rental April-Labor Day. Ice-skating and cross-country skiing during winter, weather permitting.

This well-kept park becomes a bird-watcher's paradise in early May, and August through October as migratory birds stop along their routes. Monarch butterflies are also plentiful during mid-September. A wide variety of activities are available throughout the year that appeal to children of all ages.

Queen Elizabeth II Gardens
Tecumseh Road and Ouellette Street
Windsor
519-255-6270

This formal flowering garden located five minutes from the tunnel includes a six-acre rose garden with 450 different varieties. Kids will enjoy the maze-like shrubbery and the grounded Lancaster Memorial Bomber, a large World War II Royal Air Force Bomber.

Adventure Parks

Amusement rides, family entertainment, a trip back to the wild west and to prehistoric times — Michigan's adventure parks offer hours of fun for children of all ages.

Boblo Island
4401 West Jefferson, Detroit
313-843-0700

Location: There are three docks. Detroit dock — Jefferson and Clark Streets, near the Ambassador Bridge. Gibraltar dock — I-75 south to exit 29A. Amherstburg, Ontario, dock — Off Kings Highway 18.

Hours: Hours vary. Park is open weekends, May-Memorial Day and after Labor Day; daily, Memorial Day-Labor Day. Generally 9:30 a.m. is the first Detroit departure, daily.

Admission: Tickets cover both boat ride and admission to the Island Theme Park. They vary in price depending on dock, day, and time. Season passes available from Detroit dock.

Ages: All ages

Plan: Full day

Parking: $3 Detroit dock, $2.50 Gibraltar dock, $2.50 (U.S. dollars) Amherstburg dock

Lunch: Food concessions, restaurants, picnic sites

Facilities: Bathrooms, rides, food, and gift concessions

Boblo is Detroit's floating pleasure island, with enough rides and fun to last an entire day. There are two special children's play areas. Fort Fun offers cargo nets, ball crawl, air bounce, teepee maze, and other energy-venting activities for children under 48 inches. Kiddieland has six rides suitable for two to five year olds. Children of all ages will want to watch "Ski Fever," a water-skiing stunt show; "Captain Andy's Rivertown Review," a computerized show of 14 animated, singing animals; and the special-effect shows new each year in the Carrousel Theatre. Even if your kids are too old for the kiddie areas, but too young for the really scary rides, they'll enjoy the train, Pirate Ship, and Log Flume. Families can also rent roller skates and bicycles.

Illuminated Cascades
1992 Warren Avenue, Jackson
517-788-4320 day
517-788-4227 night

Location: Exit 138 at junction of I-94 and US-127

Hours: Illuminated Cascades: 7:30-11 p.m., Memorial Day-Labor Day. All other park facilities: Noon-dark, Memorial Day-Labor Day.

Admission: $2 adults and children 6 and up, children 5 and under free. Group rates available.

Ages: All ages

Plan: Half day visit; spend an evening

Parking: Free on site

Facilities: Picnic and playground areas, paddleboats and miniature golf, Cascades museum and gift shop.

Summer evenings, the Cascades, a 500-foot hill of six spraying fountains, comes to life in vivid color. Live bands, fireworks, and entertainment add to the thrill. Beginning at noon, families can enjoy paddleboats, miniature golf, and other park facilities.

Penny Whistle Place
G-5500 Bray Road, Flint
313-785-8066

Location: I-475 and Carpenter Road (exit 11)

Hours: 10 a.m.-8 p.m., Monday-Saturday. Noon-8 p.m., Sunday, Memorial Day-Labor Day, weather permitting.

Admission: $2.50, children 3 and under free. Group rates available.

Ages: 3-10 year olds

Plan: Half day visit

Parking: Free on site

Lunch: Concessions, picnic tables

Facilities: Bathrooms, drinking fountains, benches for parents

At Penny Whistle, a creative playground, children can explore, climb, and become daring adventurers in a safe environment. Toddlers play in a sandbox with creative dump trucks large enough to sit on, zoom down the

Tube Slides, and march around the Punch Bag Forest. Older children will love diving into layers of orange balls in the Ball Crawl, soaring over an abyss in the Cable Glide, and pumping water and sound at the Music Pump. Parents can sit up close to watch, give their children a hand, or become adventurers themselves. Attendants are also on hand to help children.

Prehistoric Forest
US-12, Onsted (Irish Hills)
517-467-2514

Location: On US-12 in Irish Hills

Hours: 10 a.m.-6 p.m., daily, Memorial Day-Labor Day

Admission: $3.50 adults, $3 children 4 to 16, 3 and under free.

Ages: Preschoolers

Plan: Short visit

Parking: Free on site

Lunch: Picnic sites. Stagecoach Stop U.S.A. is down the road.

Facilities: Bathrooms, gift shop

Prehistoric Forest, a kitschy representation of Mesozoic life, is for dinophiles with a taste for the tacky. The safari train takes you "deep" into the forest where more than 40 prehistoric beasts dwell in different stages of decomposition. Some are tall and ferocious, their scales barely covering chicken wire frames. For young children, such details don't count; they'll be amazed and delighted.

Stagecoach Stop, U.S.A.
7203 US-12, Onsted (Irish Hills)
517-467-2300

Location: On US-12 in Irish Hills, seven miles west of M-50 and M-52 intersection

Hours: 10:30 a.m.-6:30 p.m., Tuesday-Sunday, June-August. Closed Mondays.

Admission: $6 adults, $5 children. Group rates available.

Ages: All ages

Plan: Half day visit

Parking: Free on site

Lunch: Restaurant, ice cream parlor, concessions, fudge shop, picnic tables

Facilities: Bathrooms, gift shop

Walk along an 1880s Wild West town. Visit the general store, carriage house, saw mill, and blacksmith shop. Take a wild game train ride. Visit the petting farm and kiddie rides. Don't be surprised if the townfolks get rowdy and a street fight begins. Just sit on the bleachers and see who's going to win.

Water Parks

Buck the wild waves, whoosh around the curves of a monster slide, take a bumper boat ride, and watch a sea lion show — Michigan's water parks keep you cool.

Four Bears Water Park
3000 Auburn Road, Utica
313-739-5863

Location: Auburn Road, between Ryan and Dequindre, seven miles east of I-75, just off M-59

Hours: 11 a.m.-7 p.m., Monday-Thursday and Sunday; 11 a.m.-8 p.m., Friday, Saturday and holidays, Memorial Day-Labor Day.

Admission; $10.95 over 48 inches, $5.95 under 48 inches, under 3 years and over 65 years free. Group rates and season pass available.

Ages: All ages

Plan: Full day visit

Parking: Free. Next to entrance and across the street.

Lunch: Restaurant, vending machines, concessions, picnic tables

Facilities: Bathrooms, beach house with showers and lockers. Gift shop selling beach paraphernalia and Four Bears souvenirs.

Wear your bathing suit, pack a change of clothes and a picnic lunch, and plan on a full day of water activities at Four Bears. Young children will enjoy the kiddie rides and playground, bumper boats and miniature water slide. Older children will want to play miniature golf, practice their swings at the batting cages, take a turn on the 50-foot triple water slide, or ride the go-carts. The whole family will enjoy the sea lion show, paddle boats, and man-made lake. Four Bears is the area's best full-service water park and well worth the admission price.

Groveland Oaks Water Slide
5990 Grange Hall Road, Holly
313-634-9811

Location: Groveland Oaks County Park, Dixie Highway at Grange Hall Road

Hours: 10 a.m.-4 p.m., daily, Memorial Day-Labor Day

Admission: Water slide 50 cents/ride or $3/day. Oakland County residents vehicle entry fee $3 weekday ($4 weekend); non-residents $5 weekday ($6 weekend).

Ages: Recommended 5 and up

Plan: Half day-full day visit

Parking: Free on site

Lunch: Concession stands

Facilities: Bathrooms, beach, paddleboat, canoe, rowboat and waterbug (1-person paddleboat) rental

Groveland Oaks offers an added attraction to family beach visits. Now you can ride a water slide and splash right into the lake.

Lake Erie Metropark Wave Pool
32481 West Jefferson, Rockwood
313-379-5020

Location: Brownstown Township between Gibraltar and Rockwood, along Lake Erie

Hours: Memorial Day-Labor Day: 9:30 a.m.-7 p.m., weekdays. 9:30 a.m.-8 p.m., weekends and holidays.

Admission: $2.50. $1.50 twilight (6 p.m.-closing). Raft rental $1 per raft. $2 daily vehicle permit, $10 annual vehicle permit.

Ages: All ages. Small children need to be closely supervised.

Plan: Half day-full day visit

Parking: Free on site

Lunch: Snack bar and picnic tables adjacent to pool area

Facilities: Bathrooms, coin lockers, wet shop with beach paraphernalia and rafts

Throughout the day, the pool alternates periods of three-foot waves with intervals of calm. Be sure to arrive early enough to rent a raft. It's more fun to ride the wild waves on a raft.

Michigan Waterworld
56558 Pontiac Trail, New Hudson
313-437-7550

Location: I-96 at New Hudson-Milford exit, four miles from Kensington Metropark

Hours: Memorial Day-Labor Day: 11 a.m.-7 p.m., Monday-Thursday. 11 a.m.-8 p.m., Friday and Saturday. Noon-8 p.m., Sunday.

Admission: Call for current prices. Group rates available.

Ages: 5 and up

Plan: Half day-full day visit

Parking: Free on site

Lunch: Concessions, picnic area
Facilities: Bathrooms

Michigan Waterworld offers families lots of activities including two giant water slides, little Indy cars, bumper boats, miniature golf, and moon-walk.

Red Oaks Waterpark
Thirteen Mile Road, Madison Heights
313-858-0906

Location: Between John R and Dequindre
Hours: 11 a.m.-8 p.m., Memorial Day-Labor Day
Admission: $5 per person, $3 seniors, $3 twilight (6-8 p.m.). Children 5 and under free.
Ages: All ages. Supervise small children closely.
Plan: Half day-full day visit
Parking: Free on site
Lunch: Concessions, picnic areas, and grills
Facilities: Bathrooms, beach house, carpeted pool deck, raft rental at admission window

Red Oaks offers the largest wave-action pool in Michigan. Be sure to arrive early to rent a raft. It's more fun to ride the waves on a raft. The 3,360-foot water slides splash down into a separate pool and are the longest in the Midwest. What a wild way to beat the summer's heat.

Waterford Oaks Wave Pool and Water Slide
1700 Scott Lake Road, Pontiac
313-858-0918

Location: Waterford Oaks County Park, Dixie Highway and Telegraph Road
Hours: 11 a.m.-8 p.m., daily, Memorial Day-Labor Day

Admission: $5 per person, 5 and under free, $3 twilight (after 6 p.m.)

Ages: All ages. Supervise small children carefully.

Plan: Half day-full day visit

Parking: Free on site

Lunch: Snack bar, grills, and picnic areas

Facilities: Bathrooms, inflatable rafts available for purchase, beach house. Also in park—tennis, shuffleboard, and volleyball courts.

Take the plunge from Waterford Oaks' dual flume, 340-foot long "Slidewinder" water slide. Or body surf in the three-foot waves that alternate with calm periods in the large wave-action pool.

9
PEOPLE MOVERS

Motion and excitement. That's what this chapter is all about. Here are all the best rides in town — on land, sea and air. There are urban trolleys, miniature trains, old-fashioned stern-wheelers, country hay wagons, sleighs, and Detroit's own People Mover. Even when the planes and cars are anchored to the ground in a museum setting, your child will be soaring in his mind's eye.

Abbreviations: SP — site offers school programs; T — site offers group tours; H — wheelchair accessible.

SP H	Passenger Steamship

Boblo Boat
313-843-8800, 519-252-4444

Location: There are three docks. Detroit dock — Jefferson and Clark streets; 90-minute boat ride. Gibraltar dock — I-75 to exit 29A; 45-minute boat ride. Amherstburg, Ontario, dock — Off Kings Highway 18; 10-minute boat ride.

Hours: Hours vary, May-September

Admission: Tickets cover both boat ride and admission to the Island Theme Park. They vary in price depending on dock and day.

Parking: Each dock charges nominal parking fee

Facilities: Snacks, drinks, and sandwiches are available on the boat as well as on the island

Sure, there are lots of rides, shows, and excitement on Boblo Island, but for some, the main attraction is the windy 90-minute steamship ride from the Detroit dock, across the Detroit River, aboard the historic *S.S. Columbia* or *S.S. Ste. Claire*.

SP	Historic Steam Engine

Coe Rail
840 North Pontiac Trail, Walled Lake
313-669-1248, 313-851-7957

Location: On Pontiac Trail, just north of Maple Road

Hours: 1 and 2:30 p.m., Sunday, mid-April-November

Admission: $5 adults, $4 children 2 to 10 and seniors. Group rates and group charters available.

Parking: Free on site

Facilities: Gift shop sells chips and candy, engineer hats, train whistles, and train items

All aboard for a one-hour ride on a restored 1917 Erie Lakawanna passenger train, with narration and magic show, compliments of Judy and Larry Coe. School groups and birthday parties welcome.

T	Trolley

Dearborn Trolley Company
23500 Park Avenue, Dearborn
313-274-6300

Location: Southfield Freeway and Michigan Avenue

Hours: Every 33 minutes, 10 a.m.-5 p.m., Monday-Saturday. Every 60 minutes, noon-5 p.m., Sunday.

Admission: $1 adults, 75 cents children 6 to 12 and seniors, children 5 and under free. Exact change is needed.

The Dearborn Trolley's route includes major Dearborn hotels, the downtown shopping district, Fairland Shopping Center, Henry Ford Museum and Greenfield Village, and Henry Ford Estate-Fairlane. Take the entire loop around Dearborn or use the trolley to conveniently go from one place to the next. Tours of Metro Detroit are also available, as well as group charters for special occasions.

H	Downtown Transit System

Detroit People Mover
313-962-7245

Location: There are 13 stations long the 2.9 mile route around downtown Detroit

Hours: 7 a.m.-11 p.m., Monday-Thursday. 7 a.m.-midnight, Friday. 9 a.m.-midnight, Saturday. Noon-8 p.m., Sunday. Round-trip rides are approximately 15 minutes long.

Admission: 50 cents, children 5 and under free. Exact change is needed, although token machines selling 50-cent coupons for dollar bills are in the works.

Parking: Many people find it convenient to park in Greektown and use the station on the third floor of Trapper's Alley, or park in RenCen lots off Jefferson and use the station on the second level of the Millender Center

There's nothing that will make you feel more like a tourist than sailing above the street level and catching a brilliant view of the Detroit River. The People Mover is one of Detroit's best thrills. For a mere 50 cents, you can ride as much as you want, peek into office buildings, view each station's wonderful public art, and feel on top of the world.

Trolley

Detroit Trolley
1301 East Warren, Detroit
313-933-1300

Location: The trolley runs from Washington and Grand Circus Park to the RenCen and along Jefferson

Hours: Every 12-15 minutes, 7:10 a.m.-5:40 p.m., Monday-Friday. 10 a.m.-5:40 p.m., Saturday, Sunday and holidays. Doesn't run Christmas or New Year's Day.

Admission: 45 cents, exact change

Parking: Best bet — park in RenCen lots and catch the trolley in front of the Visitor's Center at Jefferson, east of Beaubien

Ride the red trolleys and experience downtown Detroit by land after cruising by air on the People Mover. Kids will especially enjoy the old-fashioned pace and the bells.

Miniature Train

Detroit Zoo Train
8450 West Ten Mile Road, Royal Oak
313-398-0903

Pay zoo admission an you can ride the train for free, all day. There are two stations, one at the entrance, the other at the back of the zoo, near the Log Cabin Learnng Center. *For complete information, see* Science and Nature.

Hay & Sleigh Rides

Domino's Farms Hay and Sleigh Rides
24 Frank Lloyd Wright Drive, Ann Arbor
313-995-4258

Say hello to the animals at the petting farm and then enjoy a free, slow-paced 15-minute ride through Domino's Farms. *For complete information, see* Science and Nature.

Ships

Dossin Great Lakes Museum
100 Strand
Belle Isle Park, Detroit
313-267-6440

Pretend you're on the hull of a great liner or in the cabin of a Detroit River barge. Experience shipping without getting sea sick. *For complete information, see* Museums.

SP   Antique Vehicle Rides

Greenfield Village
20900 Oakwood Boulevard, Dearborn
313-271-1976 (24-hour information)
313-271-1620

During the season (April-Labor Day), visitors can choose a variety of old-fashioned rides, each at an additional fee above admission. There are narrated carriage tours, 30-minute steam engine train rides (the train is open through October), antique car rides, and a 15-minute ride on a old-fashioned sternwheeler, the *Suwanee*. I would recommend the train ride. For $1.50, you can ride back and forth through the village all day. During the winter (January-mid-March), there are sleigh rides, weather permitting, through the closed village. *For complete information, see* Historic Sites.

Historic Vehicles

Henry Ford Museum
20900 Oakwood Boulevard, Dearborn
313-271-1976 (24-hour information)
313-271-1620

Where else can you learn about the automobile in American life and see such popular culture items as the first McDonald's sign, Texaco service station original pumps, and a 1940s diner? There are also impressive steam trains, motorcycles, airplanes, bicycles, coaches and buggies, as well as antique autos. *For complete information, see* Museums.

Old-fashioned Train

Huckleberry Railroad
Crossroads Village
G-5055 Branch Road, Flint
313-736-7100

Lean out the windows and catch a breeze; keep a lookout for robbers and villains. The Huckleberry Railroad is a delightful 45-minute ride on an old-fashioned steam engine. *For complete information, see* Historic Sites.

SP   **Steamboat**

Island Queen
Kensington Metropark
2240 West Buno Road, Milford
313-685-1561
1-800-47-PARKS

Location: Kensington Boat Rental
Hours: Noon-6 p.m., daily, June-Labor Day. Weekends only, mid-May-June, and Labor Day-Early October. Group charters available at other times.

Admission: $2 adults, $1.50 children, 12 and under

Parking: Free on site

Step back into history on the 66-passenger, diesel-powered paddlewheel. The 45-minute ride on Kent Lake is a refreshing and relaxing change of pace during summer's dog days.

Old-fashioned Train

Junction Valley Railroad
7065 Dixie Highway, Bridgeport
517-777-3480

Location: Five miles west of Frankenmuth

Hours: 10 a.m.-6 p.m., Monday-Saturday; 1-6 p.m., Sunday, Memorial Day-Labor Day. 1-5 p.m., weekends only, September and October.

Admission: $2 adults, $1.50 chilren

Parking: Free on site

Kids will love riding 22 feet down a steep grade into a valley on this quarter-size train as lights flash and bells clang. In the valley, there is a railroad-inspired playground.

Hay & Sleigh Rides

Kensington Farm Center's Hay and Sleigh Rides
2240 West Buno Road, Milford
1-800-47-PARKS

Location: Farm Center

Hours: Every 30 minutes, 12:30 p.m.-4:30 p.m., weekends. Group charters available at other times.

Admission: $1.50 adults, $1 children

Parking: Free on site

Ride through Kensington's fields, ripe with shimmering corn during the fall, the bare skeletal corn shucks silhouetted against the white sky in winter. Kids love the sturdy horses, the old-fashioned hay wagon, and red sleigh. Each ride is approximately 30-minutes long. Warm up and have a snack at the Country Store.

Mount Clemens Train Ride
Gratiot Avenue, Mount Clemens
313-465-5035

Location: Gratiot Avenue and Joy Boulevard

Hours: 1, 2, 3, and 4 p.m., every Sunday, mid-May-September 25

Admission: $3 adults, $1.75 children 4 to 12, 4 and under free

Parking: Free on site

Take a 45-minute ride back into time on the 1924 diesel locomotive. Banjo and harmonica music crackles over the loudspeaker; inside the train car are faded ads: "Lux soap flakes — only 10 cents a box." The train goes through the Selfridge Military Base and stops at the Selfridge Military Air Museum for those who want to get off. Passengers are picked up one hour later.

Pelee Island Cruises
Pelee Island, Ontario, Canada
519-724-2115

Location: Docks are located in Kingsville and Leamington

Hours: Boats leave three times a day — morning, noon, and late afternoon during spring and summer. Call for specific times and location.

Admission: $8 adults, $4 child, under 6 free

Parking: Free on site

Take a 1½ hour round trip cruise across Lake Erie from Kingsville or Leamington to Pt. Pelee Island and back. Or take a ride along with your car and spend some time exploring

Pt. Pelee by car. Vehicle reservations must be made in advance.

R.E. Olds Transportation Museum
240 Museum Drive, Lansing
517-372-0422

Automobile lovers will enjoy all the antique cars. *For complete information, see* Museums.

Romeo Horse Drawn Hayrides
64040 Mount Road, Romeo
313-752-6328

Location: Mound Road, just north of Twenty-Nine Mile Road, just northeast of Stony Creek Nature Center.

Hours: Call to reserve group ride (minimum: 13 people)

Admission: $3 per person includes ride, cider, and donuts

Parking: Free on site

Facilities: Bathrooms

Two strapping Belgian horses pull the straw-filled wagon on a scenic back-roads route. Evening rides are also available. After the ride, relax with a cup of hot cider and donuts.

Selfridge Military Air Museum
Selfridge Air Base, Mt. Clemens
313-466-5035

Airplanes are everywhere, majestically grounded in the museum's field and roaring through the sky on Sunday maneuvers. *For complete information, see* Museums.

Hay & Sleigh Rides

Silver Saddle Hay and Sleigh Rides
2991 Oakwood, Ortonville
313-627-2826

Location: M-24 and Oakwood

Hours: Noon-5 p.m., Saturday and Sunday. Groups of 15 or more may schedule rides 10 a.m.-midnight, daily.

Admission: $4 for an hour ride before 5 p.m.; $8 after 5 p.m.

Parking: Free on site

Take an hour ride through the country on Silver Saddle's 150 acres. Kids will also enjoy seeing the farm animals and several unusual animals — buffalo, llama, and ostrich.

Train

Southern Michigan Railroad
320 South Division Street, Clinton
517-456-7677

Location: Three blocks south of US-12

Hours: Trains leave at noon, 12:45, 1:30, 2:15, 3, 3:45, and 4:30 p.m., Saturday, Sunday, and holidays, May-October. Group rides may be scheduled at other times.

Admission: $4 adults, $2 children, round-trip fare

Parking: Free on site

The Southern Michigan Railroad takes you on a one-hour-and-20-minute ride between Clinton and Tecumseh, two charming small towns. It is a wonderful way to introduce your children to train travel, enjoy fall scenery, and browse through Tecumseh's restored shopping disrict.

Transportation Museum

Southwestern Ontario Heritage Village
Essex County Road 23
Essex, Ontario, Canada
519-776-6909

A transportation museum that documents the progress from foot power to modern-day vehicles. *For complete information, see* Historic Sites.

H   Boat

Star of Detroit Cruises
20 East Atwater Street, Detroit
313-259-9160, 313-465-7827

Location: Docked at Hart Plaza

Hours: Lunch 11 a.m.-1:30 p.m., Monday-Friday. Brunch: 11 a.m.-1:30 p.m., Saturday and Sunday. Dinner: 7-10 p.m., daily, May-August.

Admission: Cruise admission varies depending on meals served. Six years old and under are free.

Parking: Use Joe Louis Arena

Cruise the Detroit River while enjoying a deluxe multi-course meal and music. The Star of Detroit is Detroit's largest restaurant on water.

Miniature Train

Starr-Jaycee Park Train
Thirteen Mile Road, east of Crooks
Royal Oak

Free train rides are offered noon-5 p.m. on the first full weekend of every month, April-November, weather permitting.

Airplanes

Yankee Air Force Museum
Willow Run Airport, Ypsilanti
313-483-4030

Kids with a passion for planes will love this hangar full of World War II planes and colorful aviation memorabilia. *For complete information, see* Museums.

10
THAT'S
ENTERTAINMENT

Children love live performances. Whether it's a folk concert, puppet show, classic holiday play, or outdoor concert, Detroit has it all. For first time theater-goers, check the local library or parks and recreation department for a children's theater series. These shows are especially geared for preschoolers and usually last less than an hour. The Summer Children's Concert Series at Meadow Brook Music Festival is also a good bet. The audience is very informal; you can sit up close and munch on a peach while listening to Prokofiev's *Peter and the Wolf*.

The biggest children's show in town is the Detroit Youtheatre, offering October to May Saturday performances of the best in mime, drama, dance, music, and puppetry from around the country. The Youtheatre's Wiggle Club is a series designed for three to five year olds. Older children find plenty of interest in the remaining lineup.

Children of all ages enjoy the Peanut Butter Players, a troupe of professional child actors who serve lunch and then perform Saturdays and Sundays during the school year. For older children, watch for matinee concerts, dances, and shows at Detroit's legitimate theaters. Children will never forget their first trip to Detroit's grand theaters—the Fisher, Fox, Masonic Temple, Music Hall, or Orchestra Hall.

Family Shows

Ann Arbor Parks and Recreation
Junior Theatre
Pioneer High School Little Theatre
601 Stadium, Ann Arbor
313-994-2326
(Parks and Recreation number)

Location: Corner of Stadium Boulevard and Main Street

Showtime: 7:30 p.m., Friday. 1 and 3:30 p.m., Saturday and Sunday. There are usually two productions a year.

Tickets: $3 adults, $2 children

Ages: Elementary school children

Parking: Free on site

Classic fairy tales are brought to the stage by talented Ann Arbor-area school children.

Family Shows

Ann Arbor Parks and Recreation
Mini-Matinee Club
2800 Stone School Road, Ann Arbor
313-994-2326

Location: Stone School Auditorium, Packard and Stone School Roads

Showtime: 2 p.m., Sunday. Eight performances during the school year.

Tickets: $4 adults, $3 children

Ages: 4 and up

Parking: Free on site

Each Sunday performance, geared to families with young elementary-aged children, includes a short play or puppet show plus an additional entertainer—either magic, music, dance, mime, or juggling. A playground on the grounds can be used before or after the show.

SP   Music

Ann Arbor Symphony Orchestra
Michigan Theatre
603 East Liberty, Ann Arbor
313-994-4801

Location: Liberty and State Streets
Showtime: Once a month, selected weekend evenings or matinees, September-April
Tickets: $11-$6 adult, $5-$4 child. Special children's concert, $1.50 per person.
Ages: 5 and up
Parking: Street parking, nearby lots

Children will especially enjoy the early December concert, "Caroling by Candlelight," a lively sing-along with refreshment and a visit with Santa. "Caroling" has three Sunday performances, two of them matinees. In February, the Symphony performs a children's concert, featuring youth soloists and youth artists in a multi-media presentation.

                                       Music

The Ark
637½ South Main, Ann Arbor
313-761-1451

Location: Between Hill Street and Madison. Entrance is on Moseley. The Ark is above the South Main Market.
Showtime: Matinee performances, Sunday afternoons
Tickets: $5 adults, $3 children
Ages: Preschool and up

Parking: Free on site

Peter "Madcat" Ruth, the Song Sisters, the Chenille Sisters, Gemini, and other Ann Arbor and national folk notables make annual appearances at this small, intimate folk club, which offers children's concerts almost once-a-month.

Fun & Games

The Art Castle
1061 East Long Lake Road, Troy
313-680-1127

Location: Long Lake Plaza, east of Rochester Road

Showtime: During the school year: Noon-5:30 p.m., Monday-Friday. 10 a.m.-5:30 p.m., Saturday. Noon-4 p.m., Sunday. During the summer: 10 a.m.-5 p.m., Monday-Saturday. Noon-5 p.m., Sunday.

Tickets: Molds are $2.75 and up; magnets and pins are 50 cents each

Ages: All ages from preschool through adult

Parking: Free on site

Children of all ages will enjoy painting a plaster mold or splatter-painting a t-shirt or sweatshirt. The Art Castle also offers birthday party and group discounts.

Theater

Attic Theatre
7939 Third, Detroit
313-875-8284

Location: Third and West Grand Boulevard

Showtime: 8 p.m., Wednesday-Sunday. 5:30 and 9 p.m., Saturday. 2:30 and 7 p.m., Sunday.

Tickets: $11-$19

Ages: Most plays are geared for an adult audience; occasionally there are family plays during December

Parking: Use street parking or the Fisher Building lot

Dinner Theater

Baldwin Public Library
300 West Merrill, Birmingham
313-647-1700

Location: Downtown Birmingham

Showtime: 7-8 p.m., selected Thursdays

Tickets: Free

Ages: 6 and up

Parking: Use metered adjacent lots or street parking

Advance registration is necessary for this free family dinner theater. Bring a picnic supper; the library provides punch and an hour's worth of fun from local performers.

Music

Birmingham-Bloomfield Symphony Orchestra
Several locations in the
Birmingham-Bloomfield area
313-643-7288

Location: "Classical Series" at Temple Beth El, 7400 Telegraph Road, Birmingham. "Pops Series" at Roma's of Bloomfield, 2101 South Telegraph Road, Bloomfield Hills. "Cranbrook Festival" at Christ Church Cranbrook, 470 Church Road, Bloomfield Hills. "Nutcracker Ballet" at West Bloomfield High School, Orchard Lake Road, West Bloomfield.

Showtime: Weekend evenings and matinees, October-May

Tickets: $10-$12

Ages: Children will enjoy the December "Holiday Family Pops" and the Nutcracker

Parking: Free at each site

Birmingham Community House
380 South Bates, Birmingham
313-644-5832

Location: Woodward and Maple Roads

Showtime: 1 p.m., Saturday matinees throughout the year

Tickets: $3

Ages: Preschool and up. Children under 5 must have adult chaperones.

Parking: Use street parking or nearby lots

    The Community House offers families a variety of mime, music, magic, dance, storytelling, and drama performed by traveling troupes and local entertainers.

Birmingham Theatre
211 South Woodward, Birmingham
313-644-1096

Location: ½ block south of Maple on South Woodward

Showtime: 8 p.m., Tuesday-Saturday. 2 p.m., Wednesday and Sunday. 7 p.m., Sunday.

Tickets: $13-$26

Ages: Most plays are geared for an adult audience; occasionally a family show will play during the holiday season

Parking: There is a lot north of the theater on South Woodward and a structure immediately behind the theater on Brownlee Street.

SP   Theater

Bonstelle Theatre
3424 Woodward Avenue, Detroit
313-577-2960

Location: Woodward and Elliott, one block south of Mack

Showtime: 8 p.m., Friday and Saturday. 2 p.m., Sunday

Tickets: $8 adults, $6 student

Ages: Generally, shows for adult audience with a family show each holiday season. Every other year *A Christmas Carol* is performed.

Parking: Lot adjacent to theater on Elliott

H   Music

Brunch with Bach
Detroit Institute of Arts
5200 Woodward, Detroit
313-833-2323

Location: Kresge Court Cafe

Showtime: 10 and 11:30 a.m., Sundays

Tickets: $11.50, concert and full brunch; $10 concert and continental brunch. Reserve tickets at least a week in advance. $4 concert-only tickets available on a first-come, first-served basis.

Ages: Primarily an adult activity available to mature children, recommended ten years and older.

Parking: Use Detroit Science Center parking lot ($2) on John R

   Mature children with a penchant for classical music and adult foods (like quiche and Boston endive) will enjoy sitting in the hushed Kresge Court, quietly eating brunch while watching a piano or string concert. Come prepared with pencil and paper for sketching, a perfect antidote for the young and sometimes, restless.

Family Shows

Cleary Auditorium
201 Riverside Drive West, Windsor, Ontario
519-252-8311

Location: Riverside Drive West and Ferry Street, one block west of Ouellette Avenue

Showtime: 7:30 p.m., Thursday evenings. Matinee performances available for holiday show.

Tickets: $7

Ages: Preschool and elementary school

Parking: Metered street parking, lots across the street near the river, also in back of the auditorium

Several children's shows are offered each season as part of the Cleary Stage Series, appealing to families with young children. The Windsor Symphony Orchestra also offers a family concert series at Cleary.

Special Events

Cobo Arena
600 Civic Center Drive, Detroit
313-567-6000

Sesame Street Live! comes to Cobo Arena every January.

Special Events

Cobo Hall
1 Washington Boulevard, Detroit
313-224-1010

Cobo Hall hosts the annual Autoshow in January, Home Furniture and Flower Show in March, and the Christmas Carnival in December.

Fun & Games

Colors
2520 West Twelve Mile Road, Berkley
313-546-5566

Location: At northwest intersection of Twelve Mile and Coolidge Roads

Showtime: 10 a.m.-7 p.m., Monday-Saturday. Noon-4 p.m., Sunday.

Tickets: $1 for the paint. $3-$9 for each plaster mold. Group and birthday party rates available.

Ages: Preschool-adult

Parking: Free on site

Colors is a great place for families to spend an hour or two creating in a stress-free environment. Put on a smock, become a Picasso, and paint a cute plaster mold, t-shirt, or sweatshirt as creatively as you want. One lucky bonus — kids always like the finished product.

Family Shows

Concerts-For-Youth
Oakland University Center
for the Arts
231Varner Hall, Rochester
313-370-3018 (information)
313-370-3013 (box office)

Location: I-75 and University Drive, Oakland University campus

Showtime: 10 a.m., eight Mondays performances, October-May

Tickets: $4. Group admission available.

Ages: 6 to 12 years

Parking: Free on site

Oakland Schools and the Oakland Center for the Arts sponsor a children's concert series of poetry, music, magic, storytelling, theater, and a special holiday show in December. Performances are open to school groups and the public. Oakland Center for the Arts also offers an adult season of dramas and musicals that would interest older children.

Cranbrook Summer Children's Theatre
Annetta Wonnberger
313-644-9065, 313-645-3679

Location: Cranbrook Education Community, 500 Lone Pine Road, Bloomfield Hills

Showtime: Public performances held at the end of summer classes in late July, early August. One set of performances involve students in third through seventh grades, the other 14 years and older.

Tickets: Moderate prices

Ages: Preschool and up

Parking: Free on site

Your children will enjoy watching their peers perform folk and fairy tales or modern musicals.

Croswell Opera House
129 East Maumee Street, Adrian
517-263-5674

Location: M-52 and Business US-223

Showtime: 8 p.m., Friday and Saturday. 3 p.m., Saturday and Sunday. Winter and summer theater.

Tickets: Winter: $6 adults, $5 children. Summer: $8 adults, $6 children.

Ages: While most shows are geared for an adult audience, a family holiday musical is always offered at the end of November and beginning of December

Parking: Metered street parking, large metered lot behind the theater

The Croswell Opera House, the oldest continuously operating theater in Michigan, is a historic site worth seeing. Drive out for the holiday musical or a light musical during the summer. Call ahead to arrange a tour of the building.

SP **Theater**

Detroit Center for
the Performing Arts
Eastown Theatre
8041 Harper Avenue, Detroit
313-961-7925

Location: Two blocks north of I-94 at the Van Dyke exit

Showtime: 10 a.m., Wednesday, Thursday, Friday. 2 p.m., Saturday and Sunday. 8 p.m., Friday and Saturday. Times vary with production.

Tickets: $2.50-$14. Group rates available.

Ages: Preschool and up

Parking: Free parking in three lighted, secure lots within a block of the theater

Detroit Center for the Performing Arts offers five children's theater touring productions, plus weekday matinees at the Eastown, open to school groups and the public. There are also weekend matinees and evening performances of their regularly scheduled adult season, including several musicals appropriate for family entertainment.

SP **Dance**

Detroit Dance Collective
Lila Jones-Johnson Theater
Oakland Community College
739 South Washington, Royal Oak
313-548-9664

Location: Corner of Lincoln and Washington, downtown Royal Oak

Showtime: Annual Danceabout performances usually the second weekend in February

Tickets: $10 adults, $8 students

Ages: 8 and up

Parking: Free parking in structure and open lots on both sides of the theater

The Detroit Dance Collective offers highly creative and imaginative numbers in their annual Danceabout. It's a concert perfect for children who haven't had much exposure to dance as well as those who are dancers themselves. The group also travels to schools with a program of concerts and classes.

Omnimax Theater

Detroit Science Center
5020 John R, Detroit
313-577-8400

The Omnimax Theater's 360° domed ceiling draws you into the movie, creating a sense that you are moving with the motion on the screen. Children will enjoy this excitement. *For more information, see* Museums *and* Science and Nature.

Theater for Hearing Impaired

Detroit Sign Company —
Deaf Theater
313-588-2295

The Detroit Sign Company sponsors one annual spring concert for a hearing/hearing impaired audience, held in the Lila R. Jones-Johnson Theater, Oakland Community College, 739 South Washington, Royal Oak. For more information, contact Larry Walatkiewicz, 288-5598 TDD/V, or Dave Barrett, 588-2295 TDD/V.

Detroit Symphony Orchestra
Young People's Concerts
Orchestra Hall
3711 Woodward Avenue, Detroit
313-833-3700

Location: Between Warren and Mack, one mile south of the DIA

Showtime: 11:30 and 2 p.m., Saturday. Usually four concerts each season.

Tickets: $9, $8, $6

Ages: All ages, but 6 to 12 would derive the greatest enjoyment

Parking: $3, lots on Parsons and on Woodward.

These light classical concerts are designed to familiarize children with serious music in a fun way. The Detroit Symphony plays along with dance, mime, puppets, and guest conductors.

Detroit Youtheatre
Detroit Institute of Arts
5200 Woodward, Detroit
313-833-2323

Location: The theater entrance is on John R

Showtime: 11 a.m. and 2 p.m., Saturdays, October-May. Additional matinees are scheduled during vacation weeks. School matinees are held during the week.

Tickets: $4 for most shows; $5 for special shows. Group rates and discount passes available.

Ages: 5 and up. "Wiggle Club" series for 3 and up.

Parking: Use the lot adjacent to the Science Center on John R, $2.

The Detroit Youtheatre offers the finest and largest children's theater season in the Detroit area, every Saturday from October to May. Once you see one, you'll want to spend every Saturday at the Youtheatre. Birthday party and group packages are also available.

Special Event

Disney's
Magic Kingdom on Ice

Mickey and his friends fill the ice in Joe Louis Arena for an early November week of matinee and evening performances.

Dessert Theater

Farmington Community Center —
Family Dessert Theater
24705 Farmington Road, Farmington
313-477-8404

Location: Farmington Road, just north of Ten Mile Road

Showtime: 7-8:30 p.m., once-a-month on Wednesday, September-April

Tickets: $4 individual, $12 family, includes dessert and show

Ages: 4 and up

Parking: Free on site

The whole family will enjoy an hour of children's theater, puppet shows, or family entertainment followed by desserts.

Theater

Fisher Theatre
West Grand Boulevard at Second, Detroit
313-872-1000 (information)
313-871-1132 (group sales)

Location: West Grand Boulevard and Second Avenue

Showtime: 8 p.m., Tuesday-Saturday. 2 p.m., Saturday and Sunday. 7 p.m., Sunday.

Tickets: $20-$35

Ages: Most plays are geared for an adult audience; occasionally there are plays and musicals appropriate for a young audience.

Parking: Use lots adjacent to the theatre, $2-$5.

The Fisher Theatre is housed in a landmark building (*See* Historic Sites) and is Detroit's major "Broadway" playhouse.

Family Shows

Flint Youth Theatre
924 East 6th Street, Flint
313-762-1018

Location: Whiting Auditorium, downtown Flint

Showtime: 4:30 and 7 p.m., weekday performances

Tickets: $2.50. Group rates available.

Ages: Preschool and up

Parking: Free on site

The Flint Youth Theatre offers puppets, plays, and musical tales in three productions during the year.

Theater

Fox Theatre
2211 Woodward, Detroit
313-567-6000 (information)
313-645-6666 (tickets by phone)

Location: On Woodward, two blocks south of I-75

Showtime: Evening and matinee performances

Tickets: Prices vary with performances

Ages: While most shows are geared for an adult audience, family holiday concerts are scheduled for December and *Muppet Babies Live!* for April

Parking: Lot across the street between John R and Woodward, Fox parking tower on north side of theater, underground lot at Grand Circus Park

The Fox is an opulently beautiful, landmark Detroit theater you won't want to miss. *See also* Historic Sites.

Music

Freedom Hill
15000 Metroparkway, Sterling Heights
313-979-8750

Location: On Metroparkway (Sixteen Mile) between Utica and Schoenherr Roads

Showtime: Concerts are scheduled May-September

Tickets: Price varies with concert

Ages: Varies depending on type of concert

Parking: $2 on site

Freedom Hill books concerts throughout the summer and offers families a chance to sit up on a hill and enjoy an outdoor concert. Ethnic festivals are also held here during the summer.

Theater

Greenfield Village Theatre Company
Henry Ford Museum, Dearborn
313-271-1620

Location: Henry Ford Museum

Showtime: Matinee and evening performances throughout the year. Most plays are geared for an adult audience, but children are welcome. During December, a special children's classic is usually performed.

Tickets: December show: $4. Other shows: $8. Dinner and show: $23.

Ages: 6 and up

Parking: Free on site

Think carefully before bringing small children to a Greenfield Village Theatre Company play. We found the holiday performances slow paced and long, even though they were adaptations of classic children's stories. Older children who enjoy live performances will still enjoy the costumes, scenery, and meeting the performers up close after the show.

Family Shows

Grosse Pointe Children's Theatre
Grosse Pointe War Memorial
32 Lakeshore Drive, Grosse Pointe Farms
313-881-7511, 313-885-6219

Location: William Fries Auditorium, Grosse Pointe War Memorial, Lakeshore Drive near Fisher Road

Showtime: Matinees and evenings, selected Saturdays and Sundays

Tickets: $5 adults, $4 children and seniors

Ages: All ages

Parking: Free on site

The Grosse Pointe Children's Theatre, made up of school-aged children, performs several energetic shows throughout the year, including one for the December holidays. Birthday parties and groups receive special recognition before the performance.

Dance

Harbinger Dance Company
Smith Theatre
Oakland Community College Campus
27055 Orchard Lake Road, Farmington Hills
313-477-7014

Location: Campus entrance on Orchard Lake Road, just south of I-696

Showtime: Evenings and matinees. Fall and spring concerts at Smith Theatre. Winter or spring concerts at Music Hall.

Tickets: $8-$22, depending on concert location

Ages: 5 and up

Parking: Free on site

Detroit's oldest professional modern dance troupe offers a fresh and innovative approach to dance that will appeal to children. The company also offers touring school programs.

Theater

Hilberry Theatre
Corner of Cass and Hancock, Detroit
313-577-2972

Location: Cass is one block west of Woodward; Hancock is one block south of Warren.

Showtime: The Hilberry offers first rate adult shows in evening and matinee performances, October-May and during the summer. A children's show is performed 10:30 a.m. and 1 p.m., Monday-Saturday, and 8 p.m., Wednesday-Saturday, during July.

Tickets: $14-$10 for regular series; $2.50 for July's children's show. Group rates available.

Ages: 3 to 13 years for the children's show

Parking: Two lots across Cass from the theater, $1.75 fee

Children will enjoy July's special children's play, performed in the Hilberry's intimate Studio Theatre. After the performances, cast members are on hand to give autographs.

Ice Capades

During March, Olympic gold medalists and other outstanding skaters perform their annual extravaganza of skill and beauty at Joe Louis Arena.

Independence Oaks Nature Center Amphitheatre
9501 Sashabaw Road, Clarkston
313-858-0906

Location: 2½ miles north of I-75, on Sashabaw Road

Showtime: Matinees and evening performances throughout the year

Tickets: $1

Ages: All ages

Parking: Vehicle entry fee: $5 weekdays, $6 weekends and holidays

The Independence Oaks Amphitheatre offers a variety of entertaining and educational family shows that focus on Michigan history and its natural resources.

Theater, Music

Jewish Community Center
Aaron DeRoy Theatre
6600 West Maple, West Bloomfield
313-661-1000

Location: Maple Road, just west of Drake Road

Showtime: Evening and Sunday matinee performances, depending on show

Tickets: $3-$8.50, depending on show

Ages: Preschool and up

Parking: Free on site

Family shows and concerts are offered throughout the year. During November's Jewish Book Fair week, there are children's programs held on Sunday afternoon.

Family Shows

Jewish Community Center
15110 West Ten Mile Road, Oak Park
313-967-4030

Location: Ten Mile Road, just east of Greenfield Road

Showtime: Sunday matinees, year-round

Tickets: $4 adults, $3 children

Ages: Preschool to 7

Parking: Free on site

Throughout the year, the center offers afternoon performances of local storytellers, children's theater, and puppetry.

Special Events

Joe Louis Arena
600 Civic Center Drive, Detroit
313-567-7333

The arena hosts Ringling Bros. and Barnum & Bailey Circus, Walt Disney's Magic Kingdom On Ice, and the Ice Capades.

Kids Koncerts
Southfield Parks and Recreation
26000 Evergreen Road, Southfield
313-354-4717

Location: Room 115, Parks and Recreation Building, Evergreen Road, just north of Ten Mile Road

Showtime: 1:30-2:15, once-a-month on Saturday

Tickets: $2

Ages: 4 to 10

Parking: Free on site

Once-a-month, throughout the year, Southfield Parks and Recreation brings to the stage a series of clowns, mimes, musicians, and magicians to entertain area families.

Lathrup Youth Theatre—
Lathrup Village
Recreation Department
Southfield-Lathrup High School
19301 West Twelve Mile Road, Southfield
313-559-3893

Location: Just east of Evergreen Road

Showtime: 8 p.m., Thursday-Saturday; 2 p.m., Sunday, last weekend in July

Tickets: $5 adults, $2.50 children

Ages: All ages

Parking: Free on site

The Lathrup Youth Theatre is an enthusiastic troupe of 300 children ages 5-18 who audition the last weekend in May for a part in the summer's performance of a children's musical.

MacKenzie Hall
Children's Concert Series—
"The Peanut Gallery"
3277 Sandwich Street
Sandwich, Ontario, Canada
519-255-7600

Location: From the bridge, take Riverside Drive west until it becomes Sandwich Street. MacKenzie Hall is located at Sandwich and Brock.

Showtime: 2 p.m., three Sundays throughout the year

Tickets: $4

Ages: Preschool-11

Parking: Free on site

Mimes, musicians, puppeteers, and dancers entertain children, who are sitting informally on the floor in a bright and modern gallery.

Macomb Center for
the Performing Arts
44575 Garfield Road, Mount Clemens
313-286-2141

Location: Garfield and Hall (M-59) Roads, near Lakeside Mall

Showtime: 10 a.m. and 1 p.m., one Saturday a month, September-April

Tickets: $4 adults, $3.50 children

Ages: Preschool-adult

Parking: Free on site

The Sunshine Series brings national and local children's theater troupes to the Macomb Center stage, performing classic fairy tales and magic. In addition, there are December holiday shows, including *A Christmas Carol.*

Maplewood Family Theatre
31735 Maplewood, Garden City
313-525-8846

Location: Maplewood Community Center
Showtime: 6 p.m., once a month on Tuesdays, throughout the year
Tickets: $5 includes dinner and show
Ages: All ages
Parking: Free on site

Enjoy a light meal and a performance by a local children's theater troupe.

Marquis Theatre
135 East Main, Northville
313-349-8110, 313-349-0868

Location: Downtown Northville
Showtime: Selected matinee and evening performances for the public and school groups throughout the year
Tickets: $5 adults, $4 children
Ages: Preschool and up
Parking: Metered parking on street or in municipal lots

Come to the Marquis Theatre, a national historic landmark in Northville, sink into plush red velvet seats and munch on buttery popcorn as you watch a lively rendition of a children's classic, or a popular musical. All shows are suitable for families; three are geared specifically to children and performed during spring, summer, and winter.

Fun & Games

Marvin's Marvelous
Mechanical Museum and Emporium

Hunter's Square Shopping Plaza
31005 Orchard Lake Road, Farmington Hills
313-626-5020

Location: On Orchard Lake Road, just south of
Fourteen Mile Road

Showtime: 10 a.m.-9 p.m., Monday-Thursday.
10 a.m.-midnight, Friday and Saturday. Noon-8
p.m., Sunday.

Tickets: 25 cents for most machines and rides.
A dollar bill changer is located near the rides.

Ages: Preschool and up

Parking: Free lot on site

Line your pockets with quarters and come
to Detroit's only indoor ride emporium. Over
300 mechanical games, kiddie rides, and authentic old-fashioned pinball machines make
this a child's dream come true. Toddlers will
love the variety of rides, the circus atmosphere, and the continuous bells and bleeps.
Older children will want to try to outwit the
"metal grabbers" and snag a special prize, or
shoot ducks and enemies on beautifully restored machines, many built in the early part of
the century. There's plenty of room for birthday parties.

Theater

Masonic Temple

500 Temple, Detroit
313-832-2232 (information)
313-871-1132 (group sales)

Location: Temple and Second

Showtime: Matinee and evening performances
depending on show

Tickets: Vary, depending on show

Ages: Generally geared to an adult audience, although many shows are of interest to children of all ages

Parking: Use area lots, $2-$5

The Masonic Temple Theatre, a designated historic building with a seating capacity of over 4,000 seats, is one of the area's most beautiful and largest theatrical houses. It hosts the Michigan Opera Theatre, dance concerts, and touring shows, including musicals with spectacular sets.

Music

Meadow Brook Music Festival
Oakland University, Rochester
313-377-2010

Location: Walton Boulevard, between Adams and Squirrel Roads

Showtime: Children's concerts: 11 a.m., Saturday. Gates open at 10 a.m. Children's concerts are scheduled June-August. The Festival also includes weekday and weekend matinee and evening concerts for families and adults.

Tickets: $3-$10 children's concerts, $10-$27.50 adult concerts

Ages: Preschool and up

Parking: $3 parking on site

Children love the informality of the outdoor concerts. Sit up close in the pavilion or high up on the hill, munch on snacks and listen to famous classical children's pieces, watch a musical fairy tale, puppets, or mime.

From June to September the Music Festival also offers a full season of classical, jazz, and pops, with matinee and evening performances. Families are welcome; they may picnic on the lawn before and after the concert. At Thursday and Sunday concerts, children 12 and under are admitted free on the lawn when accompanied by paying adults (one child per adult, additional children receive 50 percent discount).

Meadow Brook Theatre
Oakland University, Rochester
313-377-3300
313-370-3318 (group sales)

Location: Walton Boulevard between Adams and Squirrel Roads, on the campus of Oakland University

Showtime: Matinee and evening performances depending on play. Student performances and post-play discussions, Wednesday and Saturday matinees, Tuesday and Wednesday evenings.

Tickets: $13-21. Student tickets are discounted.

Ages: Generally an adult audience, but many plays are appropriate for 11 and up

Parking: Free on site

Eight plays are offered each season; each offers special school matinees. The annual December favorite, *A Christmas Carol*, is fun for the entire family.

Michigan Opera Theatre
313-874-SING (information)
313-874-7878 (group sales)

Location: The season is split between Masonic Temple (500 Temple Avenue) and the Fisher Theatre (West Grand Boulevard)

Showtime: 1 p.m. matinees and 8 p.m. evenings for selected shows. Usually six shows in a season.

Tickets: $10-$40. 50 percent discount for students and seniors one-half hour before show. Group rates available.

Ages: 7 and up

Parking: $4, lots adjacent to theater

Each season, the Michigan Opera Theatre offers a special student matinee for one of its shows with great appeal for children. A question-and-answer session follows the performance. The MOT also provides a traveling "Overture to Opera" for performances in the schools and special American Sign Language performances for the hearing-impaired.

Special Event

Michigan Renaissance Festival
Holly
313-645-9640

Location: One mile north of Mt. Holly, Inc., on Dixie Highway (US 10) between Pontiac and Flint

Showtime: 10 a.m.-7 p.m., weekends, mid-August-late September

Tickets: $9.95 adult, $4.95 children. Group prices available.

Ages: All ages

Parking: Free on site

Enter a sixteenth-century village dell and take part in the merrymaking. Children will enjoy old-fashioned rides and entertainment—puppet shows, dance, juggling, jousting, and more.

Family Shows

Michigan Theater
603 East Liberty, Ann Arbor
313-668-8397

Location: West of State Street, just off the U of M campus

Showtime: Weekend afternoons

Tickets: $7-$8.50

Ages: Preschool and up

Parking: Use parking lot on Maynard and East Liberty

The "Not Just For Kids" series offers children an introduction to the performing arts by bringing to the stage nationally prominent singers, dancers, actors and puppeteers.

Special Event

Muppet Babies Live!

The Fox Theatre hosts the Saturday morning cartoon crew during its annual visit in April.

Dance, Theater

Music Hall
350 Madison Avenue, Detroit
313-963-7680
313-963-7622 (group sales)

Location: Madison Avenue exit off I-75

Showtime: 2 or 8 p.m., depending on performance

Tickets: $16-$30, depending on performance

Ages: 5 and up

Parking: Lighted parking on all four sides of theater

Music Hall offers Detroiters a first-rate dance concert series, including legendary modern dance and classical dance companies. Throughout the year, it also hosts a music series, theater series, and well-known entertainers.

Family Shows

Novi Parks and Recreation Special Events
45175 West Ten Mile Road, Novi
313-347-0400

Location: On Ten Mile Road, between Taft and Novi Roads

Showtime: 3 p.m., selected Sundays
Tickets: $2-$5
Ages: All ages
Parking: Free on site

Leading local musicians, magicians, and children's theater troupes entertain the entire family.

Family Shows

Oak Park Family
Entertainment Series
14300 Oak Park Boulevard, Oak Park
313-545-6400

Location: Community Center, Oak Park Boulevard, just west of Coolidge
Showtime: 2 p.m., selected Sundays throughout the year
Tickets: $1.50
Ages: 12 and under
Parking: Free on site

The Oak Park Department of Recreation has put together a series of Sunday concerts with well-known local musicians, puppeteers, and magicians, perfect for a family afternoon.

Music, Dance

Orchestra Hall
3711 Woodward Avenue, Detroit
313-833-3700

Location: Between Warren and Mack, one mile south of the DIA
Showtime: 8 p.m.
Tickets: $8-$16
Ages: All ages
Parking: $3, lots on Parsons and on Woodward

Historic Orchestra Hall is once again the proud home of the Detroit Symphony Orchestra. In addition, it sponsors three cultural series a season. The "Guest Performers Series," a lineup of ethnic dance and music, would be of interest to children.

Music, Special Events

The Palace
One Championship Drive, Auburn Hills
313-377-8600,
313-377-0100 (group sales)

Nationally known rock groups and entertainers, plus dazzling special events, take center stage at the Palace. During selected rock concerts, parents without tickets may stay and relax in the "Quiet Room," a banquet room equipped with refreshments. For easiest access to the room, parents should park in the lot north of the auditorium, entrance 3 off Lapeer Road, then bring the kids through the East Foyer, the place to meet them after the concert. The Palace Gardens, an outdoor amphitheater with both a covered pavillion and outdoor lawn seating, is scheduled to open May 1991. It will offer a variety of family and adult entertainment from May through September.

Lunch Theater

Peanut Butter Players
Players Club
3321 Jefferson Avenue East, Detroit
313-559-6PBP

Location: 2½ miles east of the Renaissance Center
Showtime: Lunch at noon, show at 1 p.m., Saturday and Sunday, September-May
Tickets: $6 includes lunch. Group admissions and birthday packages available.

Ages: Preschool and up

Parking: Free, behind the club

This talented troupe of children, ages 9 to 17, first act as servers, bringing the audience their hot dog, apple, and donut lunch. Then they change into costumes and engergetically burst forth with song and dance. The Peanut Butter Players offer two musical productions during the school year, plus a holiday musical revue during December, which is presented free of charge in the New Center One atrium on West Grand Boulevard.

Theater

The Performance Network
408 West Washington, Ann Arbor
313-663-0681

Location: 2½ blocks west of Main Street

Showtime: Shows are scheduled 48 weekends a year. Times vary; children's matinees are usually Sunday afternoon.

Tickets: Prices vary with each show but are generally moderate

Ages: Preschool-adult, depending on show

Parking: Free on site

The Performance Network is a 150-seat "black box" theater, nestled in among artists' studios in a converted factory building. It hosts a variety of performances by area talent, including dance, puppet shows, and experimental theater.

Music

Pine Knob Music Theatre
Clarkston
313-645-6666 (Ticketmaster)
313-625-0511 (group sales)

Location: Sashabaw Road, off I-75

Showtime: Evenings, late May-early September

Tickets: Both pavillion and lawn tickets are available

Ages: Concerts are geared to an adult audience but many may interest older children

Parking: $5 on site

Pine Knob offers outdoor music and entertainment throughout the summer. Relax on the lawn with a picnic or sit in the pavillion.

Fun & Games

Plaster Playhouse
6629 Orchard Lake Road, West Bloomfield
313-851-8650

Location: Maple at Orchard Lake, next to Farmer Jack

Showtime: Noon-6 p.m., weekdays. 11 a.m.-6 p.m., weekends.

Tickets: $1 for the paint. $3 and up for the plaster molds. Group rates and birthday party packages available.

Ages: Preschool-adult

Parking: Free on site

At the Plaster Playhouse, kids of all ages can choose a modern plaster mold and in less than an hour, turn it into a colorful work of art. The atmosphere is informal, and the adult supervision encouraging.

Music, Special Events

Pontiac Silverdome
1200 Featherstone, Pontiac
313-456-1600

A variety of concerts and special events play throughout the year.

Theater, Dance

Power Center
121 Fletcher, Ann Arbor
313-763-333

Ann Arbor's modern facility hosts concerts, dance, theater, and music series. The kids will love the reflecting glass windows.

Family Shows

Puppets in the Park
Bloomer Park
7581 Richardson Road, West Bloomfield
313-334-5660

Location: Richardson Road, ½ mile east of Haggerty Road

Showtime: 1-2 p.m., one weekday in July and August

Tickets: Free

Ages: Preschool and early elementary

Parking: Free on site

Enjoy a balmy summer day, watch a puppet show, and eat a picnic lunch.

Theater

Quirk Theatre
124 Quirk, Ypsilanti
313-487-1221

Location: On the Eastern Michigan University campus

Showtime: Evenings and matinees

Tickets: $3.50-$6

Ages: While most shows are geared for an adult audience, there are several children's shows offered throughout the year.

Parking: On site

The EMU Players perform a holiday play in December and several adaptations of children's classics throughout the year.

Special Event

Ringling Bros.
and Barnum & Bailey Circus

The beginning of October is the time the "Greatest Show On Earth" comes to the Joe Louis Arena.

Special Event

Royal Hanneford Circus

This circus comes to The Palace in March with lots of animal acts plus death-defying stunts, clowns, and glitter.

Special Event

Sesame Street Live!

The Sesame Street gang takes the stage at Cobo Arena for a wild and noisy show, held for almost two weeks during the end of January.

Music

Shaine Park Concerts
Shaine Park
Martin and Henrietta, Birmingham
313-644-1807 (Public Services)

Location: Two blocks west of Woodward, one block south of Maple

Showtime: 7:30 p.m., every Thursday, June-August

Tickets: Free

Ages: All ages

Parking: Use metered lots and street parking

Pull up a patch of earth and settle in for a lively outdoor concert in the middle of downtown Birmingham. Kids can play on the climbers and swings in the park while you listen to the music.

Special Event

Shrine Circus
The State Fairgrounds Coliseum hosts the colorful and noisy annual Shrine Circus in March.

Family Shows

Smith Theatre
Oakland Community College
27055 Orchard Lake Road, Farmington Hills
313-471-7700

Location: Campus entrance on Orchard Lake Road, just south of I-696

Showtime: 7:30 p.m., Fridays and Saturdays during the school year

Tickets: Approximately $3

Ages: Preschool and up

Parking: Free on site

Smith Theatre offers a "Kids Series" of local puppetry, mime, dance, music, and theater troupes.

Family Shows

Stagecrafters Youth Theatre
Baldwin Theatre
415 South Lafayette, Royal Oak
313-541-6430

Location: Between Ten and Eleven Mile Roads

Showtime: 1, 4, and 7 p.m., weekdays during December

Tickets: $3

Ages: Preschool and up

Parking: Free on site

Young children will enjoy watching their favorite fairy tales and children's musicals performed by drama students ages 8 to 17, during the Youth Theatre's winter and summer productions. The Stagecrafters also offer an adult season of drama and musicals, September-April. Older children would enjoy many of these productions.

Family Shows, Special Events

State Fairgrounds
1120 West State Fair Avenue, Detroit
313-368-1000

The State Fairgrounds hosts children's theater performances and dog and horse shows throughout the year, the Shrine Circus in March, and the annual Michigan State Fair at the end of August.

Family Shows

Troy Parks and Recreation Family Playhouse
Troy Community Center
520 West Big Beaver, Troy
313-524-3484

Location: Between Livernois and Crooks on Big Beaver

Showtime: 2 p.m., Saturday

Tickets: $2.50

Ages: Preschool-12

Parking: Free on site

Throughout the year, Troy Parks and Recreation brings to the stage a series of clowns, mime, musicians, and magicians to entertain area families.

Music

West Bloomfield
Parks and Recreation
Concerts
Marshbank Park
Hiller Road, West Bloomfield
313-334-5660

Location: Hiller Road, north of Commerce Road

Showtime: 7:30 p.m., Sunday, June-August

Tickets: Free. $2 vehicle entry fee.

Ages: For the entire family

Parking: Free on site

Bring blankets, lawn chairs, and picnic hampers and enjoy outdoor concerts with the entire family.

Music

Windsor Symphony Orchestra
201 Riverside Drive
Windsor, Ontario, Canada
519-973-1238

Location: Cleary Auditorium, Riverside Drive West and Ferry Street, one block west of Ouellette Avenue

Showtime: 3 p.m., Saturday or Sunday. A three-concert family series is offered.

Tickets: $8 adults, $5 students

Ages: 2 and up

Parking: Metered street parking, lots across the street near the river and in back of the auditorium

The emphasis is on fun as classical music is brought to life with art, mime, and humorous conducting.

Young People's Theater
1035 South Main Street, Ann Arbor
313-996-3888 (ticket information tape)

Location: Downtown Ann Arbor in the Ann Arbor Civic Theatre Building

Showtime: Four or five family shows a year, evening and weekend matinee performances. YPT also offers year-round acting classes.

Tickets: $5 adults, $3 children

Ages: Shows are geared to an audience of all ages. Children 5 and up perform and act as stagehands.

Parking: Free, behind building

Young People's Theater offers talented children a chance to perform in a variety of shows, from folk and fairy tales to modern musicals. Performances are energetic and creative and perfect for the entire family.

11
CHEERING FOR
THE HOME TEAM

Ask any preteen or teenage boy in the Detroit area where he'd like to go for a family outing, and it's fairly certain he'll mention a sporting event. Tigers in the summer; Lions, Spartans and Wolverines in the fall; Red Wings and Pistons in the winter. Detroit's sports fans are loyal and tenacious, and they train their children early.

To avoid disappointing your children, send away for tickets early, or ask your friends with season tickets if they'll sell you a few. And when you go, be ready to part with a lot of cash. Most children go to sporting events as much for the food as for the game.

Don't forget to check the team schedules for special promotions. Many sponsors offer free gifts to the first several thousand patrons at a certain game. Your children will be thrilled to leave with a free calendar, mug, t-shirt, visor, cap, ball, or notebook.

Pro Arena Football

Detroit Drive
Joe Louis Arena
600 Civic Center, Detroit
313-567-6000 (information)
567-7350 (box office)
567-7474 (group rates)
645-6666 (Ticketmaster
to charge tickets by phone)

Location: Civic Center at the Riverfront, Downtown Detroit

Season: May-August

Tickets: $8-$17

Lunch: Lots of food concessions, including Little Caesar's Pizza. Our family's favorite is the large soft ice cream cone with chocolate and nutty topping for $1.50.

Parking: Use Joe Louis parking lot, adjacent to arena on Atwater Street. $5 fee.

Pro Football

Detroit Lions
Pontiac Silverdome
1200 Featherstone Road, Pontiac
313-335-4151

Location: M-59 and Opdyke Road

Season: September-January

Tickets: $6-$15.50

Lunch: The Main Event, a full service restaurant, plus lots of concessions including Elias Brothers

Parking: Lot on site. $5 fee.

Highlights: Occasional promotions offer free calendars, posters, or growl towels

Detroit Lions Training Camp
Pontiac Silverdome
1200 Featherstone Road, Pontiac
313-335-4131

Location: M-59 and Opdyke Road

Season: 9-11:15 a.m., 3-5 p.m., daily mid-July-mid-August. No morning practice on Sunday.

Tickets: Free

Lunch: Restaurants are located along Walton Blvd.

Highlights: Visitors are allowed to watch the Lions practice. Arrive a half-hour early, and you might be able to catch a few autographs as the players come out to practice.

Detroit Pistons
The Palace
One Championship Drive, Auburn Hills
313-377-0100 (information)
313-377-8201 (group sales)
313-645-6666 (Ticketmaster
to charge tickets by phone)

Location: I-75 and M-24

Season: November-April

Tickets: $5-$19

Lunch: Lots of choices including McDonald's, pizza, and Best kosher hot dogs

Parking: Lot on site. $5 fee.

Highlights: There are special promotions throughout the season when fans 14 and younger receive Pistons t-shirts, basketballs, mugs, wristbands, baseball caps, gym bags, or pennants. We took three boys to one game and came home with three new basketballs. Try to attend one of these games!

Pro Hockey

Detroit Red Wings
Joe Louis Arena
600 Civic Center Drive, Detroit
313-567-6000 (information)
313-567-7350 (box office)
313-567-7474 (group rates)
313-645-6666 (Ticketmaster
to charge tickets by phone)

Location: Civic Center at the Riverfront, downtown Deroit

Season: October-March

Tickets: $8-$16

Lunch: Lots of concessions, including Little Caesar's Pizza

Parking: Use Joe Louis parking lot, adjacent to arena on Atwater Street. $5 fee.

Highlights: There are several special games when fans are given calendars or pucks

---

Pro Baseball

Detroit Tigers
Tiger Stadium, Detroit
313-962-4000 (information)
313-963-7300 (charge by phone)
313-963-9944 (hotline)

Location: Michigan and Trumbull

Season: April-October

Tickets: $4-$10.50. To mail-order tickets, send money order or check with self-addressed envelope, plus specific information regarding number of tickets, game, etc., to: Ticket Dept., P.O. Box 77322, Detroit, MI 48277.

Lunch: Lots of food choices, including Domino's Pizza

Parking: Use lots surrounding stadium. $4-$8 fee.

Highlights: The Tigers also have a schedule of special games when gifts of t-shirts, mugs, tote bags, notebooks, and baseball cards are given out.

Pro Indoor Lacrosse

Detroit Turbos
Joe Louis Arena
600 Civic Center Drive, Detroit
313-567-6000 (information)
313-567-7350 (box office)
313-567-7474 (group rates)
313-645-6666 (Ticketmaster
to charge tickets by phone)

Location: Civic Center at the Riverfront, downtown Detroit

Season: January-February

Tickets: $10-$15

Lunch: Many concessions including Little Caesar's Pizza

Parking: Use Joe Louis parking lot, adjacent to arena on Atwater Street. $5 fee.

Auto Racing

Flat Rock Speedway
14041 South Telegraph Road, Flat Rock
313-782-2480, 313-847-6726

Location: One mile south of Flat Rock on Telegraph Road

Season: 7-10 p.m., Saturday. 1:30-5:30 p.m., Sunday. May-September 18.

Tickets: $7 adults, $2 children 6 to 12, under 6 free

Lunch: Concessions
Parking: Free on site

Basketball

Harlem Globetrotters
Both the Joe Louis Arena and The Palace host the hilarious hoopsters in their annual Motown visit. Dates vary each season.

Harness Racing

Hazel Park Raceway
1650 East Ten Mile Road, Hazel Park
313-398-1000

Location: Ten Mile and Dequindre Roads
Season: 7:30 p.m., Monday-Saturday, early April–mid-October
Tickets: $3.50 clubhouse, $2.50 grandstand. Must be at least 12 years old to enter grandstand.
Lunch: Two clubhouse restaurants, grandstand concessions
Parking: Use lots surrounding raceway. $1.50 and up fees.

Thoroughbred Racing

Ladbroke Detroit Race Course
28001 Schoolcraft Road, Livonia
313-525-7300, 313-525-7312

Location: Schoolcraft and Middlebelt Roads
Season: 2:30 p.m., Wednesday-Friday. 1 p.m. Sunday. 6 p.m., Sunday. Late March-Late November
Tickets: $4 clubhouse, $2.50 grandstand. Family discounts on Saturday.
Lunch: Clubhouse restaurants, grandstand concessions

Parking: On site. There is a fee.

Rodeo

Longhorn World Championship Rodeo
Saddle up the gang and bring them to The Palace for the annual rodeo every February.

Auto Racing

Michigan International Speedway
12626 US-12, Brooklyn
313-592-6671, 313-961-1922

Location: M-50 and US-12

Season: Special event races are held on weekends, June-August

Tickets: $20-$65 depending on event. Discounts for children 12 and under.

Lunch: Elias Brothers Big Boy concession.

Parking: Free on site

College Sports

Michigan State University
Spartans — Go Spartans!
220 Jenison Field House, East Landing
517-355-1610

Location: MSU Campus: Football — Spartan Stadium. Basketball — Jack Breslin Student Events Center. Hockey — Munn Arena.

Season: Football—September-November. Basketball—November-March. Hockey—October-March.

Tickets: Football $16, basketball $7, hockey $6 and $5

Lunch: Concessions

Parking: Most lots around the Football Stadium and Jennison Field House charge $3

Harness Racing

Northville Downs
301 South Center, Northville
313-349-1000

Location: Seven Mile and Seldon Roads

Season: 7:30 p.m., Monday-Saturday, October-December. 1 p.m., Saturday, Thanksgiving-December 31. 7:30 p.m., Wednesday-Monday; 1 p.m., Saturday, January-April.

Tickets: $3.50 clubhouse, $2.50 grandstand. Children must be 12 years or older.

Lunch: Clubhouse restaurant, grandstand concessions

Parking: Use lots surrounding site. $1.50 and up fees.

College Sports

University of Detroit Titans
4001 West McNichols Road, Detroit
313-927-1700

Location: Livernois and McNichols (Six Mile Road), Calihan Hall

Season: December-March

Tickets: $6 and $4

Lunch: Concessions

Parking: Use adjacent lot. $3 fee.

College Sports

University of Michigan
Wolverines — Go Blue!
1000 South State Street, Ann Arbor
313-764-0247

Location: UofM Campus: Football—UofM Stadium. Basketball—Crisler Arena. Hockey—Yost Field House.

Season: Football—September-November, Basketball—November-March. Hockey—October-March.

Tickets: Football $18, basketball $10, hockey $6 (reserved) and $4 (general admission)

Lunch: Concessions

Parking: Use lots surrounding sites or park on campus and walk

---

College Sports

Wayne State University Tartars
Detroit
313-577-4280

Location: Lodge Expressway (M-10) and Warren: Football—WSU Stadium. Basketball — Matthaei Building

Season: Football—September-November. Basketball—November-March.

Tickets: Tickets are available at box office on day of game. Football: $5 adults, $3 students, $1 children 12 and under. Basketball: $3 adults, $2 students, $1 children 12 and under.

Lunch: Concessions

Parking: Use street along Lodge Service Drive or adjacent to sports facilities

---

Harness Racing

Windsor Raceway
Windsor, Ontario, Canada
313-961-9545 or 519-969-8311

Location: Highway 18 and Sprucewood, about three miles from the Ambassador Bridge

Season: 7:30-10:30 p.m., Tuesday, Thursday, Friday, and Saturday. 1 p.m., Saturday. 7 p.m., Sunday. October-July.

Tickets: $2.50 adults, children under 13 free

Lunch: Concessions and restaurant

Parking: Lot on site, $1.25 U.S. fee.

Wrestling

World Wrestling Federation
The Palace, 3777 Lapeer Road, Auburn Hills
313-377-0100 (information)
313-377-8201 (group sales)
313-645-6666 (Ticketmaster)

Location: I-75 and M-24

Season: Hulk Hogan and his gang of comic wrestlers invade The Palace once a month

Tickets: $9-$16

Lunch: Lots of choices, including McDonald's, pizza, and Best kosher hot dogs

Parking: Lot on site. $5 fee.

12
BURNING
OFF ENERGY
A Sampling of
Participant Sports

If your kids are like mine, they are always full of energy and raring to play. Here's a sampling of sites where they can burn off one or two hours of energy, without signing up for costly lessons. There are places for Little Leaguers' batting and fielding practice, a friendly fishing hole where kids are assured of a catch, area municipal pools, and ice-skating rinks. You have your pick of places that rent canoes and offer bumper bowling, sledding, horseback riding, go-karts, and miniature golf.

To help your selection, sports are listed alphabetically. I have intentionally omitted specific hours and prices because they fluctuate so rapidly. Please call for directions, hours, and fees.

Archery

It's ok for Jason to play William Tell, just don't fall for the apple-on-the-head trick. You can rent equipment and play for one hour during open shooting.

Starlight Archery Co.
3001 Rochester Road, Royal Oak
313-585-1818

Starlight Archery Co.
21570 Groesbeck, Warren
313-771-1580

Batting Cages

Here's your chance to be MVP (Most Valuable Parent) and indulge your child in a Tiger fantasy. Most area batting cages are open April to October and offer slow-pitch and fast-pitch in both softball and hardball. The sites provide bats and batting helmets; bring mitts if there are fielding cages.

C.J. Barrymore's Sports Center
21750 Hall Road, Mount Clemens
313-469-2800

Features: Batting cages, softball diamonds, go-carts, kiddie karts, miniature golf, video arcade, driving range, pro shop, family restaurant, indoor/outdoor concessions

---

Four Bears Water Park
3000 Auburn Road, Utica
313-739-5863

Features: Batting cages, miniature golf, water slides, bumper boats, go-carts, sea lion show, restaurant. *For full information, see* Parks.

Grand Slam Baseball
Training Center
3530 Coolidge Highway, Royal Oak
313-549-7100, 313-353-8067

Features: Batting cages, fielding cages, pro shop, snack bar

Home Plate Sports Center
32909 Harper, St. Clair Shores
313-296-5655

Features: Batting cages

Marino Sports Center, Inc.
38951 Jefferson, Mount Clemens
313-465-6177

Features: Batting cages, miniature golf, driving range, pro shop

Oasis Golf/Tru Pitch Batting Cages
39500 Five Mile Road, Plymouth
313-420-4653

Features: Batting cages, miniature golf

Red Oaks Golf Dome and Sports Village
29601 John R, Madison Heights
313-548-1857

Features: Batting cages, go-carts, miniature golf, indoor and outdoor driving range, playscape and snack bar

Sport-Way
38520 Ford Road, Westland
313-728-7222

Features: Batting cages, go-carts, miniature golf

Van Dyke Sport Center
32501 Van Dyke, Warren
313-979-2626

Features: Batting cages, go-carts, miniature golf, indoor/outdoor driving range, video arcade, restaurant, concessions, pro shop

Bicycling

Rent bicycles-built-for-two or single seaters and take a spin with the kids, April-October

---

Gallup Park Livery
3000 Fuller Road, Ann Arbor
313-662-9319

Stony Creek Metropark
4300 Main Park Road, Washington
313-781-4242

For full information, see Parks

Boating

Take your children out to sea every summer on a wild boat ride. Paddle under bridges, talk to the fish, spin some yarns, have a picnic. Surrounded by lakes and rivers, Metro Detroit offers a variety of boat rentals.

Addison Oaks
1480 West Romeo Road, Oxford
313-693-2432

Features: Rowboat and paddleboat rental on Buhl Lake and Adams Lake. *For full information, see* Parks.

Belle Isle Canoe Livery
Belle Isle, Detroit
313-267-7115

Features: Canoe and paddleboat rental on the Detroit River. *For full information, see* Parks.

Delhi Metropark
8801 North Territorial Road, Dexter
313-426-8211

Features: Canoe rental on Huron River. *For full information, see* Parks.

Dodge Park No. 4
4250 Parkway, Pontiac
313-682-0800

Features: Rowboat, paddleboat, and canoe rental on Cass Lake. *For full information, see* Parks.

Great Lakes Yachts
24400 East Jefferson, St. Clair Shores
313-778-7030

Features: Yacht rental on Lake St. Clair

Groveland Oaks
5990 Grange Hall Road, Holly
313-634-9811

Features: Paddleboat, canoe, rowboat, and one-person "waterbug" rental on Stewart Lake. *For full information, see* Parks.

Heavner's Canoe and Cross Country Ski Rentals
2775 Garden Road, Milford
313-685-2379

Features: Canoe rental on the Huron River

Independence Oaks
9501 Sashabaw Road, Clarkston
313-625-0877

Features: Rowboat, paddleboat, waterbug, canoe rental on Crooked Lake. *For full information, see* Parks.

Kensington Metropark
2240 West Buno Road, Milford
313-685-1561

Features: Canoe, paddleboat, and rowboat rental on Kent Lake. *For full information, see* Parks.

Orchard Lake Boats and Windsurfing
3840 Orchard Lake Road, Orchard Lake
313-682-1990

Features: Rowboat, windsurfer rental on Orchard Lake

Pine Lake Marina
3714 Elizabeth Lake Road, Waterford
313-682-2180

Features: Pontoon boat, motorboat, and rowboat rental on Pine Lake

Stony Creek Metropark
4300 Main Road, Washington
313-781-4242

Features: Paddleboat, sailboat, rowboat, and canoe rental on Stony Creek Lake. *For full information, see* Parks.

Sun and Ski Marina
3981 Cass Elizabeth Road, Pontiac
313-681-7100

Features: Pontoon boat rental on Cass Lake

Bumper Bowling

For preschoolers, bumper bowling is the greatest invention since Sesame Street. Children are protected against bowling gutter balls by plastic tubing that sits in the gutters. Throw the ball any which way, and it's bound to bounce off the bumper, careen down the lane and knock off a few pins. Here is a sampling of area lanes offering bumper bowling on a regular basis. For more information, call the Bowling Proprietors Association of Greater Detroit, 559-5207.

Astro Lanes
32388 John R, Madison Heights
313-585-3131

Belmar II
3351 West Road, Trenton
313-675-8319

Bowl One
1639 East Fourteen Mile, Troy
313-588-4850

Cherry Hill Lanes
300 North Inkster Road
Dearborn Heights
313-278-0400

Liberty Bowl
17580 Frazho, Fraser
313-778-6390

Recreation Bowl
40 Crocker Boulevard, Mount Clemens
313-468-7746

Regal Lanes
27663 Mound Road, Warren
313-751-4770

Universal Lanes
2101 East Twelve Mile, Warren
313-751-2828

West Bloomfield Lanes
6800 Orchard Lake Road, West Bloomfield
313-855-9555

Cross-Country Skiing

It's possible to cross-country ski almost everywhere in metro Detroit, from city, county, state, and national parks, to golf courses, ski resorts, and nature preserves. Many area ski shops and resorts rent equipment on a daily basis. Here is a sampling of sites that rent equipment and offer scenic trails.

Addison Oaks
1480 West Romeo Road, Oxford
313-693-0220

For full information, see Parks

Glen Oaks
30500 Thirteen Mile Road
Farmington Hills
313-851-8356

For full information, see Parks

Heavner's Canoe and
Cross Country Ski Rentals
2775 Garden Road, Milford
313-685-2379

Independence Oaks
9501 Sashabaw Road, Clarkston
313-625-0877

For full information, see Parks

Kensington Metropark
2240 West Buno Road, Milford
313-685-1561

For full information, see Parks

Lake Erie Metropark
32481 West Jefferson, Rockwood
313-379-5020

For full information, see Parks

Metro Beach Metropark
Metropolian Parkway, Mount Clemens
313-463-4581

For full information, see Parks

Plymouth Orchards and Cider Mill
10685 Warren Road, Plymouth
313-455-2290

For full information, see Seasonal Harvest

White Lake Oaks
991 South Williams Lake Road, Pontiac
313-698-2700

For full information, see Parks

Downhill Skiing

Five area ski resorts offer southeastern Michiganians an easy escape to the slopes. Generally open from November to March, they offer rental, instruction, ski shop, and restaurant.

Alpine Valley
6775 East Highland, Milford
313-887-4183

Mt. Brighton Ski Area
4141 Bauer Road, Brighton
313-229-9581

Mt. Holly, Inc.
13536 South Dixie Highway, Holly
313-634-8260
582-7256 (snowline)

Pine Knob Ski Resort
Sashabaw Road and I-75, Clarkston
313-625-0800

Riverview Highlands Ski Area
15015 Sibley Road, Riverview
313-479-2080

Fishing

Sure you can rent a rowboat and take along all your fishing gear. But if you want a hassle-free fishing trip, head over to the Spring Valley Trout Farm in Dexter (*see* Science and Nature), where fishing is fun, quick, and everyone is guaranteed a catch.

Go-Carting

Treat your little daredevils to a fast ride around the go-cart track. Children under 51 inches can ride around only on an adult's lap.

C.J. Barrymore's Sports Center
21750 Hall Road, Mount Clemens
313-469-2800

Features: Batting cages, softball diamonds, go-carts, kiddie karts, miniature golf, video arcade, driving range, pro shop, family restaurant, indoor/outdoor concessions

---

Four Bears Water Park
3000 Auburn Road, Utica
313-739-5863

Features: Batting cages, miniature golf, water slides, bumper boats, go-carts, sea lion show, restaurant. *For full information, see* Parks.

Red Oaks Golf Dome and Sports Village
29601 John R, Madison Heights
313-548-1857

Features: Batting cages, go-carts, miniature golf, indoor and outdoor driving range, playscape and snack bar.

Sport-Way
38520 Ford Road, Westland
313-728-7222

Features: Batting cages, go-carts, miniature golf

Van Dyke Sport Center
32501 Van Dyke, Warren
313-979-2626

Features: Batting cages, go-carts, miniature golf, indoor/outdoor driving range, video arcade, restaurant, concessions, pro shop

Hiking

The area's many arboretums, parks, and nature centers offer a variety of self-guided hiking trails. *See* Science and Nature *and* Parks.

Horseback Riding

Get along little doggies, time for some horsing around. Here is a sampling of area ranches that offer riding by the hour. Many are open year-round, weather permitting.

Bald Mountain Riding Stables
3085 South Lapeer Road, Pontiac
313-391-1553

For full information, see Parks

Hell Creek Ranch
10866 Cedar Lake Road, Pinckney
313-878-9658

Highland Recreation Area
5200 East Highland Road, Milford
313-887-5135

For full information, see Parks

Lucy's Livery
6386 Shea Road, Marine City
313-765-9910

Maybury State Park
20145 Beck Road, Northville
313-349-8390

For full information, see Parks

Pontiac Lake Recreation Area
7800 Gale Road, Pontiac
313-666-1020

For full information, see Parks

Silver Saddle Riding Stable
2991 Oakwood, Ortonville
313-627-2826

For full information, see People Movers

Willowbrook Farms
47430 Ten Mile Road, Novi
313-349-3220

Ice-Skating

Celebrate winter all year round by taking a twirl on the area's many indoor rinks during family open skating. Or enjoy the real thing— bundle up and skate out in the open, with snowflakes falling all around you. Here is a sampling of the area's indoor and outdoor rinks. Skate rental is noted.

Adams Ice-Skating Area
10500 Lyndon, Detroit
313-935-4510

Features: Indoor rink, skate rental

Addison Oaks
1480 West Romeo Road, Oxford
313-693-2432

Features: Outdoor rink. *For full information, see* Parks

Adray Ice Arena
14900 Ford Road, Dearborn
313-582-7470

Features: Indoor rink

Bald Mountain Recreation Area
1330 Greenshield, Lake Orion
313-693-6767

Features: Outdoor rink. *For full information, see* Parks

Berkley Ice Arena
2300 Robina, Berkley
313-546-2460

Features: Indoor rink, skate rental

Birmingham Ice Sports Arena
2300 East Lincoln, Birmingham
313-645-0730
313-645-0731

Features: Indoor rink

Clark Park
1400 Scotten, Detroit
313-297-9330

Features: Outdoor rink, skate rental

Compuware-Oak Park Arena
13950 Oak Park Boulevard, Oak Park
313-543-2338
313-543-2339

Features: Indoor rink, skate rental

Devon-Aire Arena
9510 Sunset, Livonia
313-425-9790

Features: Indoor rink

Eddie Edgar Arena
33841 Lyndon, Livonia
313-427-1280

Features: Indoor rink

Ella Mae Power Park
45175 West Ten Mile Road, Novi
313-347-0400

Features: Outdoor rink

Garden City Ice Arena
200 Long Cabin Drive, Garden City
313-261-3490
Features: Indoor rink

Hart Plaza
Jefferson at Woodward, Detroit
313-224-1185

Features: Outdoor rink, skate rental

Highland Recreation Area
M-59 east of US-23, Milford
313-887-5136

Features: Outdoor rink. *For full information, see* Parks

Holly State Park
8100 Grange Hall Road, Holly
313-634-8811

Features: Outdoor rink

Independence Oaks
9501 Sashabaw Road, Clarkston
313-625-0877

Features: Outdoor rink. *For full information, see* Parks

Inkster Civic Arena
20277 South River Park, Inkster
313-277-1001

Features: Indoor rink, skate rental

John Lindell Ice Arena
1403 Lexington, Royal Oak
313-544-6690

Features: Indoor rink

Kennedy Ice Rink
3131 West Road, Trenton
313-675-7300

Features: Outdoor rink

Kensington Metropark
2240 West Buno Road, Milford
313-685-1561

Features: Outdoor rink. *For full information, see* Parks

Lakeland Ice Arena
7730 Highland (M-59), Pontiac
313-666-1911

Features: Indoor rink, skate rental

Lincoln Park Community Center
3525 Dix, Lincoln Park
313-386-0137

Features: Indoor rink, skate rental

Lower Huron Metropark
17845 Savage Road, Belleville
313-697-9181

Features: 3 outdoor rinks. *For full information, see* Parks

Melvindale Ice Arena
4300 South Dearborn, Melvindale
313-928-1200

Features: Indoor rink

Metro Beach Metropark
Metro Parkway at Jefferson
Mount Clemens
313-463-4581

Features: 2 outdoor rinks. *For full information, see* Parks

Palmer Park
Third Avenue and Merrill Plaisance, Detroit
313-935-4350

Features: Outdoor rink

St. Clair Shores Civic Arena
20000 Stephens, St. Clair Shores
313-445-5350

Features: Indoor rinks

Southfield Sports Arena
26000 Evergreen Road, Southfield
313-354-9357

Features: Indoor rink, skate rental

Veterans Ice Arena
2150 Jackson Road, Ann Arbor
313-761-7240

Features: Indoor rink, skate rental

Westland Multi-Purpose Arena
6210 North Wildwood, Westland
313-729-4560

Features: Indoor rink, skate rental

Yack Arena
3131 Second, Wyandotte
313-246-4515

Features: Indoor rink

Yost Ice Arena
State and Hoover, Ann Arbor
313-763-0064

Features: Indoor rink

Miniature Golfing

Test your putting skills against green hills, blue lagoons, colorful windmills, or wishing wells. Time to show the kids the difference between a bogey and a boogie. Here is a sampling of area miniature golf sites. Most are open seasonally during the summer and early fall. At Recreation Bowl you won't have to worry about the weather; the summer-only golf course is indoors.

Captain's Cove Adventure Golf
3409 Edgar Street, Royal Oak
313-549-7676

C.J. Barrymore's Sports Center
21750 Hall Road, Mount Clemens
313-469-2800

Four Bears Water Park
3000 Auburn Road, Utica
313-739-5863

For full information, see Parks

Marino Sports Center, Inc.
38951 Jefferson, Mount Clemens
313-465-6177

Metro Beach Putt-Putt
Metro Parkway at Jefferson, Mount Clemens
313-963-3022

For full information, see Parks

Oasis Golf/Tru-Pitch
Batting Cages
39500 Five Mile Road, Plymouth
313-420-4653

Putt-Putt Golf and Games
30749 Grand River, Farmington Hills
313-471-4700

Recreation Bowl
40 Crocker Boulevard, Mount Clemens
313-468-7746

Red Oaks Golf Dome and Sports Village
29601 John R, Madison Heights
313-548-1857

Royal Oak Putt Putt
1025 North Campbell Road
Royal Oak
313-1893

Sport-Way
38520 Ford Road, Westland
313-728-7222

Ted's Southgate Golf Center
11125 Reeck Road, Southgate
313-374-2211

Van Dyke Sport Center
32501 Van Dyke, Warren
313-979-2626

Roller-Skating

The music's on, the lights are blinking. Put the kids into continuous motion at the roller rink. Here is a sampling.

Ambassador Roller Rink
96 West Fourteen Mile, Clawson
313-435-6525

Bonaventure Roller Skating Center
24505 Halstead Road
Farmington Hills
313-476-2201

Skateworld of Troy
2825 East Maple Road, Troy
313-689-4100

Skateworld of Woodhaven
23911 Allen Road, Woodhaven
313-671-0220

Skateboarding

Bring your skateboard and required safety equipment—helmet, knee pads, elbow pads, and shoes. Try your skill on the area's newest skateboarding ramps. All participants (parental signatures required for minors) must register and sign a waiver form before using the skateboard ramps.

Sports Afield 2
216 Patilla Road, Hwy. 2
Tecumseh, Ontario, Canada
519-727-3967, 519-727-6604

A large, year-round, indoor complex with a variety of half-pipe, mini, wall-ride, fly and rail-slide ramps, just 10 miles outside of Windsor.

Veterans Park
2150 Jackson Road, Ann Arbor
313-761-7240

A large outdoor ramp open April-October.

Sledding

Many city and country parks, nature preserves, arboretum and golf courses offer toboggan runs and sledding sites. (*For full information, see* Parks *and* Science and Nature). Here is a sampling.

Addison Oaks
1480 West Romeo Road, Oxford
313-693-2432

Bald Mountain Recreation Area
1330 Greenshield, Lake Orion
313-693-6767

Bloomer State Park
John R at Bloomer Road, Rochester
313-739-1600

Highland Recreation Area
M-59 east of US-23, Milford
313-887-5135

Holly State Park
8100 Grange Hall Road, Holly
313-634-8811

Kensington Metropark
2240 West Buno Road, Milford
313-685-1561

**Middle Rouge Parkway
(Edward Hines Parkway)**
Cass-Benton area between Six and
Seven Mile Roads, Northville
313-224-7733
313-224-7734

Pontiac Lake Recreation Area
7800 Gale Road, Pontiac
313-666-1020

**Southfield Civic Center—
Evergreen Hills**
26000 Evergreen Road, Southfield
313-354-9603

Stony Creek Metropark
4300 Main Park Road, Washington
313-781-4242

Willow Metropark
I-275 at South Huron Road, Flat Rock
313-697-9181

Swimming

Municipal pools, recreation centers, and area YMCAs—for a small fee you can beat the heat in both indoor and outdoor pools. Even with lifeguards on duty, be sure to supervise your kids. (*See* Parks for a listing of water parks). Here is a sampling.

Beech Woods Recreation Center
22200 Beech Road, Southfield
313-354-9510

Features: Outdoor pool. Non-resident must be accompanied by a Southfield resident.

Detroit Recreation Department Pools
313-224-1184

There are 19 locations.

Brewer Recreation Center
4535 Fairview, Detroit
313-267-7152
Features: Indoor pool

Butzel Family Center
7737 Kercheval, Detroit
313-267-7125
Features: Indoor pool

Butzel Recreation Center
10536 Lyndon, Detroit
313-935-3319
Features: Indoor pool

Chandler Park
313-876-7150
Features: Outdoor pool

Heilmann Recreation Center
19601 Crusade, Detroit
313-267-7153
Features: Indoor/Outdoor pool

Johnson Recreation Center
8640 Chippewa, Detroit
313-935-3121
Features: Indoor pool

Kemeny Recreation Center
2260 South Fort, Detroit
313-297-9332
Features: Indoor pool

Kronk Recreation Center
5555 McGraw, Detroit
313-898-6359
Features: Indoor pool

Lipke Recreation Center
19320 Van Dyke, Detroit
313-876-0312
Features: Outdoor pool

Maheras Recreation Center
12550 Avondale, Detroit
313-267-7155
Features: Outdoor pool

Palmer Park
313-876-0428
Features: Outdoor pool

Patton Recreation Center
2301 Woodmere, Detroit
313-297-9337
Features: Indoor/Outdoor pool

Rouge Park
313-935-3761
Features: Outdoor pool

Wheeler Recreation Center
637 Brewster, Detroit
313-833-9777
Features: Indoor pool

Williams Recreation Center
8431 Rosa Parks Boulevard, Detroit
313-898-6584

Young Recreation Center
2751 Robert Bradby Drive, Detroit
313-224-0530

Jewish Community Center Pool
6600 West Maple Road, West Bloomfield
313-661-1000

Features: Indoor/Outdoor pool. Non-member must be accompanied by member and pay a fee.

Mercy Center Pool
28600 Eleven Mile Road, Farmington Hills
313-476-8010

Features: Indoor pool

Metro Beach Metropark Pool
Metro Parkway at Jefferson, Mount Clemens
313-463-4581

Features: Indoor pool. *For full information, see* Parks.

YMCA Pools

Eleven area YMCAs have indoor pools. Non-members pay a fee.

Birmingham
400 East Lincoln, Birmingham
313-644-9036

Downriver
3211 Fort Street, Detroit
313-281-2600

Downtown
2020 Witherell Street, Detroit
313-962-6126

Eastside
10100 Harper, Detroit
313-921-0770

Farmington
28100 Farmington Road, Farmington Hills
313-553-4020

Livonia Family
14255 Stark Road, Livonia
313-261-2161

Northside
13220 Woodward, Detroit
313-868-1946

Northwestern
2175 West Seven Mile Road, Detroit
313-533-3700

South Oakland
1016 West Eleven Mile Road, Royal Oak
313-547-0030

Wayne/Westland
827 South Wayne Road, Westland
313-721-7044

Western
1601 Clark Street, Detroit
313-554-2136

Whirlyball

If you're looking for something different, this new sport is a combination bumper car, basketball, and jai-alai. Kids age ten and up can participate. Prices run approximately $100/hour (ten people share the court and the cost).

Whirlyball of Michigan
19781 Fifteen Mile Road, Mount Clemens
313-792-4190

13
DETROIT AT WORK
Tours

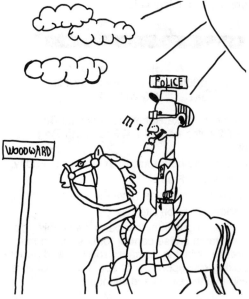

Everyone enjoys peeking behind the scenes. Children especially benefit from seeing people at work and watching made-in-Michigan products being born. Unfortunately, the rising insurance costs of the last few years have forced many companies to discontinue their tours. This chapter lists Michigan companies and cottage industries that still welcome families and groups with a regularly scheduled tour. While most of the tours are within a two-hour drive from Detroit, I have also included tours farther away to help you plan your overnight adventures.

There are also many community sites that will take small groups on a tour, provided you call first and arrange a mutually convenient time. Try police and fire stations, courthouses, hospitals, theaters, fast-food restaurants, grocery stores, butcher shops, radio and TV stations, even your own job site. Many of the museums and historic sites listed in this book offer tours to school and civic groups; several theaters offer school field trips. You are limited only by your imagination.

Industry

AC Spark Plug Tour
1300 North Dort Highway, Flint
313-257-7722

Location: Take Robert T. Longway Boulevard exit 2 miles east of I-475 to North Dort Highway

Hours: One-hour tour. 1 p.m., Monday-Friday.

Admission: Free

Ages: Minimum age 12 years

Parking: Free on site

Walk right into the parts assembly room and watch cruise control "brains" being made, presses clinking, furnaces roaring, and people boxing row upon row of spark plugs. Children will love the sights and sounds.

Farming

Ammon's Orchard Tours
7407 North US-31, Traverse City
616-938-1644

Location: 1½ miles north of Acme on US-31

Hours: Call for tour reservation, May-October

Admission: $10 family, $4 adult, $2 children

Ages: All ages

Parking: Free on site

Freebies: Complimentary hot or cold cherry drink and dessert

Tour the cherry orchard, watch the mechanical harvesting of cherries, and learn why Tra-

verse City is the Cherry Capital of the World.
After the tour, you can purchase a wide selection of specialty cherry foods and freshly
picked fruits in the farm market.

Amway Corporation
7575 East Fulton Road, Ada
616-676-6701

Location: M-21 (Fulton Road), 12 miles east of
downtown Grand Rapids and 11 miles west of
the I-96 Lowell exit

Hours: One-hour tour. 9-11 a.m., 1-3 p.m.,
Monday-Friday. Closed holidays and mid-
June. Two-week advance reservations are required for groups of ten or more. Tours for the
handicapped are available upon advance request.

Admission: Free

Ages: Minimum age 6 years

Parking: Free on site

Freebies: Amway product (shampoo or
mouthwash) for adults, and Amway coloring
book and crayons for children

Tour the extensive Amway World Head-
quarters and learn all about the growth, products, and markets of one of the world's largest
direct-selling companies. The tour includes a
slide presentation, product showcase room,
bus trip of the grounds, and guided tour of
printing department, computer area, and administration building. Kids will enjoy the printing room, bus tour, and slide show.

Arts & Scraps
4719 Cadieux, Detroit
313-881-7840

Location: One mile south of the I-94 Cadieux

exit, in the basement of the First Lutheran Church

Hours: 10 a.m.-2 p.m., Tuesday. 4-7 p.m., Thursday. 10 a.m.-1 p.m., Saturday. Also by appointment.

Admission: Free. Children can stuff a bag full of artistic scraps for a very modest price.

Ages: Preschool and up

Parking: Free in church parking lot

Arts & Scraps offers parents and early elementary teachers a rainy day treasure trove of scraps and odds and ends—everything that children need for creative expression. Kids will enjoy peeking into barrels and looking through boxes, "shopping" for items they can paint, color, glue, and cut into special projects.

Food

Big Boy Warehouse
4199 Marcy, Warren
313-759-6000

Location: Off Ryan Road, south of Ten mile Road

Hours: One-hour tour. 10 a.m. and 12:30 p.m., weekdays except Tuesday.

Admission: Free

Ages: Minimum age 6 years

Parking: Free on site

Freebies: Before the tour, everyone is treated to juice and homemade sweet rolls. After the tour, adults are given a loaf of freshly baked bread and a Big Boy coffee mug; children receive Big Boy banks.

After a slide show and treat, the tour starts in the bakery distribution center where sweet rolls, buns, pie crusts, and breads are sliced, frosted, and packaged. Walk through the cool ice cream room, marvel at the spice bins in the pungent seasonings room, continue through the stocked warehouse, meat and vegetable processing rooms, and end up in the bakery—

a warm, wonderful-smelling room. This is a tour that makes your nose come alive.

Industry

Bissel, Inc.
2345 Walker NW, Grand Rapids
616-453-4451

Location: Take I-96 west past Grand Rapids to exit 28. Turn left on Walker.

Hours: 1½ hour tour, 10 a.m., weekdays. Schedule three weeks ahead

Admission: Free

Ages: Recommended 12 and up

Parking: Free on site

Freebies: After the tour, visitors can go to the adjacent factory outlet store and receive a discount on their purchases

Tour the factory that manufactures home care products. Watch shampoo bottles blown, metal parts pressed, and sweeper motors assembled.

Food

Brooks Beverages Plant
777 Brooks Avenue, Holland
616-396-1281

Location: 32nd Street and US-31

Hours: For small groups, 10 to 30 minute self-guided tour. 8:30 a.m.-5 p.m., Monday-Friday. For groups of 20 or more, call to schedule a guided tour

Admission: Free

Ages: All ages

Parking: Free on site

Freebies: Free sample of pop

Tour a soft-drink bottling factory and watch production of various soft drink brands from the syrup room to the finished product.

Industry

Buick City Tour
902 East Hamilton, Flint
313-236-4494

Location: North side of Flint, Broadway-Stever exit off I-475

Hours: 1½ hour tour, 9:45 a.m. or 12:30 p.m., Tuesday and Thursday. Call to reserve a space.

Admission: Free

Ages: Minimum ages 6 years

Parking: Free on site

Freebies: Children can keep their Mickey Mouse "safety" sunglasses

Watching a car being born is a hometown treat. Kids will be amazed at the hi-los, levers, robots, sparks, noises, and conveyor belts. You will too. This is one tour that shouldn't be missed.

Farming

Calder Brothers Dairy Farm
9334 Finzel Road, Carleton
313-654-2622

Location: South Stoney Creek and Finzel Roads. Carleton is about 70 minutes south of downtown Detroit, off I-75 south.

Hours: 10 a.m.-8 p.m., Monday-Saturday. 11 a.m.-8 p.m., Sunday. Closes at 9 p.m. during the summer. Call ahead to schedule tours.

Admission: $2

Ages: All ages

Parking: Free on site

Freebies: Ice cream cone

Milk a cow by hand, bottle feed a calf, watch a cow being machine milked, and see how milk is stored for transport to the Calder

Bros. processing plant. Kids will also enjoy petting the other animals—peacocks, dogs, burros, and geese.

The Candle Factory
301 Grand View Parkway
Traverse City
616-946-2280, 616-946-2850

Location: South side of Grandview Parkway, one block west of downtown
Hours: Summer: 10 a.m.–10:00 p.m., Monday-Saturday. Noon–6 p.m., Sunday. Fall and Christmas season: 10 a.m.–6 p.m., Monday-Wednesday. 10 a.m.–9 p.m., Thursday-Saturday. Noon–5 p.m., Sunday. January-May: 10 a.m.–6 p.m., Monday-Saturday. Noon–5 p.m., Sunday.
Admission: Free
Ages: All ages
Parking: Free on site

Surround yourself with candles and their heavenly fragrance. Kids will enjoy peeking into the candlemaking area to see how candles are handcarved and hand-dipped. The Candle Factory sells a wide variety of hand-made candles.

Channel 50 WKBD
26905 West Eleven Mile Road
Southfield
313-444-8500

Location: Between Inkster and Telegraph
Hours: 9 a.m.–5 p.m., Monday-Friday. Call several weeks in advance to arrange an appointment
Admission: Free
Ages: All ages

Parking: Free on site

Freebie: Items with Channel 50 logo

Walk through the TV station, peeking into sales and business offices, engineering and news rooms. See the news set and weather board up close, and sit in on a taping if your tour corresponds to show time.

Children's Museum—
Junior Leaders of Detroit
Saturday Adventures
67 East Kirby, Detroit
313-494-1223

Location: Selected cultural institutions in the Detroit area

Hours: 10 a.m.–noon, selected Saturdays throughout the school year

Admission: $20 for four visits

Ages: 11 to 14 years

This Saturday morning adventure series offers children a chance to visit leading cultural institutions, observe first-hand how they operate, and talk to the people who run them.

Chocolate Vault, Ice Cream Parlour
and Candy Shoppe
110 West Chicago, Tecumseh
517-423-7602

Location: Downtown Tecumseh

Hours: 10 a.m.-10 p.m., Monday-Saturday. Noon-10 p.m., Sunday

Admission: Free

Ages: All ages

Parking: Metered lots and street parking

Kids will enjoy watching owner Jim McCann hand dip a variety of centers and other goodies into an 80-pound chocolate melter.

Cook's Farm Dairy
2950 Seymour Lake Road, Ortonville
313-627-3329

Location: Take I-75 north to M-15 north. Go one mile east on Seymour Lake Road

Hours: One-hour tour. Summer: 9 a.m.-10 p.m., Monday-Saturday. 2-9 p.m., Sunday. Winter: 9 a.m.-8 p.m., Monday-Saturday. 2-8 p.m., Sunday. Call to schedule tours for groups of ten or more.

Admission: $2

Ages: All ages

Parking: Free on site

Freebies: Ice cream cone and glass of Cook's chocolate milk

Tours start in the cow barn. After meeting newborn calves, you are taken into the production plant for a dry run of the process that turns cows' milk into ice cream and chocolate milk. The tour ends in the ice cream parlor/farm store.

Davisburg Candle Factory
634 Davisburg Road, Davisburg
313-634-4214

Location: I-75 north to exit 93 (Dixie Highway), downtown Davisburg

Hours: May-December 25: 10 a.m.-4:30 p.m., Monday-Saturday. Noon- 4 p.m., Sunday. January-May: 10 a.m.-4:30 p.m., Tuesday-Saturday. For groups of ten or more, schedule in advance. Also call in advance to be sure the taper line is running.

Admission: Free

Ages: All ages

Parking: Free on street

Watch tapers being dipped into hot wax colors and suspended to dry. This is done courtesy of a wonderful home-made taper line contraption. Kids will enjoy watching it run. You'll love the sweet musky, cinnamon smell of the candles. A candle shop with a variety of candles and accessories is located upstairs.

Police

Detroit Police Horse Stables
100 East Bethune, Detroit
313-876-0061

Location: North of East Grand Boulevard and east of Woodward. There are two other police horse stables. One is located on Belle Isle. The other is in Rouge Park on Joy and Southfield Roads, Detroit. Call 876-0061 to schedule a visit to any of the three.

Hours: One-hour tour, 11 a.m., Monday-Friday. Call to schedule tour several weeks ahead.

Admission: Free

Ages: 5 and up. Group maximum is 20 people

Parking: Free on site

Walk through the stables and meet regal police horses. See where they sleep, eat, and exercise. The stable on Bethune also houses blacksmith and leatherworks shops.

Utilities

Detroit Water Department—
Springwell Water Plant
8300 West Warren, Detroit
313-224-3834

Location: Warren and Wyoming, just east of Ford Road

Hours: One-hour tour, 9 a.m.-2 p.m., Monday-Friday

Admission: Free

Ages: Minimum age 12 years. Group maximum is 20 people; minimum is 5 people.

Parking: Free on site

Watch the pumps and cisterns working as they bring in raw water, purify, and filter it and pump it out to metro Detroit households. The plant is an architectural wonder.

                                    Transportation

Detroit-Windsor Tunnel
100 East Jefferson, Detroit
313-567-4422

Location: Jefferson Avenue and Randolph. Report to entrance on Detroit side.

Hours: By appointment only, April, May, and September

Admission: Free

Ages: Minimum age 9 years

Parking: Free on site

Have a snack, watch a film about the tunnel's history and construction, and then take a tour of tunnel offices. (*See* Historic Sites).

                                          Industry

Dow Visitor's Center
500 East Lyon Road, Midland
517-636-8658

Location: East Lyon Road and Bayliss Street

Hours: 1½ hour tour, 10 a.m. and 2 p.m., Monday-Friday. Call at least two weeks in advance to schedule tour.

Admission: Free

Ages: Minimum age 12 years

Parking: Free on site

Freebies: A roll of Saran Wrap

Tour one of the world's largest and most diversified specialty chemical production facilities. Watch a slide presentation about Dow's earliest beginnings and learn about the many chemical, plastic, and agricultural products manufactured at this site. Then walk through the Saran Wrap plant and see production and shipping first hand.

Ecology

Ecology Center of Ann Arbor
2050 South Industrial, Ann Arbor
313-665-6398

Location: Stadium and South Industrial
Hours: 9:30 a.m.-4:30 p.m., Friday and Saturday. Call for an appointment
Admission: Free
Ages: K-12th grade
Parking: Free on site

Watch recycling equipment in use and learn about ecology and recycling.

Farming

Erie Orchards and Cider Mill
1235 Erie Road, Erie
313-848-4518

Location: Just west of Telegraph Road on Erie Road, south of Monroe
Hours: Call to arrange one-hour tour, Monday-Friday
Admission: $2 per person includes tour, hayride, one pumpkin, glass of cider, and donut
Ages: Preschool and up
Parking: Free on site
Freebies: Children receive coloring books. Adults are given fruit fact sheets and recipes.

Look behind the scenes at an apple orchard, starting with a hayride through the orchard full of 3,500 dwarf trees. Walk into the grading room and cold storage room. Watch how cider and donuts are made, pick apples and pumpkins, and then relax with a complimentary glass of cider and a fresh donut.

Library

Farmington Library Tours
Farmington Hills Branch Library
32737 West Twelve Mile Road
Farmington Hills
313-553-0300

Location: West of Orchard Lake Road

Hours: Call to arrange a tour and program in the Children's Department during library hours. 10 a.m.-9 p.m., Monday-Thursday. 10 a.m.-5 p.m., Friday and Saturday. 1-5 p.m., Sunday.

Admission: Free

Ages: Preschool and up

Parking: Free on site

Hear a story, play on the creative climbers, and explore the children's department resources—computers, puppets, puzzles, hands-on realia collection, and, of course, books.

Utilities

Fermi 2 Power Plant
6400 North Dixie Highway, Newport
586-5228

Location: I-75 exit 21 Newport Road to North Dixie

Hours: 9 a.m.-5 p.m., by reservation. Call 3 to 5 weeks in advance.

Admission: Free

Ages: 5 and up. At least one adult must accompany every 25 children.

Parking: Free on site

Freebies: Free literature on Fermi 2 and nuclear power

Watch a videotape about the future of nuclear power, take a bus tour of the cooling towers, walk through the control room, play energy-related video games, and use a power-generating bicycle.

Art Tours

Forum for Art
Sally Kaplan, Birmingham
313-644-4394

Location: Art tours at area cultural institutions and artists' studios

Hours: Saturday afternoons

Admission: $75 per session for two participants (one adult/one child)

Ages: Preschool-adult

Sally Kaplan, an instructor at Detroit's Center for Creative Studies, takes families behind the scenes into the studios and workshops of area artists, theater troupes, musicians and dancers. Participants are often offered hands-on experiences.

Food

Gerber Products Company
445 State Street, Fremont
616-928-2000

Location: Main Street, Fremont (northeast of Muskegon)

Hours: 9 a.m.-5 p.m., Monday-Friday. Call for specific information and times. Gerber's new format for visitors, including a video and 3-D movie, should be in place by fall 1990.

Admission: Free
Ages: All ages
Parking: Free on site

Visit the home of America's most recognized baby food and watch a step-by-step video describing how baby food is made. Next, don 3-D glasses and settle in for a humorous 3-D look at one day in the life of a baby, from the baby's point of view. Afterwards, shop for some Gerber "souvenirs" to take home.

Food

Guernsey Farm Dairy
21300 Novi Road, Northville
313-349-1466

Location: Between Eight and Nine Mile Roads
Hours: 1-5 p.m., the Sunday before St. Patrick's Day only
Admission: Free
Ages: All ages
Parking: Free on site

Enjoy a tour of the plant, clowns and balloons for the kids, and samples of homemade dairy products. Browse in the general store, and stay for a meal in the restaurant or an ice cream from the ice cream parlor.

Mining

Gypsum Mine Tour
Michigan Natural Storage
1200 Judd SW, Grand Rapids
616-241-1619

Location: Chicago and Burlingame Drives
Hours: 1¼-hour tour, 8 a.m.-5 p.m., Tuesday-Friday, by appointment only
Admission: $1.50 adults, $1.25 junior high students, $1 elementary students and seniors. $25 minimum charge.

Ages: All ages

Parking: Free on site

Freebies: You can keep the rocks you find

Go down into the mine, hear about the history and geology of gypsum mining, and spend some time exploring for rocks. The mine is currently used by local businesses for natural cold storage.

Cultural

Japanese Cultural Center and Tea House
315 South Washington Avenue, Saginaw
517-776-1648

Location: Ezra Rust Drive and South Washington Street, across from the Saginaw Zoo

Hours: One-hour tour, every half hour. Spring and summer: Noon-6 p.m., Tuesday-Sunday. Fall and winter: Noon-4 p.m., Wednesday-Sunday. Call ahead to schedule groups of 15 or more.

Admission: Tour of garden and tea house only: $2 per person, children 12 and under free when accompanied by an adult. Tour of garden and tea house plus informal tea service (green leaf tea and sweets): $3 adults, $1 children. School children tours: $2 per child includes tea service, origami craft, and video.

Ages: All ages

Parking: Use zoo parking lot across the street

Experience the serenity and simple beauty of the Japanese garden and tea house. Children will especially enjoy creating an origami figure and, if they are adventurous, tasting a sweet gelatin candy and green tea.

Toys

Kalamazoo Toy Train Factory
541 Railroad Street, Bangor
616-427-7927

Location: One block north of M-43 in old restored depot. Bangor is approximately 20 miles west of Kalamazoo.

Hours: 30-minute tour, 10 a.m.-4 p.m., Monday-Friday

Admission: Free

Ages: All ages

Parking: Free, across the street from depot

The tour begins with a short video explaining the manufacturing process of gauge-one toy trains. Visitors then walk through the restored depot and watch workers put train parts together by hand. In the gift shop, four different Kalamazoo train sets are arranged on a multi-level track, chugging along to music and sounds. This tour is a must for model train collectors.

Food

Kilwins Candy Kitchens, Inc.
200 Division Road, Petoskey
616-347-4831

Location: Northeast of the downtown shopping district

Hours: 30-minute tour, 10 a.m., Monday-Friday

Admission: Free

Ages: All ages

Parking: Free on site

Freebies: A sample chocolate

This is a heavenly tour for chocoholics. Walk through the candy-making rooms and drool over 500-pound chocolate melters, watch the candy conveyor belts merrily chugging along, and then (yum!) taste a special sample. After your tour, you can buy candy in the gift shop.

Farming

Langerderfer Poultry Farm
11844 Strasburg Road, Erie
313-856-4283

Location: Take Telegraph Road six miles south of Monroe to Woods Road. Go west one mile to Strasburg Road. Go south ¼ mile to farm.

Hours: March-June: 9 a.m.-6 p.m., Monday-Friday. 1 a.m.-5 p.m., Sunday. For a tour, call ahead.

Admission: $1.75

Ages: All ages

Parking: Free on site

Freebies: A snack of hot chocolate and farm fresh hard boiled eggs

What better way to celebrate spring! The Langenderfer Poultry Farm is a working farm full of baby chicks and ducklings. Children can hand feed the animals, learn about the incubation process, and visit a nursery full of baby animals. The farm also offers a "Rent-an-Animal" program. Families can take home baby chicks and ducks for Easter and then return them to the farm through June, provided they keep their receipts.

Animals

Leader Dog for the Blind
1039 South Rochester Road, Rochester
313-651-9011

Location: Adams and Rochester Roads

Hours: Two-hour tour, held one Sunday afternoon each month except June, July. August, and December. Call for exact dates. Tour registration is requested.

Admission: Free
Ages: All ages
Parking: Free on site

This tour offers an in-depth look at the dogs and the training program that creates seeing-eye dogs. Visitors are taken through the kennels, infirmary, training areas, and people dormitories. A 20-minute movie explores the special bond between seeing-eye dogs and their blind owners.

Arts & Crafts

Little Dipper Shoppe
415 North Fifth Street, Ann Arbor
313-994-3912

Location: Kerrytown
Hours: 9:30 a.m.-5:30 p.m., Monday-Friday. 9 a.m.-5 p.m., Saturday.
Admission: $1.04 for one pair of dipped candles
Ages: All ages
Parking: Use metered lot adjacent to Kerrytown

Kids will enjoy choosing their own small tapers and then dipping them in the color of their choice. The store's fragrance is a pleasure for the noses in your family.

Industry

Lorann Oils, Inc.
4518 Aurelius, Lansing
517-882-0215

Location: Jolly and Mt. Hope Roads
Hours: Half-hour tour, 9 a.m.-5 p.m., Monday-Friday. Call to schedule. Tours are arranged according to the group's needs and when the production line is running.
Admission: Free

Ages: School-age through adult

Parking: Free on site

Freebies: Visitors receive a small souvenir

Walk through the plant and watch small, one gram bottles being filled, capped, sealed, labeled, and packed. Lorann Oils, Inc., manufactures and bottles food flavoring and pharmaceuticals.

Arts & Crafts

Mary Maxim, Inc.
2001 Holland Avenue, Port Huron
313-987-2000

Location: Holland and Pine Grove Avenue

Hours: 9:30 a.m.-5:30 p.m., Monday-Saturday. Noon-5 p.m., Sunday. Call at least one week in advance to arrange a tour. A minimum of 12 people are needed for a tour.

Admission: Free

Ages: School-age children through adult

Parking: Free on site

Freebies: Coffee and cookies, a special tour bag with a complimentary needlework gift, and Mary Maxim catalog

Enjoy a snack and watch a demonstration of needlework at this leading manufacturer of needlecraft kits.

Animals

Michigan Humane Society— Genesee County
G-3075 Joyce Street, Flint
313-744-0511

Michigan Humane Society-North
3600 Auburn Road, Auburn Heights
313-852-7420

Michigan Humane Society-West
37255 Marquette, Westland
313-721-7300

Each office will take children through the kennels, infirmary and office, 10 a.m.-5 p.m., Monday-Friday. Call to arrange a convenient tour time for your group.

Animals

Michigan State Veterinary School
Vet-A-Visit Veterinary Clinical Center
Michigan State University, East Lansing
517-353-5420

Location: Bogue and Wilson, near Wharton Center
Hours: 9 a.m.-4 p.m., Saturday, usually held mid-April
Admission: Free
Ages: All ages
Parking: Use Wharton Center lot

Take a peek behind the scenes at MSU's Veterinary School. This is a perfect tour for veterinary-wannabe's and animal lovers.

Animals

Oakland County Care Center
1700 Brown, Auburn Hills
313-858-0863

Location: West of M-24 on Brown Road
Hours: ½-hour tour, 10 a.m.-5 p.m., Tuesday-Friday. Call to schedule a tour.
Admission: Free
Ages: All ages
Parking: Free on site

Tour the kennels and meet the dogs who are waiting for adoption.

Arts & Crafts

O'Neill Pottery
1841 Crooks Road, Rochester
313-375-0180

Location: Between Avon and M-59

Hours: Call two weeks in advance to schedule a tour or hands-on workshop

Admission: Tour free. 1½-hour hands-on workshop: $4 per person to create a ceramic work and have it glazed and fired (work is ready two weeks from date of workshop).

Ages: All ages

Parking: Free on site

Children will enjoy visiting this 125-year-old home, now the studio of working potter Helen O'Neill. Learn about clay work, watch her work on the potter's wheel, and then walk around the two-acre grounds and feed the farm animals living in the 120-year-old barn. Older children or adults may choose the hands-on workshop and create their own ceramic work.

Sports

The Palace
One Championship Drive, Auburn Hills
313-377-8200

Location: Take exit 81, Lapeer Road, off I-75

Hours: 10 a.m., 11 a.m., noon, and 1 p.m., Tuesdays. Call ahead to arrange a tour. Groups of 10 to 40 can be accommodated. Families can be added on to larger groups.

Admission: Tour prices include guided tour, lunch in the Palace Grille, and a souvenir item (we received a photograph of Isiah Thomas). $4.75 children, $7.95 or $9.75 for adults depending on menu selection.

Ages: Preschool and up

Parking: Free on lot

Immerse yourself in Pistons glory, peek behind the scenes into the multimillion dollar Pistons broadcast center and, if it's empty, walk through the Pistons' locker room. If you're lucky, you might even catch a glimpse of a player or coach. Your preteen sons will nominate you best parent of the year.

Food

Pelee Island Winery
455 Highway 18, East Kingsville
Ontario, Canada
519-733-6551, 519-776-6898

Location: Downtown Kingsville. Take Ambassador Bridge over and follow the Huron Line to Highway 3, all the way to Kingsville (about 40 minutes from the bridge).

Hours: One-hour tours. May-December: Noon, 2, and 4 p.m., Monday-Saturday. January-April: Noon, 2 and 4 p.m., Saturday.

Admission: $3 adults, $2 seniors, 18 and under free

Ages: All ages

Parking: Free on site

See a slide presentation of the history of Pelee Island and its winery, walk through the processing plant, see rooms used for bottling, fermentation, and laboratory. After the tour, sample the wines and browse in the gift shop.

Arts & Crafts

Pewabic Pottery
10125 East Jefferson, Detroit
313-822-0954

Location: On East Jefferson between Cadillac and Hurlbut Streets, 3½ miles east of downtown Detroit

Hours: 10 a.m.-5 p.m., Tuesday-Saturday. Call two weeks in advance to schedule a tour or hands-on workshop.

Admission: Tour: $2 adults, $1 students. 1½ hour hands-on workshop: $5 children for the experience only, $8 children to have work glazed and fired (work is ready four weeks from date of workshop).

Ages: Minimum 5 years for tour, 6 years for workshop.

Parking: Free on site

Pewabic Pottery is a historic, turn-of-the-century pottery, famous for its contemporary ceramics. Children are allowed to tour the workshops and galleries, but they will benefit more from participating in hands-on workshops that explore clay works.

Utilities

Phoenix Memorial Laboratory
230 Bonisteel Boulevard, Ann Arbor
313-764-6220

Location: Bonisteel Boulevard and Murfin

Hours: 9 a.m.-4 p.m., Monday-Friday. Call to arrange a tour.

Admission: Free

Ages: 1st grade and up

Parking: Free on site

Tour the nuclear reactor plant and laboratory. Kids will enjoy peering into the azure pool surrounding the nuclear reactor and watching demonstrations that show the radioactivity of various materials.

Utilities

Saginaw Water Works
522 Ezra Rust, Saginaw
517-776-1450

Location: Across from the Saginaw Zoo

Hours: One-hour tour, 9 a.m.-3:30 p.m., Monday-Friday. Call two weeks in advance to reserve tour.

Admission: Free

Ages: Minimum age - second grade

Parking: Free on site

Watch a movie that explains how water is treated and purified, then walk through the treatment plant. Kids will enjoy the sights and sounds of pumps and gushing water.

Food

St. Julian Winery
716 South Kalamazoo, Paw Paw
616-657-5568

Location: ¼ mile north of I-94 on M-40. Paw Paw is about 15 miles west of Kalamazoo.

Hours: 20-minute tour held every hour 9 a.m.-4 p.m., Monday-Saturday. Noon-5 p.m., Sunday. Call to schedule a large tour.

Admission: Free

Ages: All ages

Parking: Free on site

Freebies: Wine tasting for adults, non-alcoholic juice for kids

Walk through the cellars, crushing room, bottling room, and warehouse in this guided tour that shows you how wine is made using both state-of-the-art equipment and old world methods.

Food

Sander's, Inc.
100 Oakman Boulevard, Highland Park
313-868-5700

Location: Oakman and Hamilton

Hours: 1½-hour tour, 9:30 a.m., Monday-Friday. Minimum tour group size 10, maximum size 25.

Admission: Free

Ages: Minimum 18 years

Parking: Free on site

Freebies: A homemade cake and coffee snack, plus seasonal candy treats to take home

Watch the production of your favorite Sander's products, including ice cream, topping, bumpy cakes, candies, donuts, and cookies. Visit the design center and see seasonal candies and special treats being made. Perfect for all Sander's aficionados.

Arts & Crafts

Scrap Box
2455 South Industrial, Ann Arbor
313-994-4420

Location: South Industrial and Eisenhower

Hours: 10 a.m.-2 p.m., Tuesday. 2-6 p.m., Thursday. 10 a.m.-2 p.m., Saturday. Arrange for group workshops during hours the store is closed to regular business.

Admission: Free

Ages: Preschool and up

Parking: Free on site

At the Scrap Box, junk comes in all sizes and shapes. Children can look through bins and boxes of foam, wood, plastic, paper, cardboard, and cork discards and fill a grocery bag for $2. Creativity and playfulness will turn the scraps into treasures. This is the perfect place to stock up on materials for rainy day projects.

Food

Stahl's Bakery
51021 Washington, New Baltimore
313-725-6990

Location: Washington and Main Streets, downtown New Baltimore

Hours: Call several weeks ahead to arrange a Monday-Friday morning tour

Admission: Free

Ages: All ages

Parking: Free on site

Freebies: A "belly button cookie" (chocolate chip butter cookie)

Step into the sweet, humid cloud of Stahl's Bakery and watch bread made the old-fashioned way, by a fraternity of flour-dusted young men wearing white aprons. Kids will enjoy watching large batches of dough kneaded by hand and made into loaves, and watching the bakers take out finished loaves with long bread oars called "peels."

Government

State Capitol
Capitol Avenue, Lansing
517-335-1483 (Monday-Friday)
517-373-0183 (weekends)

Location: Between Allegan and Ottawa Streets

Hours: 8 a.m.-4 p.m., Monday-Friday. 10 a.m.-4 p.m., Saturday. Noon-4 p.m., Sunday. Groups of ten or more must schedule a tour several weeks in advance of visit.

Admission: Free

Ages: 3rd grade and up

Parking: Meters on street, reserved areas for buses behind Capitol on Walnut Street

Tour the elegant state capitol, recently restored to its 1879 splendor. Visit Senate and House viewing galleries and committee rooms and take a look at our lawmakers' workplace. Don't forget to notice the portraits of former Michigan governors, located on the second floor rotunda, near the Governor's executive office and reception rooms.

Food

Superior Fish Company
309 East Eleven Mile Road, Royal Oak
313-541-4632

Location: Downtown Royal Oak
Hours: ½–hour tour, 2-5 p.m., Monday-Friday
Admission: Free
Ages: All ages. Ten people minimum needed for a tour.
Parking: Free, park behind store
Freebies: Children are often given a clam shell as a souvenir

Peek into the glass-enclosed cutting room and watch fish being processed. Children are also shown a table of many types of fish to identify and touch.

Food

Sutton's Candy
12740 Mansfield, Detroit
313-837-5066

Location: Glendale and Mansfield
Hours: One-hour tour, 10 a.m., Tuesday and Thursday. Call for appointment
Admission: Free
Ages: Kindergarten and up
Parking: Free on site
Freebies: Fudge samples

Small children will especially enjoy peeking behind the scenes at this wonderfully chocolate-scented, family-owned business. After the tour, visitors may buy candy.

Media

TV 2 WJBK
16550 West Nine Mile Road, Southfield
313-557-2000

Location: Just east of Southfield Road

Hours: Call to arrange a time

Admission: Free

Ages: All ages

Parking: Free on site

Walk into the newsroom, offices, and onto the news set. Kids of all ages will enjoy peeking behind the scenes and talking to a station personality.

Industry

Upjohn Pharmaceutical Company
7171 Portage, Kalamazoo
616-323-5866

Location: Two miles south of airport. Going west on I-94, take exit 78 south.

Hours: One-hour tour, 8:15 and 10:30 a.m., 1:15 p.m., Monday-Friday. No 8:15 a.m. tour Tuesdays. By appointment only.

Admission: Free

Ages: All ages. Children must be accompanied by an adult.

Parking: Free on site

See a 20-minute film describing the company's history and products, then tour the plant, watching manufacturing and packaging.

Food

Warner Wine Haus
706 South Kalamazoo, Paw Paw
616-657-3165

Location: ¼ mile north of I-94 on M-40, Paw Paw is approximately 15 miles west of Kalamazoo.

Hours: 45-minute tour, held every hour. May-September: 9 a.m.-5 p.m., Monday-Saturday. Noon-5 p.m., Sunday. October-Christmas: 10 a.m.-5 p.m., Monday-Saturday. Noon-5 p.m., Sunday. Call ahead to schedule a large group and also during the winter months.

Admission: Free

Ages: All ages

Parking: Free on site

Freebies: Wine tasting for adults, non-alcoholic juice for children

See how wine is made, beginning with the grapes on the vine. Walk through the factory and see the grape holding tanks, wine processing, bottling, the champagne process, cellar and casks, shipping and handling. End the tour with a wine-tasting session.

Arts & Crafts

Wooden Shoe Factory
447 US-31 at 16th Street, Holland
616-396-6513

Location: Two miles west of I-96 from Grand Rapids

Hours: 8 a.m.-4:30 p.m., Monday-Saturday

Admission: 25 cents, children 5 and under free

Ages: 9 and above

Parking: Free on site

Kids will enjoy watching serious shoemakers turn blocks of wood into wooden shoes or "klompens" using 100-year-old machinery and old-fashioned hand carving. After the tour, browse around the gift shop, full of Dutch imports, wooden toys, and homemade fudge.

Wright & Filippis, Inc.
2845 Crooks Road, Rochester
313-853-1855

Location: M-59 and Crooks

Hours: 8 a.m.-4:30 p.m., Monday, Tuesday, Thursday and Friday. 8 a.m.-7 p.m., Wednesday.

Admission: Free

Ages: Minimum age 7 years

Parking: Free on site

Children acquire a better understanding of the handicapped when they visit Wright & Filippis, a firm that researches and develops high-tech products for the disabled. Tour groups learn the difference between an orthosis and prothesis, tour the workshops and computer rooms, and try out the wheelchairs. In the Future House, a lucite and glass structure showcasing the latest in home aids for the handicapped, a "genie" responds to voice commands.

14
PROGRAMS FOR
THE SCHOOLS
A Sampling of
Traveling
Programs

Michigan is full of talented actors, dancers, artists, and musicians who will bring their art into the schools. There are also traveling science and history programs, sponsored by area museums and individuals, which offer school children new ideas in an entertaining format. Here is a sampling of traveling programs available for school, church, synagogue, library, or civic organizations. Fees are not listed because they fluctuate with each booking, depending on the size of the group and traveling distance.

For additional listings, you'll want to look through "Michigan Touring Arts Attractions," a

resource directory of professional touring artists and exhibitions published by the Touring
Arts Agency, Midland Center for the Performing Arts, and the Michigan Council for the Arts.
Call 517-631-5930 to order a free copy.

Science

Al Hyams "Explorations in Chemistry"
313-357-0482

Retired science teacher Al Hyams plays his
harmonica and mixes up dramatic (and safe)
chemical explosions to turn kids on to the fun
of chemistry. Program for up to 150 students,
grades 3 to 6 or middle school.

Puppets

Ann Arbor Folk Marionettes
Rachel Urist
310 Awixa, Ann Arbor
313-662-0712

Meet two-feet-tall marionettes, created and
manipulated by a troupe of child puppeteers.
Ann Arbor Folk Marionettes perform folk tales
from around the world.

Music

Ann Arbor Symphony Orchestra
527 East Liberty, Ann Arbor
313-994-4801

During November, the Ann Arbor Symphony Orchestra offers after-school workshops for teachers in Washtenaw County. At-
tending teachers are then eligible to book
AASO ensembles to visit their schools, from
November to February.

Atlantis Expedition
Nancy Henk
313-893-6341 (11 a.m.-7 p.m., weekdays)

The Atlantis Expedition interprets classical music with unusual forms of puppetry, including giant puppets, masks, and shadow puppets. Their show is geared for grades 1 to 6 or family audiences and requires an auditorium setting.

BABES
17330 Northland Park Court, Southfield
313-443-0886 or
1-800-54-BABES

Engaging puppets teach children about drugs and encourage them to feel good about themselves when they "say no." For elementary school-age students.

Blue Pigs
Detroit Police Crime Prevention Section
313-224-4030

Through a variety of songs and musical styles, five talented Detroit Police officers offer children information about child protection, drug abuse and awareness, and crime prevention. The approximately 45-minute show is tailored to fit audiences in grades K to 12.

Theater

Bonstelle Theatre
3424 Woodward Avenue, Detroit
313-577-3010

Bonstelle Theatre offers "Movin' Theatre," a touring performance of theatrical dance, various forms of stage movement, and period styles.

Music

Chamber Music for Youth
3000 Town Center, Suite 1335, Southfield
313-357-1111

The Lyric Chamber Ensemble visits middle schools and high schools, offering concerts and workshops.

Theater, Dance

Crossroads Productions
Donald V. Calamia
13120 Nathaline, Redford
313-537-4860

This entertaining and popular touring theater company offers a wide variety of performances targeted specifically for young children, families, and young adults. The touring schedule includes "Family Classics" (fairy tale theater), "Contemporary Social Dramas" (thought-provoking dramas about divorce, AIDS, and drugs), "Storytime Theatre" (folk tales and popular children's stories), and "Showcase Presentations" (special shows for special occasions).

Dance-Theater

Dance Focus
Betsy Maxwell
Ann Arbor Parks and Recreation
313-994-2326

Dance Focus offers four original dance-theater shows—"Cinderella," "The Three Little Pigs," "Dorothy's Adventures in Oz," and "The Ugly Duckling." Each show is approximately 30 to 45 minutes long and designed for children and families.

Puppets

Daren Dundee, Entertainer
21175 Carson, Mt. Clemens
313-463-1798

Puppeteer Daren Dundee offers a variety of programs for young children, incorporating story-telling, puppetry, and magic.

Science

Detroit Audubon Society
121 South Main Street, Royal Oak
313-545-2929

Schools can subscribe to a weekly reader all about birds, created by the National Audubon Society. Speakers with a slide presentation on changing topics are also available to clubs and schools.

Dance

Detroit Dance Collective
739 South Washington, Royal Oak
313-548-9664

Detroit Dance Collective, a modern dance company made up of performers who are also dance educators, offers a variety of school performances, classes, and workshops for students. They will design programs to meet the special needs of any group.

Transportation

Detroit Department of Transportation
1301 East Warren, Detroit
313-833-1196

A mobile demonstration bus provides exhibits and skits focusing on how to ride a bus, bus safety, courtesy, and vandalism protection. Presentations are 40 minutes and children receive promotional gifts—coloring books, pencils, buttons, certificates, and game dittos.

Science

Detroit Edison — School Safety Coordinator
Public Affairs Department
2000 Second Avenue, Detroit
313-237-9213

Audio-visual presentation explaining how electricity is made and transmitted, plus safety tips. For grades 4 to 6. Free. Call to schedule, 8 a.m.-5 p.m., Monday-Friday.

History

Detroit Historical Museum — Yesterday on Tour
5401 Woodward Avenue, Detroit
313-833-1419, 313-297-9273

"Yesterday On Tour" offers several 40–

to 60–minute hands-on, living history programs for the schools. "Slave Narrative" is a 45-minute, one-act play about Michigan's role in the Underground Railroad, suitable for grades 3 and up. "Les Français a Detroit," for grades K to 8, looks at life in Michigan 250 years ago. "Hardtack and Coffee," for all ages, explores a woman's life in Michigan during the Civil War. "Search for Power," for high school and adult audiences, describes life in Detroit during the women's suffrage movement.

Art

Detroit Institute of Arts — Art to the Schools
5200 Woodward Avenue, Detroit
313-833-7883

Call 9 a.m.-5 p.m., Monday-Friday, for an "Art to the Schools," request form. Scheduling is not handled over the phone.

Free 45– to 60–minute art appreciation talks are available for grades 4 to 6, Tuesdays and Thursdays, October to May. The talks are based on the DIA's collection and are illustrated with slides and reproductions. The topics include "People of the World," "Introduction to the Museum," "American Art," "Native American Art," "Modern Art," "Arts of Asia," "African Art," and "Ancient World."

Puppets

Detroit Recreation Puppeteers
Nancy Hank
Detroit Parks and Recreation
2735 West Warren, Detroit
313-898-6341

Children's puppet shows for recreation departments, special events, and schools.

Science

Detroit Science Center
Larry Christiansen
5020 John R, Detroit
313-577-8400

Choose classroom workshops for 35, or auditorium performances for 250, or combine them. Both formats consist of demonstration and audience participation and last 45 minutes. A variety of topics include "The Magic of Science" (K to 8), "It's Electrifying" (K to 8), "Light and Laser" (K to 8), "Bones and Bodies" (1 to 6), "Sound Sensations" (1 to 6), "Daring Dectectives" (3 to 8), and Starlab Portable Planetarium.

Values

Dolls for Democracy
B'nai Brith Women's Council of
Metropolitan Detroit
25835 Southfield Road, Southfield
313-552-8150

"Doll ladies" bring into the classroom 12-inch replica dolls of famous courageous people who have worked for the betterment of humanity. The presentation teaches brotherhood/sisterhood and the importance of perseverance over adversity. The approximately 45-minute biographical presentation is geared to grades 2 to 6. It's free, but donations are accepted.

Science

Ecology Center
417 Detroit, Ann Arbor
313-761-3186

An ecology van visits schools to teach children about planting, composting, and recycling. The Ecology Center on Industrial in Ann Arbor offers tours. *See* Detroit at Work.

Music

Gemini
2000 Penncraft Ct., Ann Arbor
313-665-0165

Twin brothers Sandor and Laszlo Slomovits, professionally known as Gemini, offer concerts for elementary to high school students. They offer boisterous fun, incorporating a wide range of musical traditions and instruments into their songs.

Theater

Goodtime Players
Jan Koengeter
Ann Arbor Parks and Recreation
313-994-2326

Goodtime Players offer seven original musical shows: "Sweet Betsy From Pike," "The Secret Under the Stone in the Road," "Enchantment in the Woods," "The Peanuts Gang Goes Broadway," "The Firebird," "Rumpelstiltskin," and "Gotta Dance! Gotta Sing!" Shows are approximately 30 to 45 minutes and geared for children and families.

Science

Great Lakes Herpetological Society
Bob White
13862 Church Road, Berville
313-784-9134, 313-498-2195

The Great Lakes Herpetological Society offers free talks to schools, scouts, and clubs on the subject they love best — reptiles. Society members usually bring along a few pets, too.

Dance

Harbinger Dance Company
Oakland Community College
Farmington Hills
313-477-7014

Elementary schools can book the Harbinger Dance Company's creative program, "Dance American Style," which highlights American dance from Native American dances to Colonial minutes. A program of "Creative Resources for Educational Awareness and Training Exposure Through Dance" is also available to Detroit middle schools.

Science

Huron-Clinton Metroparks
1-800-47-PARKS

Free slide and movie programs on southeast Michigan nature for grades K to 12. Brochures are mailed in September. Act quickly; the programs are booked on a first come, first served basis.

Science

Impression 5 Museum
200 Museum Drive, Lansing
517-485-8116

Six entertaining science shows for grades K to 12, including "The Illusion Show," "Dr. Zap Explores Electronics," "Dr. Zap in Mathemagic Land," and "Annie Anatomy." Many of the shows incorporate mime and music.

Puppets

Kids on the Block
United Cerebral Palsy of Metro Detroit
17000 West Eight Mile Road,
Suite 380, Southfield
313-557-5070

Engaging puppeteers teach children about physical disabilities using almost life-size puppets.

Science

Living Science Foundation
40400 Grand River, Novi
313-348-1985

Over 40 entertaining, hands-on science shows for grades K-12, including "Animal Family," "Life on Earth," "Nature's Law," "Where in the World," "Prehistoric Life," "Ocean's Edge," and "Exploring Space." The Living Science Foundation instructors are widely known for their razzle-dazzle demonstrations and fine teaching skills.

History, Dance

Madame Cadillac Dancers
111 East Kirby, Detroit
313-875-6354

Madame Cadillac Dancers bring the French Colonial period and the history of Detroit's first settlers to life with the authentic dance, music, and costumes. Their repertoire includes "First Lady of Detroit — story of Marie Therese Guyon," "Jean Baptiste Pointe du Sable, Black Man in the Wilderness," and "Ezekiel Solomon, Michigan's First Jewish Fur Trader." Each show is 50 minutes and appeals to children of all ages.

Theater

Meadow Brook Theatre —
Costumes in the Classroom
Oakland University, Rochester
313-370-3316

Costumes in the Classroom offers a curriculum enrichment for drama, history, English, and art classes. Six to eight period costumes are brought into the classroom and modeled during an informal lecture.

Music, Theater

Michigan Opera Theatre —
Overture to Opera for Schools
6519 Second Avenue, Detroit
313-874-7850

The MOT offers top-notch creative performances geared to children of all ages, plus special educational programs such as master classes and workshops that can supplement school curriculum. School performaces include "Monkey See, Monkey Do," "The Frog Who Became A Prince," "America Works and Sings," and "Gallantry." Performances are approximately 30 minutes with an introduction to opera of about 15 minutes.

Space

Michigan Space Center
2111 Emmons Road, Jackson
517-787-4425

School children are given a look at the history and future of space exploration that includes slides and a real astronaut's suit.

Science, Literature, Values

Mobile Ed Productions
26455 Five Mile, Livonia
313-522-0044

Mobile Ed Productions offers a variety of educationally exciting programs for K to 12, including "World of Robotics," "Amazing World of Light," "Wonder and Mystery of Chemistry," "Physics is Fun," "Reptiles are Cool," "Succeeding Without Drugs," "Adventures of Huck Finn," and "Living with Abe Lincoln."

Recreation

Oakland County Mobile Recreation Units
313-858-0906

Mobile recreation units offer sports equipment, games, puppet shows, and a moonwalk.

Drug & Safety Education

Officer Ollie and Friends
Wayne County Sheriff
1231 St. Antoine, Detroit
313-224-0414, 313-224-2233

Children are active participants in a puppet show about drug abuse, stranger danger, vandalism, and bicycle safety.

Theater

Piccolo Opera Company
Marjorie Gordon
18662 Fairfield Avenue, Detroit
313-861-6930

This nationally known, professional opera

company delights in performing hilarious versions of children's classics, complete with high-quality costumes, sets, and lighting. Most performances are one hour.

Puppets

Pippin Puppets
313-533-5229

Robert Papineau performs his own children's stories at schools, festivals, and libraries with puppets and sets he has created.

Puppets

Rick's Puppet Theater
48607 Presidential, Utica
313-566-0888

Puppeteer Rick Paul has created a variety of puppet shows with large handmade puppets, which include holiday shows for Halloween, Christmas, and Easter, plus a very effective traffic and stranger safety show. For all ages.

Magic, Storytelling

Ringling Bros. and Barnum & Bailey Circus
313-567-6000

Clowns come into the classroom to perform a comic magic show while teaching the importance of reading. Children receive several reading-oriented gifts. Shows are one-half hour and take place during the week the circus is in town.

Magic

Scheer Magic Productions
Doug Scheer
20200 North Greenway, Southfield
313-353-5662

Doug Scheer and his many alter egos —
Wizzy the Wacky Wizard, Uncle Sam, Mysto
the Magic Clown, Captain Cautious, and Jingle
the Magical Elf — perform history, science,
safety, and just plain magic shows for children
of all ages.

Magic

Stevens and Associates
Bernie Stevens
747 West Maple, Suite 501, Clawson
313-288-0338

Bernie Stevens offers a fun-filled, 30- to 45-
minute family magic show with colorful effects
and balloon animals. For children 4 and older.

Creative, Writing, Theater

Storybuilders
Sue Fraley or Tom Shaker
726 Livernois, Ferndale
313-543-8300

Storybuilders will come into the classroom
with improvisational skits to help motivate creative writing. If student stories are sent at least
one week before Storybuilders' visit, they will
bring those stories to life in light-hearted vi-
gnettes. Storybuilders also performs musicals
and holiday shows, plus a rock 'n' roll "Say No
To Drugs" show.

Storytelling

Story Peddlar
William Boyce
313-886-4932, 313-577-6296

William Boyce, Wayne State University professor, is the Story Peddlar, spinning stories for children and young adults.

Animals

Upland Hills Farm
481 Lake George Road, Oxford
313-628-1611

Farmer Webster takes the animals on the road with a program that gives city children a farm experience. They will learn about poultry and the incubation of eggs, and see the processing of wool from sheep shearing and carding to spinning and weaving.

Theater

Wallace Smith Productions
Touring Chamber Theatre
P.O. Box 1101, Fenton
313-471-7705

Touring Chamber Theatre offers an eclectic program of narrative storytelling, mime, dialogue, music, and dance. Programs are 35- to 50-minutes and encourage audience participation. The company's emphasis is on conflict resolution, problem solving, and positive values. For grades preschool to high school.

Science

Weatherschool—TV 2
P.O. Box 2000, Southfield
313-552-5273

Weatherschool offers 20 weather lessons adaptable to different grade levels, employing subjects such as math, physics, geography, art, and speech. Each lesson provides thorough teacher background information, student activities, and classroom experiments. Lessons hook into a "question of the day," which is reviewed on TV 2 "First News" at 4:30 p.m., and then explained on TV 2 "Eyewitness News" at 5 p.m., Monday-Friday. Schools should begin inquiring in early September. Weatherschool begins each year in February.

Theater

Wild Swan Theater
1510 Shadford, Ann Arbor
313-995-0987

Wild Swan Theater performs children's theater for grades preschool to 6 in a storytelling style using masks, mime, music, and puppets. Their touring productions include "Owl's Winter," "Tales of Tricks and Trouble," and "Hawk, I'm Your Brother." Their productions are also accessible for sight and hearing-impaired children through sign language interpretation and audio-description.

Theater, Dance, Music

Young Audiences, Inc.
Historic Fort Wayne
6325 West Jefferson, Detroit
313-843-6940

This non-profit agency represents many individual artists and performing troupes and offers a variety of dance, music, theater, and creative writing programs.

15
OVERNIGHT
ADVENTURES

Michigan is waiting for you. Its waterways and forested trails, historic sites and museums are yours to explore. Pack the car with an overnight case, camera, and treats. Let the kids pile in and you're off. Here are a variety of overnight adventures, arranged geographically, that received "thumbs up!" from Jordan, Andrew, and Garrett, the three junior Field travelers. We hope your family has as much fun traveling together and sharing memories as we do.

Along I-75

Turn your next trip "Up North" along I-75 into an adventure by making a few well-chosen stops.

Frankenmuth (Exit 136 off I-75 north)

Children can eat their way along Frankenmuth's Main Street tasting samples of sausage, cheese, or fudge. They can also watch woodcarving and leather-making demonstrations. Most stores are open 10 a.m.-5 p.m., daily, Labor Day-May, and 10 a.m.-8 p.m., daily, Memorial Day-Labor Day. Here are some highlights.

Antique Auto Village
576 South Main Street, Frankenmuth
517-652-2669

Have some fun in this old-fashioned, mechanized toy museum-store, complete with player piano, Lionel Train City, and juke box.

Folkswagon Tours
Bavarian Inn, Frankenmuth
517-652-9941

45-minute conducted tours of historic Frankenmuth leave continuously from the Leather Shop near the covered bridge.

Frankenmuth Flour Mill and General Store
701 Mill Street, Frankenmuth
517-652-8422

The General Store has barrels of penny candy; the Flour Mill offers a self-guided tour. Walk onto the balcony overlooking the Cass River and watch a waterwheel in action.

Holz-Brucke and Woodcarvers' Pavilion
Main Street, Frankenmuth

Walk across the Holz-brucke, the wooden covered bridge, spanning the Cass River. Stop for a drinking fountain break at the Woodcarvers' Pavilion, decorated with wooden scenes from Grimm's Fairy Tales.

Gaylord (Exit 282 off I-75 north)

Bavarian Falls Park
820 Wisconsin Avenue, Gaylord
517-732-4336, 517-732-4087

Adventure golf, go-cart track, bumper cars, and kiddie rides. Adjacent to the Call of the Wild. 10 a.m.-midnight Memorial Day-Labor Day.

Call of the Wild Museum
850 South Wisconsin Avenue, Gaylord
517-732-4336

You'll be surprised at the quality of this museum's wildlife displays. Your kids will be overwhelmed by the sheer number of stuffed, animated, and mounted Michigan animals. The gift shop offers kids a variety of inexpensive items. 8:30 a.m.-9 p.m., daily, June 15-Labor Day. 9:30 a.m.-6 p.m., daily, September-May.

Grayling (Exit 259 off I-75 north)

Hartwick Pines State Park
7 1/2 miles northeast of
Grayling on M-93
517-348-7068

Once a center of Michigan's lumbering industry, this state park offers a 49-acre preserve of white pines and a Lumberman's Museum and Interpretive Center with hands-on displays that tell the lumbering story.

Pinconning (Exit 164 off I-75 north)

Deer Acres Storybook Amusement Park
2346 M-13, Pinconning
517-879-2849

It's a petting zoo, children's playground, amusement park, folk art exhibit, and picnic grounds all rolled into one. Ringing the park are colorful sculptural renditions of popular nursery rhymes, rides for the whole family and a small petting farm. Kids will love the safari train, antique cars, and moon walk. They will also enjoy feeding the deer. 9 a.m.-7 p.m., daily, Memorial Day-Labor Day. 10 a.m.-6 p.m., weekends only, Labor Day-mid-October.

Saginaw (I-675 to Davenport exit)

Anderson Water Park
1830 Fordney Road, Saginaw
517-776-1386

Wave-action pool and double water slide. 11 a.m.-8 p.m., daily, Memorial Day-Labor Day.

Green Point Nature Center
3010 Maple Street, Saginaw
517-776-1669

Kids will enjoy the spacious Interpretive Center with its hands-on displays, wildlife feeding stations, beehives, live animals, and aquariums. Nature trails are open dawn to dusk. Interpretive center's hours vary; call before visiting.

Japanese Cultural Center and Tea House
1315 South Washington Avenue, Saginaw
517-776-1648

Enjoy a cultural experience. *See* Detroit at Work.

Saginaw Art Museum
1126 North Michigan Avenue, Saginaw
517-754-2491

This cosy art museum offers kids the "Vision-area," a special hands-on, creative gallery. 10 a.m.-5 p.m., Tuesday-Saturday. 1-5 p.m., Sunday. Closed August.

Saginaw Children's Zoo
1435 South Washington Avenue, Saginaw
517-776-1657

This delightful children's zoo offers a miniature train ride, petting farm, pony rides, and several creative sculptures that house animals, such as a Noah's Ark and whale's mouth. 10 a.m.-5 p.m., Monday-Saturday. Noon-7 p.m., Sunday and holidays. Memorial Day-Labor Day.

Saginaw Water Works
522 Ezra Rust, Saginaw
517-776-1450

Tour a water processing plant. *See* Detroit at Work.

Vanderbilt (Exit 290 off I-75 north)

Project Nature
4000 Whitmarsh Road, Vanderbilt
517-983-9900

A 2000-acre wilderness with a wide variety of pioneer, nature, and arts and crafts activities, including a Pioneer Center, Vistacore Theatre, Mountaintop Pavilion, Wilderness Tram, and Timber Mountain Ranch. 9:30 a.m.-7 p.m., daily. May 15-October 15.

Dunes and Harbors

Explore Michigan's dunes and harbors, its lumbering and pioneer history in these three charming and revitalized towns.

Grand Haven

Harbor Steamer
541 Gidley Drive, Grand Haven
616-842-8950

Take a 1 1/2-hour tour of the Grand Haven waterfront on an old-fashioned sternwheeler. Daily, Memorial Day-Labor Day.

Harbor Trolley
440 North Ferry, Grand Haven
616-842-3200

Take a refreshing ride along Lake Michigan through Grand Haven, Spring Lake, and Ferrysburg. 11 a.m.-11 p.m., daily, Memorial Day-Labor Day.

Tri-Cities Museum
One North Harbor Drive, Grand Haven
616-842-0700

Two levels chock full of tools, memorabilia, clothes, photographs, toys, and household implements tell the stories of Michigan's pioneer, railroad, and fur-trapping days. Hours vary with the seasons.

Waterfront Stadium
Washington at Harbor Drive, Grand Haven
616-842-2550

Home of summer concerts and "the world's largest musical fountain." The fountain provides a nightly sound, light, and water show during the summer.

Muskegon

E. Genevieve Gillette Nature Center
Hoffmaster State Park
6585 Lake Harbour, Muskegon
616-798-3573

The Nature Center offers hands-on exhibits, live animals, a slide show, and displays telling the story of the sand dunes. Walk out back and take the trail down to an untouched sandy beach along Lake Michigan. Then climb up the 150-step boardwalk, and you'll find yourself 190-feet above water level on a wonderfully breezy overlook. Nature Center hours: Summer: 9 a.m.-6 p.m., Tuesday-Sunday. Fall-spring: 1-5 p.m., Tuesday-Friday. 10 a.m.-5 p.m., Saturday and Sunday. Park is open 8 a.m.-10 p.m., daily, year-round.

Hackley and Hume Historic Site
430 West Clay Avenue, Muskegon
616-722-7578

Take a 40-minute tour through two beautifully ornate homes built in the late 1880s by wealthy lumber barons. Tour guides encourage children's questions. May 15-September: 1-4 p.m., Wednesday, Saturday, Sunday. Victorian Christmas: 1-5 p.m., Saturday and Sunday, Thanksgiving weekend-Christmas.

Michigan's Adventure Amusement Park
4750 Whitehall Road, Muskegon
616-766-3377

Carnival rides, live shows, refreshment stands, and gift shops. At $10 per person (children 2 and under free), it's no bargain. 11 a.m.-9 p.m., daily, Memorial Day-Labor Day.

Muskegon County Museum
430 West Clay Avenue, Muskegon
616-728-4119

This small museum offers lots of hands-on exhibits and family fun. Kids will enjoy the "Body Works," plus exhibits on Michigan lumbering, Indians, and pre-historic life. 9:30 a.m.-4:30 p.m., Monday-Friday. 12:30-4:30 p.m., Saturday and Sunday.

Muskegon Museum of Art
296 West Webster Avenue, Muskegon
616-722-2600

Ornately constructed museum houses a small permanent collection and a changing collection of interest to children. 10 a.m.-6 p.m., Tuesday-Friday. 1-5 p.m., Saturday and Sunday.

Muskegon Trolley Company
Muskegon
616-724-6420

Ride all over Muskegon on an old-fashioned trolley for 10 cents. Memorial Day-Labor Day: 11 a.m.-6 p.m., daily. Labor Day-May: 11 a.m.-5 p.m., Saturdays only.

Pleasure Island Water Fun Park
99 East Pontaluna Road, Muskegon
616-798-7857

This water amusement park offers six water slides, bumper boats, miniature golf, water cannons, picnic areas, kiddie water slide, and water play area. 10 a.m.-6 p.m., Memorial Day-mid-June. 10 a.m.-9 p.m., mid-June-Labor Day.

Port City Princess
2411 Lake Avenue, North Muskegon
616-728-8387

A variety of cruises with entertainment and/or meals are offered. Spend several hours relaxing along Muskegon Lake and Lake Michigan. Children under 4 are free; children 12 and under are half price. May-September. Hours and prices vary depending on cruise.

U.S.S. *Silversides*
349 Webster Avenue, Muskegon
616-722-3751

Kids will enjoy climbing deep into the belly of this famous World War II submarine and seeing the equipment and facilities up close. 10 a.m.-6 p.m., daily.

Waterfront Centre
1050 West Western, Muskegon
616-725-7418

Overloooking a marina, this restored curtain roll factory now houses restaurants and shops.

Queen of Saugatuck
Boat Cruises
716 Water Street, Saugatuck
616-857-4261

Take a narrated cruise on the Kalamazoo River and Lake Michigan aboard an authentic sternwheeler. May-Labor Day.

Saugatuck Dune Rides
Blue Star Highway, Saugatuck
616-857-2253

Take a narrated, scenic drive over the sand dunes between Lake Michigan and Goshorn Lake. May-October.

Magic Journey

Take a magic journey and then stop in "Turkeyville" for some old-fashioned fun.

Abbott's Magic
Manufacturing Company
124 St. Joseph Street, Colon
(southeast of Kalamazoo
between Three Rivers and Coldwater)
616-432-3235, 616-432-3236

Colon, the Magic Capital of the World, is home to the world's largest mail-order magic supply company. Visit Abbott's and treat your kids to a magic trick; salespeople will gladly demonstrate. The showroom is a magician's paradise, full of magic posters and paraphernalia. 8 a.m.-5 p.m., Monday-Friday. 8 a.m.-4 p.m., Saturday.

Marshall

American Museum of Magic
107 East Michigan Avenue, Marshall
616-781-7666, 616-781-7674

Owner Robert Lund will arrange private one-hour tours of his magic museum. He suggests children be at least 12 years old before embarking on the journey through his magic memorabilia — hundreds of tricks, books, diaries, posters, photographs, coins, statues, letters, and popular culture items with a magic theme.

Cornwell's Turkey House
18935 15 1/2 Mile Road, Marshall
616-781-4293

If you feel like talking turkey, you'll enjoy "Turkeyville, USA," the site of Cornwell's Turkey House, an ice cream parlor-restaurant-gift shop-antique barn located on a 180-acre turkey farm. Don't expect to hear much gobbling if you visit near Thanksgiving. March-December: 11 a.m.-8 p.m., Monday-Saturday. 11 a.m.-6 p.m., Sunday.

Out West

Trains, planes, animals, and nature preserves. Western Michigan offers a lot for kids to see and do.

Augusta

Kellogg Bid Sanctuary
12685 East C Avenue, Augusta
616-671-2510

Buy a bucket or two of bird seed and follow the path around the lake. You'll find yourself in the midst of geese, ducks, and swans that make their home in the sanctuary. Scatter your bird seed, stay on the trail, and you'll see caged birds of prey and wild deer. The sanctuary is located halfway between Battle Creek and Kalamazoo, 1 1/4 miles north of M-89. 8 a.m.-5 p.m. daily.

Bangor

Kalamazoo Toy Train Factory
541 Railroad Street, Bangor
(about 20 miles west of Kalamazoo)
616-427-7927

Tour a toy train factory. *See* Detroit at Work.

Battle Creek

Binder Park Zoo
7400 Division Drive, Battle Creek
616-979-1351

Children will love this small zoo. There are exotic animal settings, an area to feed and pet animals, life-sized dinosaur models, and a miniature train. Open mid-April to mid-October: 9 a.m.-5 p.m., Monday-Friday. 9 a.m.-6 p.m., Saturday, Sunday and holidays.

Kingman Museum of Natural History
175 Limit Street, Battle Creek
616-965-5117

Three floors of natural history, including hands-on dinosaurs, health, animals, and Indian exhibits. There are also planetarium shows. July and August: 9 a.m.- 5 p.m., Monday-Saturday. Rest of year: 9 a.m.-5 p.m., Tuesday-Saturday. 1-5 p.m., Sunday. Closed Monday.

McCamly Place
35 West Jackson Street, Battle Creek
616-965-7380

Downtown festival marketplace.

Coloma

Deer Forest
6800 Marquette, Coloma
(north of Benton Harbor on I-196)
616-468-4961

An animal wonderland with over 500 animals to hand feed and pet, a safari train ride to view African animals, nursery rhyme exhibits, playgrounds, and picnic tables. 10 a.m.-6 p.m., daily, Memorial Day-Labor Day.

Hastings

Charleton Park
Historic Village
2545 South Charlton Road, Hastings
(about 30 miles southeast of Grand Rapids)
616-945-3775

Eighteen restored buildings depict life in a midwestern rural village from 1850 to 1900.

Children will love the hands-on experience offered to tours and school groups. Summer tours: 10:30 a.m., 1 and 2:30 p.m., Monday-Thursday. 10 a.m., noon, 1 and 2:30 p.m., Friday-Sunday. Village is open 9 a.m.-4 p.m., daily, Memorial Day-Labor Day.

Kalamazoo

Kalamazoo Aviation History Museum
2101 East Milham Road, Kalamazoo
616-382-6555

Children's imaginations will soar when they see the colorfully restored World War II aircraft and airplane exhibits. They can also play inside several aircraft. Call ahead for tours, 10 a.m.-5 p.m., Monday-Saturday. 1-5 p.m., Sunday.

Kalamazoo Institute of Arts
314 South Park Street, Kalamazoo
616-349-7775

Children will enjoy this small art gallery with its changing exhibits and wonderful outdoor sculpture. 10 a.m.-5 p.m., Tuesday-Saturday. 1-5 p.m., Sunday. Closed August and Sundays in June and July.

Kalamazoo Nature Center
7000 Westnedge Avenue, Kalamazoo
616-381-1574

Cross a low-slung wooden bridge to enter the interpretive center, a wonderful place for kids. There are live animals, hands-on exhibits, plants, and more. Don't forget to visit the 1858 DeLano Homestead, a living pioneer farm, where children can watch demonstrations of pioneer crafts, rural Michigan history, and domestic animals.

Kalamazoo Public Museum
and Planetarium
315 South Rose Street, Kalamazoo
616-345-7092

Kids will enjoy the Egyptian Tomb Room, planetarium shows, and exhibits of Indian and pioneer implements, as well as hands-on science and technology. 9 a.m.-5 p.m., Tuesday-Saturday. 9 a.m.-9 p.m., Wednesday. 1-5 p.m., Sunday. Planetarium shows: 1:30, 2:30, 3:30 p.m., Saturday and Sunday.

Scott's Mill Park
2900 Lake Street, Kalamazoo
616-383-8778

Tour a restored, working 1870 grist mill powered by a waterwheel, see live buffalo, and walk along nature trails. 9 a.m.-9 p.m., daily, Memorial Day-Labor Day.

Train Barn
10234 East Shore Drive, Kalamazoo
616-327-4016

The top floor of this large barn is filled to the brim with intricate Lionel train layouts. The main floor is a museum displaying model trains of all varieties from the turn-of-the-century to the present. Visitors are welcome 10 a.m.-5 p.m., Saturday only.

Upjohn Pharmaceutical Company
7171 Portage, Kalamazoo
616-323-5866

Tour the Upjohn Company. *See* Detroit at Work.

Paw Paw

St. Julian Winery
716 South Kalamazoo, Paw Paw
616-657-5568

Tour a winery. *See* Detroit at Work.

Warner Wine Haus
706 South Kalamazoo, Paw Paw
616-657-3165

Tour a winery. *See* Detroit at Work.

Thumbs Up

Take a drive north on US-25 and explore the sites along Lake Huron. Michigan's thumb offers lighthouses, beaches, and state parks.

Croswell

Croswell Swinging Bridge
Howard & Maple Streets, Croswell
(10 miles north of Lexington)

Croswell city park has a very long, swinging bridge, suspended over a gorge. The bridge leads to a creative children's playground. Kids of all ages will enjoy running back and forth across the bridge. Be sure to snap a photo of Dad under the playground sign: "Be Good to Your Mother-In-Law." At the other end of the playground is more advice: "Be Good to Your Mother."

Lexington

Lexington Marina
On the shores of Lake Huron
about 25 miles north of Port Huron

Walk along an elevated, concrete board-walk that reaches out into Lake Huron. You'll hear the sounds of sail ropes clinking against boat poles.

Port Austin

Huron City Museum
7930 Huron City Road, Port Austin
(at the tip of the Thumb)
517-428-4123

This restored 1850 lumbering town has authentically furnished original buildings including a country store, log cabin, inn, church, and museum. Tour guides offer commentary. Open July and August or by special appointment.

Sanilac Petroglyphs
Port Crescent State Park, Port Austin
517-738-8663

Prehistoric people left their markings on a sandstone outcrop that can be found in the Port Crescent State Park. The park also offers picnic sites, playgrounds, swimming, and boat launch.

Port Sanilac

Sanilac Historical Museum
228 South Ridge Street, Port Sanilac
(about 40 miles north of Port Huron)
313-622-9946

The restored Loop-Harrison home includes

authentic 1870s furnishings, medical instruments, and marine, military, and Indian artifacts. On the grounds are a restored pioneer barn, log cabin, and dairy museum. 1-4:30 p.m., Thursday-Saturday, mid-June-Labor Day.

Tulips & Fish Ladders

Take a factory tour, explore "Little Holland," or enjoy the many cultural sites of Grand Rapids.

Ada

Amway Corporation
7575 East Fulton Road, Ada
(just east of Grand Rapids)
616-676-6701

Tour Amway Corporation World Headquarters. *See* Detroit at Work.

Fremont

Gerber Products Company
445 State Street, Fremont
(northeast of Muskegon)
616-928-2000

Visit the Gerber baby food plant. *See* Detroit at Work.

Grand Rapids

Bissel, Inc.
2345 Walker NW, Grand Rapids
616-453-4451

Watch home products assembled, *See* Detroit at Work.

Blandford Nature Center
1715 Hillburn Avenue NW, Grand Rapids
616-453-6192

Children will enjoy the pioneer farmstead, one-room schoolhouse, wild animal hospital, and working family farm. Several self-guided trails meander through the nature center's 143 acres, and the Interpretive Center offers many hands-on experiences. 9 a.m.-5 p.m., Monday-Friday. 2-5 p.m., Sunday.

Fish Ladder Sculpture
Front and 6th Streets, Grand Rapids

There's a special spectator's area for watching salmon whoosh over the 6th Street Dam on their way up the Grand River to spawn.

Gerald Ford Museum
303 Pearl Street NW, Grand Rapids
616-456-2675

Artifacts revealing the life and times of our 38th president are on display in this brand-new, airy museum. Be sure to watch the 28-minute movie when you first come in. 9 a.m.-4:45 p.m., Monday-Saturday. Noon-4:45 p.m., Sunday.

Grand Rapids Art Museum
155 North Division Street, Grand Rapids
616-459-4677

A large permanent collection hangs in the beautiful, turn-of-the-century Federal Building. Children will enjoy the hands-on art and color experiments in the Children's Gallery. 10 a.m.-5 p.m., Tuesday-Saturday. Noon-5 p.m., Sunday.

Grand Rapids Public Museum and Roger B. Chaffee Planetarium
54 Jefferson SE, Grand Rapids
616-456-3977

Kids will find much of interest including the Gaslight Village, a turn-of-the-century city street, Michigan mammals, Indian artifacts, and prehistoric exhibits. 10 a.m.-5 p.m., Monday-Saturday. 1-5 p.m., Sunday. The planetarium offers sky shows for children 3 and up: 1:30 and 2:30 p.m., Saturday and Sunday, October-April.

Grand Rapids Zoological Gardens
West Fulton and Valley NW, Grand Rapids
616-776-2590

This is the second largest zoo in Michigan with over 350 animals, a fresh-water aquarium, and snake house. 10 a.m.-4 p.m., daily.

Gypsum Mine Tour
Michigan Natural Storage
1200 Judd SW, Grand Rapids
616-241-1619

Tour an old gypsum mine. *See* Detroit at Work.

Splash—Family Water Park
4441 28th Street SE, Grand Rapids
616-940-3100

Several water slides, water play areas, miniature golf, scooter derby, and picnic sites.

Holland

Brooks Beverages Plant
777 Brooks Avenue, Holland
616-396-1281

Tour the plant. *See* Detroit at Work.

Deklomp Wooden Shoe and Delftware Factory and Veldheer Tulip Garden
12755 Quincy Street, Holland
616-399-1803

Watch craftspeople make wooden shoes and hand-paint Delftware. During the spring, there are two million tulips on the grounds, nestled in between windmills and drawbridges. Mid-April-May: 8 a.m.-dark, daily. June-October: 8 a.m.-7 p.m., Monday-Saturday. Noon-4 p.m., Sunday. Rest of year: 9 a.m.-5 p.m. Monday-Saturday.

Dutch Village
US-31 at James Street, Holland
616-396-1475

A quaint village complete with canals, windmills, tulips, Dutch farmhouse and barn, live animals, street organs, wooden shoe carving, folk dances, rides, and merry-go-round. June-August: 9 a.m.-6 p.m., daily. April-June and September-October: 9 a.m.-4:30 p.m., daily.

Windmill Island
Windmill Island Municipal Park, Holland
616-396-5433

A 36-acre island with canals, drawbridge, miniature Dutch village, tulip gardens, and "De Zwaan," a 200-year-old operating windmill from the Netherlands. Kids will enjoy climbing up to the top of the windmill on a guided tour, browsing through the gift shops of the Dutch village, and watching "Klompen" dancing presentations. May and July-Labor Day: 9 a.m.-6 p.m., Monday-Saturday. 11:30 a.m.-6 p.m., Sunday. June: 10 a.m.-5 p.m., Monday-Saturday. 11:30 a.m.-5 p.m., Sunday. Limited hours after Labor Day.

Wooden Shoe Factory
447 US-31 at 16th Street, Holland
616-396-6513

Tour the shoe factory. *See* Detroit at Work.

Twin Cities

Paul Bunyan legends could have started in either of these two cities, once bustling lumbertowns.

Bay City

Historical Museum of Bay County
321 Washington, Bay City
517-893-5733

Learn about the area's lumbering and fur trading eras, shipbuilding industry, and Indian heritage. 10 a.m.-5 p.m., Monday-Friday.

Jennison Nature Center
Bay City State Park
3582 State Park Drive, Bay City
517-667-0717

Located in the middle of a wetland and marsh, the park offers tours of the marshes and a chance to watch migrating waterfowl from a 30-foot tower during spring and fall. 10 a.m.-4 p.m., Tuesday-Saturday. Noon-5 p.m., Sunday.

Midland

Automotive Hall of Fame
3225 Cook Road, Midland
517-631-5760

The men and women who advanced the automobile industry are immortalized on the walls of this museum. Older children might enjoy a short visit. 9 a.m.-4 p.m., Monday-Friday.

Chippewa Nature Center
400 South Badour Road, Midland
517-631-0830

One thousand acres of woods with 14 miles of nature trails, museum with hands-on exhibits and discovery room, restored homestead farm, log schoolhouse, maple sugarhouse, and arboretum of Michigan trees. Children can explore the past. 8 a.m.-5 p.m., Monday-Friday. 9 a.m.-5 p.m., Saturday. 1-5 p.m., Sunday.

Dow Gardens
1018 West Main, Midland
517-631-2677

Sixty acres of streams, trees, flowers, waterfalls. Children will enjoy walking over many small bridges. 10 a.m.-sunset, daily.

Dow Visitor Center
500 East Lyon Road, Midland
517-636-8658

Tour the Saran Wrap production plant. *See* Detroit at Work.

Midland Center for the Arts
1801 West St. Andrews Drive, Midland
517-631-5930

Don't miss the Hall of Ideas, full of hands-on exhibits of science, technology, and health. Children will enjoy learning about Michigan's past from the colorful Indian, fur trading, farming, and lumbering exhibits. 9 a.m.-6 p.m., Monday-Friday. Noon-5 p.m., Saturday and Sunday.

Up North

Michigan's favorite resort area has many attractions in addition to sand, water, and fudge.

Acme

Music House
7377 North US-31, Acme
(northeast of Traverse City
on the East Arm of Grand Traverse Bay)
616-938-9300

You'll find old-fashioned nickelodeons, grand pianos, radios, a 97-key dance organ, and other antique automatic instruments. Kids will enjoy the period music in the turn-of-the-century Hurry Back Saloon, Acme General Store, and Lyric Theatre. May-October: 10 a.m.-4 p.m., Monday-Saturday. 1-6 p.m., Sunday.

Harbor Springs

Chief Blackbird Museum
SR-119, Harbor Springs
616-347-0200

This museum is full of Ottowa crafts, weavings, tools and implements. Children will enjoy the totem pole on the front lawn and the museum's showcases of traditional Indian clothes and arrowheads. July-Labor Day: 10 a.m.-noon and 1-5 p.m., daily.

Petoskey

American Spoon Foods Kitchen
411 East Lake Street, Petoskey
616-347-9030

This is one of my children's favorite stores in Petoskey. It's steamy-sweet inside; employees are preserving and canning in the kitchen. There are always free samples of preserves and crackers.

Kilwins Candy Kitchens, Inc.
200 Division Road, Petoskey
616-347-4831

Tour the candy factory. *See* Detroit at Work.

Little Traverse Historic Museum
Off Dock Street on US-31, Petoskey
616-347-2620

Children will enjoy the collection of old-fashioned items including a dentist's chair, doctor's table, wheelchair, sewing machine, and baby buggy. 9 a.m.-4:30 p.m., Monday-Saturday. 1-4:30 p.m., Sunday.

Pirate's Cove Adventure Golf
1230 US-31 North, Petoskey
616-347-1123

Eighteen-hole adventure miniature golf with waterfalls, bridges, and hills.

Sleeping Bear Dunes

Walking up the sand dunes in the hot summer sun is an experience that's all Michigan. Kids love it! Sleeping Bear Dunes, located approximately one hour west of Traverse City, is a natural wonder. The visitor center is located off SR-72 in Empire, and many dune climbs are in the general area from Empire to Glen Haven. For maps and information, call 616-326-5134.

Traverse City

Ammon's Orchard Tours
7407 North US-31, Traverse City
616-938-1644

Tour the cherry orchard. *See* Detroit at Work.

The Candle Factory
301 Grand View Parkway, Traverse City
616-946-2280, 616-946-2850

Watch candles being made. *See* Detroit at Work.

Clinch Park Zoo and
Con Foster Museum
400 Boardman Street, Traverse City
616-922-4904 (zoo),
616-922-4905 (museum)

Young children will enjoy this small zoo's Michigan animals and aquarium with Michigan fish. The Con Foster Museum has Indian and pioneer displays. April-Memorial Day and Labor Day-October 31: 9:30 a.m.-4:30 p.m., daily. Memorial Day-Labor Day: 9:30 a.m.-7:30 p.m., daily.

Pirate's Cove Adventure Golf
1710 US-31 North, Traverse City
616-938-9599

Eighteen-hole adventure miniature golf complete with waterfalls, bridges, and hills.

Upper Peninsula

Drive across the Mackinac Bridge into the ruggedly natural Upper Peninsula. Here you'll see Michigan's national treasures — Pictured Rocks along Lake Superior and Tahquamenon Falls. Summer turns into autumn earlier here, so bring along warm clothes. And don't come home without trying pasties, the Upper Peninsula's specialty food, steaming hot dough pockets filled with meat, potatoes, and onion.

Copper Harbor

Brockway Mountain Drive

You'll find the start of the nine-mile scenic drive four miles west of Copper Harbor. High above sea level, the drive offers a panoramic view of the mighty Lake Superior, as well as neighboring woodlands.

Delaware Copper Mine
Kearsarge, on the Keweenaw Peninsula
906-289-4688

Take a guided 45-minute underground copper mine tour, deep into the bowels of the earth. On the grounds you'll see a mining museum, prehistoric mining pits, and the ruins of nineteenth-century mining buildings. May-October.

Fort Wilkins State Park
East US-41, Copper Harbor
906-289-4215

In addition to scenic drives, copper mine shafts, and the Copper Harbor lighthouse, the park houses the restored Fort Wilkins Historic Complex, built in 1844 as a U.S. Army post. The fort offers exhibits, period rooms, living history, and audio-visual displays. Open daily mid-May — mid-October.

Fayette

Historic Fayette Townsite
On CR-483, off US-2, Fayette State Park
Fayette (on Big Bay de Noc)
906-644-2603

Walk through the tall grass of this ghost town, once a thriving nineteenth-century iron smelting community. Restored buildings and modern exhibits tell the story of a town's rise and fall. Daily, June-August.

Iron Mountain

Iron Mountain Iron Mine
Nine miles east of Iron Mountain on US-2
906-563-8077

Experience iron mining. Ride an underground train through 2600 feet of underground drifts and tunnels, 400 feet below the earth's surface to see strange geological formations, and watch miners operate modern mining machinery. June-mid-October.

Mackinac Island

You can tour the island many different ways — by foot, bicycle, horse, or horse-drawn carriage — but never by car. Leave your car in Mackinaw City and take the 30-minute ferry ride to the island.

Old Fort Mackinac
Mackinac Island
906-847-3328

The 300-year old fort and its 14 restored buildings, including a blacksmith shop, church, Indian dormitory, sally ports, and houses, offer children a lesson in living history. Costumed guides demonstrate cooking, spinning, musket firings, canon salutes, and military music. June 15-September 5: 9 a.m.-6 p.m., daily. May 15-June 14 and September 6-October 18: 10 a.m.-4 p.m., daily.

Mackinaw City

While technically in the Lower Penninsula, Mackinaw City's location at the foot of the Mackinac Bridge makes it the gateway to the Upper Penninsula.

Colonial Michilimackinac
and Mackinaw Maritime
Park and Museum
Exit 339 off I-75 North, Mackinaw City
616-436-5563

Costumed staff and demonstrations make this reconstructed 1715 military outpost and fur trading village come to life. A small museum inside an old lighthouse exhibits nautical history. June 15-September 5: 9 a.m.-7 p.m., daily. May-June 14 and September 6-October 16: 9 a.m.-5 p.m., daily.

Old Mill Creek State Historic Park
US-23, Mackinaw City
616-436-7301

A working sawmill, craft demonstrations, costumed guides, picnic sites, nature trails, and overlooks mark the site of a 1780s sawmill and dam. Archaeological digs are in progress June 24-Labor Day. Park hours: June 15-September 5: 10 a.m.-7 p.m., daily. May 15-June 14 and September 6-October 16: 10 a.m.-4 p.m., daily.

Revolutionary War Sloop *Welcome*
Mackinaw City Marina, Mackinaw City
616-436-5563

Guides in authentic British Navy costumes take visitors on a tour of the reconstructed 1775 British sloop. 11 a.m.-7 p.m., daily, June 15-Labor Day.

Teysen's Woodland Indian Museum
416 South Huron Avenue, Mackinaw City
616-436-7011

Michigan Indian, fur trading, and lumber era artifacts. 9 a.m.-9 p.m., daily, May 1-October 25.

Paradise

Great Lakes Shipwreck Museum
North of Paradise on US-123
at Whitefish Point
906-635-1742

Shipwrecks never seemed so real or Lake Superior so frightening. This museum, located on the tip of a jutting bay, offers 170 years of shipwreck history in stunning displays and an evocative movie. 10 a.m.-6 p.m., daily, Memorial Day-October 15.

Tahquamenon Falls State Park
On SR-123, between Paradise
and Newberry
906-492-3415

Walk the trails of the Upper Falls and the Lower Falls and see the second largest waterfalls in North America (Niagara Falls is numero uno). Bring rain slickers; it seems to rain whenever we visit!

Pictured Rocks National Lakeshore

Children will not easily forget the crashing waves and jutting rock formations along the 42-mile Lake Superior shoreline that makes up Pictured Rocks National Lakeshore. Although there are several excellent lookouts, boat cruises offer the best view of the cliffs. Pictured Rocks Boat Cruises go out daily weather permitting. June: 10 a.m. and 2 p.m. July 1-August 31: 9 and 11 a.m., 1, 3, and 5 p.m. September-mid-October: 10 a.m. and 2 p.m. Call 906-387-2379 for reservations.

St. Ignace

Father Marquette
Memorial and Museum
Straits State Park
720 Church Street, St. Ignace
906-643-9394, 906-643-8620

Learn about Father Marquette and Michigan Indian life in state-of-the-art audio-visual exhibits. The park offers a great view of the Mackinac Bridge. 8 a.m.-8:30 p.m., daily, mid-June-Labor Day.

Marquette Mission Park and
Museum of Ojibwa Culture
500 N. State Street, St. Ignace
906-643-9161

An Indian longbarn shares a city corner with a small museum dedicated to chronicling the Ojibwa way of life. 11 a.m.-9 p.m., daily, Memorial Day-Labor Day. Reduced hours to mid-October.

Sault Ste. Marie

Soo Locks
St. Marys Falls Canal, Portage Avenue
Sault Ste. Marie
906-362-3311

An observation platform overlooks the world's busiest and largest locking system, first built in 1855. The Visitor Center houses a film about the locks, artifacts, and a working lock model. Park is open 6 a.m.-midnight, daily, in the summer. Visitor Center is open 7 a.m.-11 p.m., daily, May-November.

Soo Locks Boat Tours
Dock 1 at 1157 East Portage Avenue
Dock 2 at 500 East Portage Avenue
Sault Ste. Marie
906-632-6301

Two-hour narrated tours travel through the locks and pass the St. Mary's Rapids. July-August: 9 a.m.-7 p.m., daily. May 15-June 30 and September 1-October 15: 9 a.m.-5:30 p.m., daily.

Soo Locks Train Tours
317 West Portage Avenue, Sault Ste. Marie
906-635-5912

Tour (1¼ hour) describes historic sites along the 15-mile route. Departures every half hour, 9 a.m.-7:30 p.m., daily. Memorial Day-Labor Day.

S.S. *Valley Camp* and Marine Museum
Johnston and Water Streets, Sault Ste. Marie
906-632-3658

The world's largest Great Lakes maritime museum is housed in a massive Great Lakes freighter and includes aquariums, lifeboats from the sunken Edmund Fitzgerald, shipwreck displays, and other maritime displays. The Port Adventure complex includes a visitor center, picnic sites, marina, historic home park, and riverfront parks. July 1-August 31: 9 a.m.-8 p.m., daily. May 15-June 30 and September 1-October 15: 10 a.m.-5 p.m., daily.

Tower of History
Portage Avenue, Sault Ste. Marie
906-632-3658

Ride up 21 stories into Michigan's sky and see Michigan and Canadian wilderness for 20 miles in every direction from five observation platforms. Same hours as the S.S. *Valley Camp* and Marine Museum.

16
AREA LIBRARIES

Libraries are wonderful places to visit. You can borrow children's books, records, tapes and magazines for free and play with a variety of hands-on materials—puppets, puzzles, and filmstrips—while you're there. The Farmington Hills library even offers two creative wooden climbers for junior library patrons.

Most libraries offer year-round free children's activities including weekday storytimes, Saturday movies, holiday puppet shows, and summer reading programs.

Here is a listing of libraries in the tri-county area. While books and such may only be checked out by residents or those with reciprocal cities' library cards, most children's library programs are open to non-residents. Be sure to call ahead if programs require registration.

Allen Park Public Library
8100 Allen Road
313-381-2425

Ann Arbor Public Library (3 branches)
343 South Fifth Avenue
313-994-2333

Auburn Hills Public Library
1827 North Squirrel Road
313-370-9466

**Belleville—Fred C. Fischer
Memorial Library**
167 Fourth Street
313-699-3291

Berkley Public Library
3155 Coolidge Highway
313-542-3393

Birmingham—Baldwin Public Library
300 West Merrill Street
313-647-1700

**Bloomfield Hills—Bloomfield Township
Public Library**
1099 Lone Pine Road
313-642-5800

Brighton Public Library
200 North First Street
313-229-6571

Canton Public Library
1150 South Canton Center Road
313-397-0999

Chelsea—McKune Memorial Library
321 South Main Street
313-475-8732

Clarkston—Independence Township Library
6495 Clarkston Road
313-625-2212

Clawson—Blair Memorial Library
416 North Main Street
313-588-5500

Davisburg—Springfield Township Library
10900 Andersonville Road
313-625-0595

**Dearborn—Henry Ford Centennial Library
(3 branches)**
16301 Michigan Avenue
313-943-2330

Dearborn Heights—Caroline Kennedy Library
24590 George Street
313-277-7762

**Dearborn Heights—John F. Kennedy Jr.
Library**
24602 Van Born Road
313-277-7764

**Detroit Public Library—Children's Library
(25 branches)**
5201 Woodward
313-833-1490

East Detroit Memorial Library
15875 Oak Street
313-445-5095

East Lansing Public Library
950 Abbott Road
517-351-2420

Farmington Community Library
23500 Liberty
313-474-7770

Farmington Hills Community Library
32737 West Twelve Mile Road
313-553-0300

Ferndale Public Library
222 East Nine Mile Road
313-548-5959

Flint Public Library (6 branches)
1026 East Kearsley Street
313-232-7399

Franklin Public Library
32455 Franklin Road
313-851-2254

Garden City Public Library
2012 Middlebelt Road
313-525-8854

Grosse Pointe Public Library (2 branches)
10 Kercheval
313-343-2074

Hamtramck Public Library
2360 Caniff
313-365-7050

Harper Woods Public Library
19601 Harper
313-343-2575

Hazel Park Memorial Library
123 East Nine Mile Road
313-542-0940

Highland Park—McGregor Public Library
12244 Woodward Avenue
313-883-4542

Highland Township Library
205 West Livingston
313-887-2218

Holly Township Library
1116 North Saginaw Street
313-634-7331

Huntington Woods Public Library
26415 Scotia Road
313-543-9720

Inkster Public Library
2005 Inkster Road
313-563-1144

Lake Orion Township Public Library
845 South Lapeer Road
313-693-1888

Lansing Public Library (1 branch)
401 South Capitol Avenue
517-374-4058

Lincoln Park Public Library
1381 Southfield Road
313-381-0374

Livonia Public Library (2 branches)
32901 Plymouth Road
313-421-6600

Madison Heights Public Library
240 West Thirteen Mile Road
313-588-1200

Milford Township Library
1100 Atlantic Street
313-684-0845

Monroe County Library System (16 branches)
3700 South Custer Road
313-241-5277

Mount Clemens Public Library
150 Cass Avenue
313-469-6200

Northville Public Library
215 West Main Street
313-349-3020

Novi Public Library
45245 Ten Mile Road
313-349-0720

Oak Park Public Library
14200 Oak Park Boulevard
313-548-7230

Pickney Community Public Library
122 Howell Street
313-878-3888

Plymouth—Dunning-Hough Public Library
223 South Main Street
313-453-0750

Pontiac Public Library
60 East Pike Street
313-857-7167

**Port Huron—St. Clair County Library System
(10 branches)**
210 McMorran Boulevard
313-987-7323

Rochester Hills Public Library
210 West University Drive
313-656-2900

Romeo District Library
107 Church Street
313-752-2291

Romulus Public Library
11121 Wayne Road
313-942-7589

Roseville Public Library
29777 Gratiot
313-777-6012

Royal Oak Public Library
222 East Eleven Mile Road
313-541-1470

St. Clair Shores Public Library
22500 Eleven Mile Road
313-771-9020

Southfield Public Library
26000 Evergreen Road
313-354-9100

South Lyon Public Library
318 West Lake Street
313-437-6431

Sterling Heights Public Library
40255 Dodge Park Road
313-977-6270

Taylor Community Public Library
12303 Pardee
313-287-4840

Trenton Veterans Memorial Library
2790 Westfield
313-676-9777

Troy Public Library
510 West Big Beaver
313-524-3535

Utica Public Library
7530 Auburn Road
313-731-4141

Walled Lake City Library
1499 E. West Maple Road
313-624-3772

Warren Public Library (5 branches)
5951 Beebe Street
313-264-8720

Waterford Township Public Library
5168 Tubbs Road
313-674-4831

West Bloomfield Public Library (1 branch)
4600 Walnut Lake Road
313-682-2120

Wyandotte—Bacon Memorial Public Library
45 Vinewood
313-282-7660

Ypsilanti District Library
229 West Michigan
313-482-4110

17
MAPS

The maps in this chapter are intended as general guides to the area. Maps of the cities of Detroit, Windsor, Ann Arbor, Flint, and Lansing show the location of some of the highlights of these cities.

State of Michigan

Five County / Southeastern Lower Michigan

Downtown Detroit

1. Bonstelle Theatre
2. Cobo Hall and Arena
3. Detroit Free Press
4. Detroit News
5. Detroit-Windsor Tunnel
6. Eastern Market
7. Fox Theatre
8. Greektown
9. Hart Plaza
10. Joe Louis Arena
11. Masonic Temple
12. Music Hall
13. Orchestra Hall
14. Renaissance Center
15. Star of Detroit Cruises
16. Tiger Stadium
17. Trapper's Alley
18. Trolley
19. Underground Railroad–
    Second Baptist Church

Cultural Center / New Center

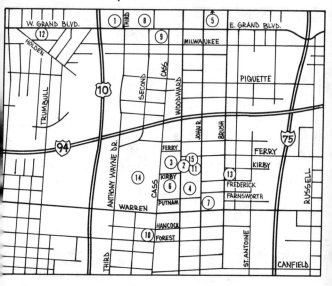

1. Attic Theatre
2. Children's Museum
3. Detroit Historical Museum
4. Detroit Institute of Arts
5. Detroit Police Horse Stables
6. Detroit Public Library
7. Detroit Science Center
8. Fisher Building
9. GM Building
10. Hilberry Theatre
11. International Institute
12. Motown Museum
13. Museum of African American History
14. Wayne State University
15. Your Heritage House

Southern Ontario

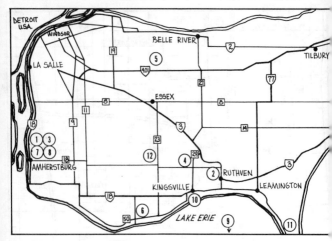

1. Amherstburg Boblo Dock
2. Colasanti's Gardens
3. Fort Malden National Historic Park
4. Jack Miner Bird Sanctuary
5. John Freeman Walls Historic Site
6. John R. Park Homestead
7. North American Black Historical Museum
8. Park House Museum
9. Pelee Island
10. Pelee Island Winery
11. Point Pelee
12. Southwestern Ontario Heritage Village

Windsor

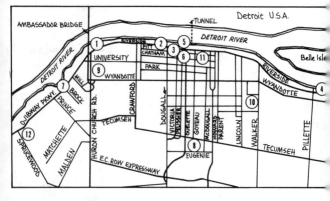

1. Ambassador Park
2. Art Gallery of Windsor
3. Cleary Auditorium
4. Coventry Gardens/Peace Fountain
5. Dieppe Gardens
6. Hiram Walker Historical Museum
7. MacKensie Hall
8. Queen Elizabeth Gardens
9. University of Windsor
10. Willistead Manor
11. Windsor City Market
12. Windsor Raceway

Ann Arbor

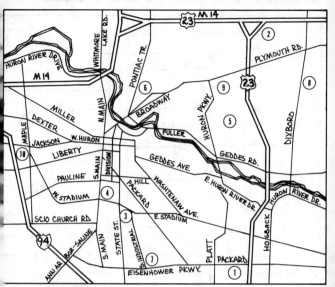

1. Cobblestone Farm
2. Domino's Farms
3. Ecology Center
4. Michigan Stadium
5. Phoenix Memorial Lab
6. Project Grow—Leslie
   Science Center
7. Scrap Box
8. U of M Matthei Botanical
   Gardens
9. U of M Music School—
   Stearns Collection of
   Musical Instruments
10. Veterans Park

Downtown Ann Arbor / U of M Campus

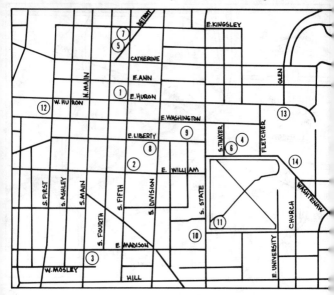

1. Ann Arbor Hands-On Museum
2. Ann Arbor Public Library
3. Ark
4. Burton Memorial Tower
5. Farmers' Market
6. Hill Auditorium
7. Kerrytown Plaza
8. Liberty Plaza
9. Michigan Theater
10. Michigan Union
11. Museum of Art
12. Performance Network
13. Power Center
14. U of M Exhibit Museum

Greater Flint Area

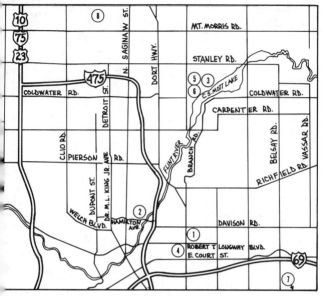

AC Spark Plug Tour
Buick City Tour
Crossroads Village /
Huckleberry Railroad
Cultural Center

5. Mott Farm
6. Penny Whistle Place
7. Symanzik's Berry Farm
8. Wolcott Orchards

Downtown Flint

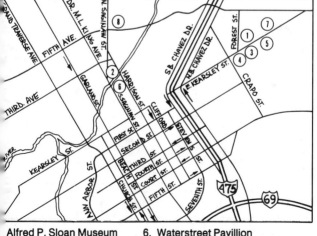

Alfred P. Sloan Museum
Children's Museum
Flint Institute of Arts
Library
Longway Planetarium

6. Waterstreet Pavillion
7. Whiting Auditorium—Youth
   Theater
8. Windmill Place

Greater Lansing Area

1. Abrams Planetarium
2. Carl E. Fenner Arboretum
3. Horticultural Gardens
4. Kresge Art Museum
5. Lorann Oils
6. Michigan Union
7. MSU Museum of Natural History
8. Potter Park Zoo

Downtown Lansing

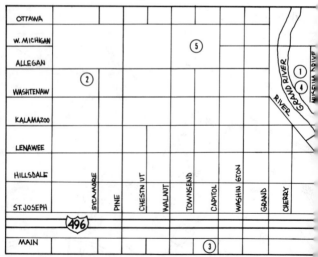

1. Impression 5 Museum
2. Michigan Historical Museum
3. Michigan Women's Historical Center and Hall of Fame
4. R.E. Olds Transportation Museum
5. State Capitol

CITY LISTING

Sites and programs described in this book are listed below by the city in which they are located.

MICHIGAN

Acme
Music House

Ada
Amway Corporation

Adrian
Croswell Opera House

Ann Arbor
Ann Arbor Farmers' Market
Ann Arbor Folk Marionettes
Ann Arbor Hands-On Museum
Ann Arbor Parks and Recreation Junior
   Theatre
Ann Arbor Parks and Recreation Mini Matinee
   Club
The Ark
Burton Memorial Tower
Cobblestone Farm
Dance Focus
Delhi Metropark
Domino's Farms
Ecology Center of Ann Arbor
Gallup Park Livery
Gemini
Kerrytown Plaza
Leslie Science Center
Little Dipper Shoppe
Michigan Theater
Museum of Art
Performance Network
Phoenix Memorial Laboratory
Power Center
Project Grow
Scrap Box
Stearns Collection of Musical Instruments
University of Michigan Exhibit Museum
University of Michigan Exhibit Museum
   Planetarium
University of Michigan Matthaei Botanical
   Gardens
University of Michigan Wolverines

Veteran's Park
Wild Swan Theatre
Yost Ice Arena
Young People's Theater

Armada
Blake's Big Apple Orchard
Blake's Orchard and Cider Mill

Auburn Heights
Michigan Humane Society-North

Auburn Hills
Detroit Pistons Basketball
Oakland County Care Center
The Palace
The Palace Gardens

Augusta
Kellogg Bird Sanctuary

Bangor
Kalamazoo Toy Train Factory

Battle Creek
Binder Park Zoo
Kingman Museum of Natural History
McCamly Place

Bay City
Historical Museum of Bay County
Jennison Nature Center

Belleville
Lower Huron Metropark
Pumpkin Factory
Thornhollow Berry Farms

Berkley
Berkley Ice Arena
Colors

Berville
Great Lakes Herpetological Society

Birmingham
Baldwin Public Library
Birmingham-Bloomfield Symphony Orchestra
Birmingham Community House
Birmingham Ice Sports Arena
Birmingham Theatre
Forum for Art
Shaine Park Concerts

Bloomfield Hills
E.L. Johnson Nature Center
Charles L. Bowers Farm
Cranbrook Academy of Art Museum
Cranbrook House and Garden
Cranbrook Institute of Science
Cranbrook Institute of Science Planetarium
Cranbrook Summer Children's Theatre

Bridgeport
Junction Valley Railroad

Brighton
Huron Meadows Metropark
Island Lake Recreation Area
Mt. Brighton Ski Area

Brooklyn
Michigan International Speedway
Walker Tavern Historic Complex

Carleton
Calder Brothers Dairy Farm

Chelsea
Waterloo Geology Center

Clarkston
Hillside Farm
Independence Oaks
Indian Springs Metropark
Pine Knob Music Theatre
Pine Knob Ski Resort

Clawson
Detroit Sign Company—Deaf Theater
Stevens and Associates

Clinton
Southern Michigan Railroad

Coloma
Deer Forest

Colon
Abbott's Magic Manufacturing Company

Copper Harbor
Brockaway Mountain Drive
Delaware Copper Mine
Fort Wilkins State Park

Croswell
Croswell Swinging Bridge

Davisburg
Davisburg Candle Factory
Springfield Oaks
Dearborn
Adray Ice Arena
Arab-American Folk Museum
Cherry Hill Lanes
Dearborn Historical Museum: McFadden Ross
    House and Exhibit Annex
Dearborn Trolley Company
Greenfield Village
Greenfield Vilage Theatre Company
Henry Ford Estate-Fairlane
Henry Ford Museum
Martinsville Cider Mill
University of Michigan-Dearborn
    Environmental Study Area
Dearborn Heights
Warren Valley Golf Course
Detroit
Adams Ice-Skating Arena
Ambassador Bridge
Anna Scripps Whitcomb Conservatory
Arts and Scraps
Atlantis Expedition
Attic Theatre
Belle Isle
Belle Isle Aquarium
Belle Isle Canoe Livery
Belle Isle Nature Center
Belle Isle Zoo
Blue Pigs
Boblo Island
Bonstelle Theatre
Brunch with Bach
Chene Park
Children's Museum
Children's Museum Planetarium
Clark Park
Cobo Arena
Cobo Hall
Detroit Center for the Performing Arts
Detroit Department of Transportation
Detroit Drive!

Detroit Edison—School Safety Coordinator
Detroit Fire Department Historical Museum
Detroit Historical Museum
Detroit Institute of Arts
Detroit Police Horse Stables
Detroit Public Library—Children's Library
Detroit Recreation Puppeteers
Detroit Red Wings
Detroit Science Center
Detroit Symphony Orchestra
Detroit Tigers
Detroit Trolley
Detroit Turbos
Detroit Water Department—Springwells Water
   Plant
Detroit-Windsor Tunnel
Detroit Youtheatre
Dossin Great Lakes Museum
Eastern Market
Fisher Building
Fisher Mansion/Bhaktivedanta Center
Fisher Theatre
Fox Theatre
GM Building
Great Lakes Indian Museum
Greektown
Hart Plaza
Hilberry Theatre
Historic Fort Wayne
International Institute
Joe Louis Arena
Madame Cadillac Dancers
Masonic Temple
Michigan Opera Theatre
Michigan Sports Hall of Fame
Motown Museum
Museum of African American History
Music Hall
National Museum of Tuskegee Airmen
Officer Ollie and Friends
Orchestra Hall
Palmer Park
Peanut Butter Players
Pewabic Pottery
Piccolo Opera Company
Renaissance Center

St. Aubin Park
Star of Detroit Cruises
State Fairgrounds
Sutton's Candy
Trapper's Alley Festival Marketplace
Underground Railroad-Second Baptist Church
University of Detroit Titans
Wayne State University Tartars
Young Audiences, Inc.
Your Heritage House

Dexter
Dexter Area Museum
Dexter Cider Mill
Dexter-Huron Metropark
Hudson Mills Metropark
Lakeview Farm and Cider Mill
Spring Valley Trout Farm

Drayton Plains
Drayton Plains Nature Center

Dryden
Seven Ponds Nature Center

East Lansing
Abrams Planetarium
Horticultural Gardens
Kresge Art Museum
Michigan State University Museum of Natural
    History
Michigan State University Spartans
Michigan State Veterinary School Vet-A-Visit

Erie
Erie Orchards and Cider Mill
Langerderfer Poultry Farm

Farmington Hills
Bonaventure Roller Skating Center
Farmington Community Center—Family
    Dessert Theater
Glen Oaks
Harbinger Dance Company
Marvin's Marvelous Mechanical Museum and
    Emporium
Mercy Center Pool
Putt-Putt Golf and Games
Smith Theatre

Fayette
Historic Fayette Townsite

Fenton
Hilltop Orchards and Cider Mill
Peabody Orchards
Wallace Smith Productions Touring Chamber
    Theatre

Ferndale
Storybuilders

Flat Rock
Flat Rock Speedway
Oakwoods Metropark

Flint
AC Spark Plug Tour
Alfred P. Sloan Museum
Buick City Tour
Children's Museum
Crossroads Village Cider Mill
Crossroads Village/Huckleberry Railroad
Flint Institute of Arts
Flint Youth Theatre
Longway Planetarium
Michigan Humane Society-Genesse County
Mott Farm
Penny Whistle Place

Frankenmuth
Antique Auto Village
Frankenmuth Flour Mill and General Store
Holz-Brucke and Woodcarvers' Pavilion

Franklin
Franklin Cider Mill

Fraser
Liberty Bowl

Fremont
Gerber Products Company

Garden City
Garden City Ice Arena
Maplewood Family Theatre

Gaylord
Bavarian Falls Park
Call of the Wild Museum

Goodelles
Ruby Farms
Goodrich
Symanzik's Berry Farm
Grand Haven
Harbor Steamer
Harbor Trolley
Tri-Cities Museum
Waterfront Stadium
Grand Rapids
Bissel, Inc.
Blandford Nature Center
Fish Ladder Sculpture
Gerald Ford Museum
Grand Rapids Art Museum
Grand Rapids Public Museum
Grand Rapids Zoological Gardens
Gypsum Mine Tour
Roger B. Chafee Planetarium
Splash—Family Water Park
Grayling
Hartwick Pines State Park
Gregory
DeGroot's Strawberries
Grosse Pointe
Grosse Pointe Children's Theatre
Grosse Pointe Shores
Edsel and Eleanor Ford House

Hamtramck
Veterans Memorial Park
Harbor Springs
Chief Blackbird Museum
Hastings
Charleton Park Historic Village
Hazel Park
Hazel Park Raceway
Highland
Ridgemere Berry Farm
Highland Park
Sander's Inc.

Holland
Brook Beverages Plant
Deklomp Wooden Shoe and Delftware Factory
    and Veldheer Tulip Garden
Dutch Village
Windmill Island
Wooden Shoe Factory

Holly
Diehl's Orchard and Cider Mill
Groveland Oaks Waterslide
Michigan Renaissance Festival
Mt. Holly, Inc.

Huron Township
Willow Metropark

Ida
Stotz's Pumpkin Farm

Inkster
Inkster Civic Arena

Iron Mountain
Iron Mountain Iron Mine

Jackson
Ella Sharp Museum
Illuminated Cascades
Michigan Space Center

Kalamazoo
Kalamazoo Aviation History Museum
Kalamazoo Institute of Arts
Kalamazoo Nature Center
Kalamazoo Public Museum and Planetarium
Scott's Mill Park
Train Barn
Upjohn Pharmaceutical Company

Lake Orion
Bald Mountain Recreation Area
Goodison Cider Mill
Middleton Berry Farm
Spezia's Strawberries

Lansing
Carl F. Fenner Arboretum
Impression 5 Museum

Lorann Oils, Inc.
Michigan Historical Museum
Michigan Women's Historical Center and Hall
   of Fame
Potter Park Zoo
R.E. Olds Transportation Museum
State Capitol
Lathrup Village
Lathrup Youtheatre—Lathrup Village Parks
   and Recreation
Lexington
Lexington Marina
Lincoln Park
Lincoln Park Community Center
Livonia
Devon-Aire Arena
Eddie Edgar Arena
Greenmead Museum and Historical Village
Ladbroke Detroit Race Course
Mobile Ed Productions

Mackinac Island
Old Fort Mackinac
Mackinaw City
Colonial Michilimackinac and Mackinaw Mari-
   time Park and Museum
Old Mill Creek State Historic Park
Revolutionary War Sloop *Welcome*
Teysen's Woodland Indian Museum
Madison Heights
Astro Lanes
Red Oaks Golf Dome and Sports Village
Red Oaks Waterpark
Marine City
Lucy's Livery
Marshall
American Museum of Magic
Cornwell's Turkey House
Melvindale
Melvindale Ice Arena
Midland
Automotive Hall of Fame
Chippewa Nature Center
Dow Gardens

Dow Visitor's Center
Midland Center for the Arts

Milford
Alpine Valley
Heavner's Canoe and Cross Country Ski Rent-
    als
Highland Recreation Area
Kensington Metropark
Kensington Nature Center and Farm Center
Proud Lake Recreation Area
Strawberry Patch

Monroe
Monroe County Historical Museum
Monroe Farmer's Market
Navarre-Anderson Trading Post and Country
    Store Museum
Sterling State Park

Mount Clemens
C.J. Barrymore's Sports Center
Crocker House
Daren Dundee, Entertainer
Macomb Center for the Performing Arts
Marino Sports Center, Inc.
Metro Beach Metropark
Metropolitan Beach Putt-Putt
Mount Clemens Farmers' Market
Mount Clemens Train Ride
Recreation Bowl
Selfridge Military Air Museum
WhirlyBall of Michigan

Mount Morris
Wolcott Orchards

Munising
Pictured Rocks National Lakeshore
Pictured Rocks Boat Cruises

Muskegon
E. Genevieve Gillette Nature Center
Hackley and Hume Historic Site
Michigan's Adventure Amusement Park
Muskegon County Museum
Muskegon Museum of Art
Muskegon Trolley Company
Pleasure Island Water Fun Park

Port City Princess
U.S.S. Silversides

New Baltimore
Stahl's Bakery
New Boston
Pumpkin Patch
New Hudson
Michigan Waterworld
Newport
Fermi 2 Power Plant
Northville
Alfonse Jacques Farm
Foreman Orchard and Cider Mill
Guernsey Farm Dairy
Marquis Theatre
Maybury State Park Petting Farm
Meyer Berry Farm
Mill Race Historical Village
Northville Downs
Parmeter Cider Mill

Novi
Ella Mae Power Park
Living Science Foundation
Novi Parks and Recreation Special Events
Willowbrook Farms

Oak Park
Compuware-Oak Park Arena
Jewish Community Center
Oak Park Family Entertainment Series
Onstead (Irish Hills)
Eisenhower Presential Car
Prehistoric Forest
Stagecoach Stop, U.S.A.
Orchard Lake
Orchard Lake Boats and Windsurfing
Ortonville
Cook's Farm Dairy
Silver Saddle Hay and Sleigh Rides
Silver Saddle Riding Stable

Owosso
Curwood Castle

Oxford
Addison Oaks
Upland Hills Farm

Paradise
Great Lakes Shipwreck Museum
Tahquamenon Falls State Park

Paw Paw
St. Julian Winery
Warner Wine Haus

Petoskey
American Spoon Foods Kitchen
Kilwins Candy Kitchens, Inc.
Little Traverse Historic Museum
Pirate's Cove Adventure Golf

Pinckney
Hell Creek Ranch

Pinconning
Deer Acres Storybook Amusement Park

Plymouth
Oasis Golf/Tru-Pitch Batting Cages
Plymouth Farmers' Market
Plymouth Historical Museum
Plymouth Orchards and Cider Mill
Roy Schultz

Pontiac
Bald Mountain Riding Stables
Detroit Lions, Inc.
Lakeland Ice Arena
Pine Grove Historical Museum
Pontiac Farmers' Market
Pontiac Lake Recreation Area
Pontiac Silverdome
Sun and Ski Marina
Waterford Oaks Wave Pool and Waterslide
White Lake Oaks

Port Austin
Huron City Museum
Sanilac Petroglyphs

Port Huron
Blue Water International Bridge
Fort Gratiot Lighthouse
Lakeport State Park

Mary Maxim, Inc.
Museum of Art and History
Port Sanilac
Port Sanilac Historical Museum

Ray Township
Wolcott Mill Metropark
Redford
Bell Creek Park and Lola Valley Park
Crossroad Productions
Riverview
Riverview Highlands Ski Area
Rochester
Bloomer State Park
Concerts for Youth, Oakland University Center
   for the Arts
Detroit Lions Training Camp
Dinosaur Hill Nature Preserve and Den
Leader Dog for the Blind
Meadow Brook Hall and Knole Cottage
Meadow Brook Music Festival
Meadow Brook Theatre
Middleton Cider Mill
O'Neill Pottery
Paint Creek Mill
Rochester Cider Mill
Sherwood Forest
Wright and Filippis, Inc.
Yates Cider Mill
Rochester Hills
Rochester Hills Museum at Van Hoosen Farm
Rockwood
Lake Erie Metropark Wave Pool
Romeo
Hy's Cider Mill
Romeo Horse Drawn Hayrides
Stony Creek Orchard and Cider Mill
Royal Oak
Captain's Cove Adventure Golf
Detroit Audubon Society
Detroit Dance Collective
Detroit Zoological Park
Grand Slam Baseball Training Center
John Lindell Ice Arena

Royal Oak Farmers' Market
Royal Oak Putt-Putt
Stagecrafters Youth Theatre
Starlight Archery Co.
Starr-Jaycee Park Train
Superior Fish Co., Inc.

Saginaw
Anderson Water Park
Green Point Nature Center
Japanese Cultural Center and Tea House
Saginaw Art Museum
Saginaw Children's Zoo
Saginaw Water Works

St. Clair Shores
Great Lakes Yachts
Home Plate Sports Center
St. Clair Shores Civic Center

St. Ignace
Father Marquette Memorial and Museum
Marquette Mission Park and Museum of
   Ojibwa Culture

St. Johns
Uncle John's Cider Mill

Saugatuck
Queen of Saugatuck Boat Cruises
Saugatuck Dune Rides

Sault Ste. Marie
Soo Locks
Soo Locks Boat Tours
Soo Locks Train Tours
S.S. Valley Camp and Marine Museum
Tower of History

Southfield
BABES
Beech Woods Recreation Center
Chamber Music for Youth
Channel 50 WKBD
Dolls for Democracy
Kids Koncerts, Southfield Parks and Recre-
   ation
Scheer Magic Productions
Southfield Civic Center-Evergreen Hills
Southfield Sports Arena

TV 2 WJBK
Weatherschool-TV 2

Southgate
Ted's Southgate Golf Center

South Lyon
Erwin Orchards

Sterling Heights
Freedom Hill
Sterling Heights Nature Center

Stockbridge
Dewey School
Waterloo Area Farm Museum

Tecumseh
Chocolate Vault

Tipton
Hidden Lake Gardens

Traverse City
Ammon's Orchard Tours
Candle Factory
Clinch Park Zoo and Con Foster Museum
Pirate's Cove Adventure Golf

Trenton
Belmar II
Elizabeth Park
Kennedy Ice Rink

Troy
Art Castle
Bowl One
Lloyd A. Stage Outdoor Education Center
Skateworld of Troy
Troy Family Playhouse
Troy Museum and Historic Village Green

Utica
Denewith's Pick Your Own Strawberry Farms
Four Bears Water Park
Rick's Puppet Theater
Rochester-Utica Recreation Area

Vanderbilt
Project Nature

Walled Lake
Coe Rail

Warren
Big Boy Warehouse
Regal Lanes
Starlight Archery Co.
Universal Lanes
Van Dyke Sport Center

Washington
Altermatt's Farm
Johnny Appleseed Cider Mill
Leo Hellebuyck Farm
Stony Creek Metropark

Waterford
Dodge No. 4 State Park
Pine Lake Marina

West Bloomfield
Holocaust Memorial Museum
Jewish Community Center
Plaster Playhouse
Puppets in the Park
West Bloomfield Lanes
West Bloomfield Parks and Recreation
  Concerts

Westland
Michigan Humane Society-West
Sport-Way
Westland Multi-Purpose Arena
William P. Holliday Forest and Wildlife
  Preserve

Woodhaven
Skateworld of Woodhaven

Wyandotte
Yack Arena

Ypsilanti
Depot Town Caboose
Makielski Berry Farm
Quirk Theatre
Ray Schultz Farm
Rowe's Produce Farm
Wizard's Orchards
Yankee Air Force Museum
Ypsilanti Farmers' Market

Ypsilanti Historical Society and Museum

SOUTHERN ONTARIO

Amherstburg
Fort Malden National Historic Park
Navy Yard Park
North American Black Historical Museum
Park House Museum

Essex
John R. Park Homestead
Southwestern Ontario Heritage Village

Kingsville
Jack Miner Bird Sanctuary
Pelee Island Cruises
Pelee Island Winery

Leamington
Pelee Island Cruises
Point Pelee National Park

Maidstone Township
John Freeman Walls Historic Site

Ruthven
Colasanti's Tropical Gardens

Sandwich
MacKenzie Hall Children's Concert Series—
    "The Peanut Gallery"

Sarnia
Kiwanis Children's Farm

Tecumseh
Sports Afield 2

Windsor
Art Gallery of Windsor
Cleary Auditorium
Coventry Gardens and Peace Fountain
Hiram Walker Historical Museum
Queen Elizabeth II Gardens
Willstead Manor
Windsor City Market
Windsor Raceway
Windsor Symphony Orchestra

THANK YOU, THANK YOU!

The artwork appearing on the Chapter openings was created by the following area students:

Chapter 1: Lori Kauffman, Detroit, Hillel Day School, grade 6.

Chapter 2: Benjamin Senopole, St. Clair Shores, James Rodgers Elementary, grade 5.

Chapter 3: Anne Jeannette LaSovage, Detroit, Burton International, grade 8.

Chapter 4: Courtney Rose, West Bloomfield, Doherty Elementary, grade 2.

Chapter 5: Philip Jackson, Lansing, Post Oak Elementary, grade 5.

Chapter 6: Owen B. Simmons, Southfield, Schoenhals Elementary, grade 4.

Chapter 7: Kyle Willette, Novi, Novi Woods Elementary, grade 4.

Chapter 8: Andrea Muzzin, Trenton, Owen Elementary, grade 5.

Chapter 9: Tiffany Miller, Dearborn, Henry Ford Elementary, grade 4.

Chapter 10: Suzy Housey, Troy, St. Hugo of the Hills, grade 5.

Chapter 11: Steve Gill, Farmington Hills, Forest Elementary, grade 5.

Chapter 12: Jeffrey Krause, Birmingham, Meadow Lake Elementary, grade 1.

Chapter 13: Mike Kegler, Grosse Pointe Woods, Ferry Elementary, grade 5.

Chapter 14: Andrew Wilkes-Krier, Ann Arbor, Burns Park Elementary, grade 4.

Chapter 15: Courtney Brown, Rochester, Meadow Brook Elementary, grade 3.

Chapter 16: Hakim Chappelle, Detroit, Davison Elementary, grade 5.

Chapter 17: Angela Oliver, Warren, Cromie Elementary, grade 5.

I'd also like to thank the following students and their art teachers for participating in the Detroit Kids Catalog Art Contest. (Students are listed according to the school they attended in spring 1989.)

Burns Park Elementary, Ann Arbor (teacher, Pat Jakunas): Andrew Cohen.

Burton International School, Detroit (teacher, Peggy Morrison): Arlyn Sartre, Belynda Black, Athena Byron, Ethan Gilbert, Heidi Letzman, Jennifer Lawson, Kiran Gill, Julian Battle, Sterling Toles, Meaghan Atkinson, Natalie Stinson, Michelle Rowland, Polly Weiss, Steve Herzberg, Titiena Swan, Vanessa Nieson.

Cromie Elementary, Warren (teacher, Sally Miller): Denise Manofsky, Eric Cronander, Andrea Rosik, Erin Shaughnessy, Heather Adkins, Jackie Birch, Mihaela Popescu, Jeremy Mazak, Rob Giese, Mike Madigan, Thomas Bilello, Nicole Gentry, Robbie Thomas, Ryan Ares.

Davison Elementary, Detroit (teacher, Rhonda Music): Cindy Flournoy, Melinda Hightower, Dondrele McFarland, Yolanda Phillips, JuJuana Johnson, Malik Chapelle.

Doherty Elementary, West Bloomfield (teacher, Linda Gold): Beverly Betel, Scott Hammond, Loren Gorosh, Julie Gold, Nick Bickes.

Ferry Elementary, Grosse Pointe (teacher, Bev Smith): Carla Pellegrino, David Dwaihy, Albert Ellis, Beth Ginger, Ilango Thirumoorthi, Jason Popham, Devan Kent, Aldo Giglio, Becky Owens, Carolyn Baiocchi, Jeff Basta, Heather Brys, Audrene Apostolos, Julie Paauola, Karin Linthorst, Kelly Kielbowicz, Melissa Palombit, Craig Hadgis, Brendan Rauss, Alex Ganum, Argie Floyd, Chris Holloway, Joseph Thompson, Fred Alvarado, Andy Picel, Evan Rouls, Emily Herodote,

Armand Bove, Joe Ahee, Chris Eder, Bob Knopf, Bradford Wheeler, Emily McLalin, Liisa Bergmann, Justin Matthews, Eric Bonten, Patricia Milne, Elizabeth Lloyd, Douglass Sul, Paul Mooney, Rochelle Bartos, Vicki Schenk, Nick Pennpage, Emily Forrest, Timothy John Peters, Michael Fine, Kathy Esselink, Lee Bryant, Jennifer Augustin, Christie Range, Becky Iskenderian, Karin Linthorst, Robin Breckenridge, Rachele Keller, Troy Bergman, Armando Apess, Ross Williams, Roberta Langlois, Katie Daniels, Lisa Unger, Lindsay Simmon, Michael Peters, Speros Dionysopoulos, Suzanne Foreman, Kim Loman, Megan Moore, Brian Bledsoe, Joe Arnone, Mark Holcomb, Nathan Wydick, Peter Torrice, Rebecca Shulman, Tammy Hendel, Steve Dube, Julia Damaha, Carolyn Pruitt, Carly Kovalcik Blagdurn, Krista Mackstaller, Mark Kelly, Peter Marks, Scott Grajek, Shane Strehler, Melissa Hirth.

Forest Elementary, Farmington Hills (teacher, Diane Russell): Jeff Leon, Gregory Evanelista, Aaron Scheinker, Mike Newman, Brad Schneider, Dayna Swarin, Ernesto Segura, Mike Tseng.

Henry Ford Elementary, Dearborn (teachers, April Beneck and Nancy Findlay): Steven Hudson, Andrew Urbiel, Chris Barretto, Michael Sinuk, Margaret Brozda, Erica Freud, Tonya Akins, Aneta Siedlecki, Karry Lips, Sandy Akins, Anna Brozda, Lane Moore, Ryan Bandy, Sakne Srour.

Hillel Day School, Farmington Hills (teacher, Carol Knoll): Ted Goodman, Karen Shalom, Jordan Field, Ami Goldfein, Elly Berger, Ilyse Broder, Owen Alterman, Maytal Samir, David Lanxner, Marah Berris, Jeremy Spoon, Laura Lubetsky, Matt Citrin.

Meadow Brook Elementary, Rochester (teacher, Julius Kusey): Beverly Emmerick, Christina Karas, Jessica Morrow, Todd Herman, Paul Etzkorn, Jennifer Nelem, Athena Leventis, Diana Pancotto, Megan Rogers, Debra Ponton, Julia Katz, Nicholas DePolo.

Meadow Lake Elementary, Birmingham (teacher, Joan Figas): David Binkley, Matt Shapiro, Alia Ahmad, Janet Yang, Debra Kim, Elaine Leung, Jason Hare, Rishi Arora, Nicole Midenberg, Brian E. Koncius, Hal DeLongchamp, Jessica Mordaunt, Jordan Winokur.

Novi Woods Elementary, Novi (teacher, Jennifer Marion): Garrett Brown, Adam Sunberg, Steve Heslip, David Galido, Sarah Park, Kimberly Lahti, Lydia Raburn, Bryan Hill, Chris Hanson, Miranda La Pan, Sophie Liao.

Owen Elementary, Trenton (teacher, Connie Cavalcante): Danny Davis, Mike Cook, Danielle Munroe, Erica Ligeski, Danny Southerby, Nicholas Watson, Scott Weston, Darin Johns, David Swenson, Rachel Quinlan, Kristy Crofut.

Post Oak Elementary, Lansing (teacher, Janet Shumaker): Mark Lucas, Veronica Salas, Brian Colon, Chris Crystal Weber, Estella Luceal Jones, Geoff McNeil, Michael Gonzales, Star De Leon, Amy Buzzitta, Antione Benson, Chris Prince, Josh Jacobsen, Sarah Williams, Shiranda Martin, Gretchen Smith, James Pyle, Starr Marie Benavides, Monique Adsit, Dan Easton, Crystal Diaz, Sandra J. Kangas, Roslyn Brown, Robyn Lovell, Ashley Taylor, Brandy Martin, Ben Diaz, Steve Borough, Roger Wickerham, Meng Xiong, John Delgado, David H. Serotkin, Erika Nelson, Joseph Crowe, Phillip Morse, Jenny Kangas, Keith Edwards, Louis Gagnon, Kha-Lihan Cross.

Rogers Elementary, St. Clair Shores (teacher, Donald Dierkes): Donald Hazel, Jeffrey Harper, Brian Neville.

Schoenhals Elementary, Southfield (teachers, Bob Crane, Carolyn Tarzyrski, Mary Kargillis): Sonia Jabiro, Eugene Zolotarevsky, Brian Williams, Dena Shammami, Fario Arabo, Tiwanna DeMoss, Jennie Collett Parchmon, Sylvia Cholak, Johnnie Wilson, Jamie Tunick, Kendrah Palk.

St. Hugo of the Hills, Bloomfield Hills (teacher, Lurlene Walls): Alissa Arnold, Lynsey Kearis, Matt Jannausch, David Reyes, Sharon Agacinski, Andrea Cuskie, Mike Shannon, Robert Wilbert, Bridgette Brennan, Megan Dietrich, Jermaine Whiting, Peter Rydesky, Nicole Hard, Lana Njor.

INDEX

Titles in the Great Lakes Books Series

Dear Reader

I'd love to hear about your experiences. How has this book helped you? Have I missed any of your favorite sites? Have you found any of the information incorrect or confusing?

Your feedback will help me with the second edition of the Detroit Kids Catalog. Write to Ellyce Field, P.O. Box 490, Franklin, Michigan 48025-0490. Be sure to include your name, address and phone so I can reach you for further clarification. Thanks!

Author Ellyce Field with husband, Steve, and sons (from left) Andrew, Jordan, and Garrett. Glenn Triest Photographic.